BROKEN GROUND

Also by William Logan

POETRY

Sad-faced Men (1982)

Difficulty (1985)

Sullen Weedy Lakes (1988)

Vain Empires (1998)

Night Battle (1999)

Macbeth in Venice (2003)

The Whispering Gallery (2005)

Strange Flesh (2008)

Deception Island: Selected Earlier Poems (2011)

Madame X (2012)

Rift of Light (2017)

CRITICISM

All the Rage (1998)

Reputations of the Tongue (1999)

Desperate Measures (2002)

The Undiscovered Country (2005)

Our Savage Art (2009)

Guilty Knowledge, Guilty Pleasure (2014)

Dickinson's Nerves, Frost's Woods (2018)

EDITIONS

Randall Jarrell, *Poetry and the Age*, expanded edition (2001)

John Townsend Trowbridge, *Guy Vernon* (2012)

WILLIAM LOGAN

Broken Ground

Poetry and the Demon of History

COLUMBIA UNIVERSITY PRESS   *New York*

COLUMBIA UNIVERSITY PRESS

Publishers Since 1893

NEW YORK   CHICHESTER, WEST SUSSEX

cup.columbia.edu

Library of Congress Cataloging-in-Publication Data

Names: Logan, William, 1950 November 16– author.

Title: Broken ground : poetry and the demon of history / William Logan.

Description: New York : Columbia University Press, [2021] |

Includes bibliographical references and index.

Identifiers: LCCN 2020048120 (print) | LCCN 2020048121 (ebook) |

ISBN 9780231201063 (hardback ; acid-free paper) | ISBN 9780231553919 (ebook)

Subjects: LCSH: American poetry—History and criticism. |

English poetry—History and criticism.

Classification: LCC PS305 .L638 2021 (print) | LCC PS305 (ebook) | DDC 811.009—dc23

LC record available at https://lccn.loc.gov/2020048120

LC ebook record available at https://lccn.loc.gov/2020048121

Columbia University Press books are printed on permanent and durable acid-free paper.

Printed in the United States of America

Cover image: Debora Greger

For Paul Bartkiewicz and Stephen Pohlman

The Advantage of it is, that the Roots will now send out new Fibres into the fresh **broken Ground**, and be well established by the Beginning of the succeeding Summer.

—John Hill, *Eden; Or, a Compleat Body of Gardening* (1758)

The owner of a place might listen with attention to the remarks of a painter . . . on the picturesque effect which projecting trees, roots, stone, and **broken ground**, with a torrent forcing its way among them, had on the eye when viewed from below.

—Uvedale Price, *Essays on the Picturesque, as Compared with the Sublime and the Beautiful*, vol. 3 (1810)

Even in the stillest evenings there is a silent and a sacred charm produced by the effect of a declining sun, whils the traveller is treading the mazes of the forest especially in **broken ground**.

—J. Hodgson and F. C. Laird, *The Beauties of England and Wales*, vol. 12, part 1 (1813)

Turn the lawn into a piece of **broken ground**, plant rugged oaks instead of flowering shrubs, break the edges of the walk, give it the rudeness of a road, mark it with wheel tracks, and scatter around a few stones and brushwood: in a word, instead of making the whole smooth, make it rough, and you make it also picturesque.

—Abraham Rees, *The Cyclopædia; Or, Universal Dictionary of Arts, Sciences, and Literature*, vol. 27 (1819)

Contents

Acknowledgments

These essays and reviews gathered themselves while I was writing the long essays for *Dickinson's Nerves, Frost's Woods*. I am indebted, as always, to editors who, unwary or unknowing, asked me to write and to those who, wary or knowing, having taken leave of their senses asked me anyway. Sometimes an editor threw a book at me, and I threw it back. Sometimes I had to shop a piece around, because occasionally a critic ought to write on whim. The Larkin essay might have been included with a pendant in *Dickinson's Nerves, Frost's Woods*; but that book was running long, and I was impatient.

These pieces appear as first published, apart from minor changes in wording and the chance improvement in style. A few lines in the review of Robert Frost's letters were rewritten where I misunderstood that he might have been joking. I would have said not; now I'll go as far as maybe.

I'm grateful to the journals in which pieces appeared in print: *New Criterion, New Walk, New York Times, New York Times Book Review, Poetry*. The gratitude is no less to the editors of various online journals and websites: *Battersea Review, Country Dog Review, The Journal, Literati Quarterly, New York Times, 92nd Street Y on Demand, Partisan, Tourniquet Review*, and *Walrus*. "A Literary Friendship" was first published as the foreword to *A Critical Friendship: Donald Justice and Richard Stern, 1946–1961*, ed. Elizabeth Murphy (University of Nebraska Press, 2013).

BROKEN GROUND

Introduction: Poetry and the Demon of History

MARINE SERGEANT. Another glorious day in the Corps. A day in the
Marine Corps's like a day on the farm. Every meal is a banquet!
Every paycheck a fortune! Every formation a parade!
—*Aliens* (1986)

Too many poetry critics sound like cheerleaders for the Dallas Cow-
boys, having signed nondisclosure agreements with the poets under
review. There's no other rational explanation for the lashings of praise
lavished week by week on poets of sublime mediocrity. In our Panglossian-
Leibnizian world, critics are rarely abused for treating poets with faith,
hope, and charity; but they're roundly attacked, these critics of temper—
these assassins, as one anthologist called them—for being critical. The
ideal critic has been recruited from Madison Avenue to provide copy for
the rear panel of a book, a panel that by long custom must collapse into
ecstasy. The trouble with contemporary criticism is that every poetry
book is a parade, a fortune, a banquet. In the cloistered world of poetry,
every book is worth reading because every poet is a genius.

The critic who stays in the trenches too long, sniping at poets, may
overrate the rare poet who does publish a good book. Like Browning's
young duchess, such a critic may briefly have a heart "too soon made
glad." We know what happened to her. Alas, such a critic may find that,
however much he loves a book, the poet's next book disappoints. Poets
are never consistent, and their talents waver under inconstant breezes.
Even in the rare exception like Auden, critics who adored the poet of the
thirties often loathed the poet of the fifties. With Lowell, some critics
who worshiped *Lord Weary's Castle* couldn't stand *Life Studies*—or, if they
liked *Life Studies*, they despised *Near the Ocean* or *Imitations* or *The Dolphin*. And everyone hated *Day by Day*.

Perhaps a poetry critic should never fall in love with his poets. There
was once a lead critic for two important journals who frequently reviewed

poet A, who could do no wrong in that critic's eyes—book after book received detailed attention and a standing ovation. Though poet A had been a remarkable and original poet in her second and third books, those afterward were an exhibition of how a superbly gifted poet could turn, by dedicated application, into a carny attraction. I recall poets B and C, about whose books I was little less than rapturous, even if to keep my sanity I allowed myself a quibble here and there. A critic may think such raptures can do nothing but continue and that the novelist, say, who wrote *The Golden Bowl* and *The Wings of the Dove* could never write a drama as leaden as *Guy Domville*. In their forties and fifties, those poets became ghosts of their former selves; and my reviews, though always mentioning the golden hours of the early books, now became surly with disappointment. What can the critic do? The critic can only be honest. The rewards of honesty are slight, but the critic can sleep at night—if he cares for sleep. Perhaps critics are lunatics. I long ago suggested that readers often like best the first book they read by a great poet. With Heaney, I prefer *Field Work* to much that came before and most after. It's not a uniform rule, but it's wise to remember that poetry that breaks ground for the poet sometimes breaks ground for the critic. A fortunate critic three or four times finds a poet who does what should have been done but hasn't been, or what should not have been done but proves everyone mistaken. There's nothing better for a critic than to discover a book that goes against all his instincts and convinces him his instincts were dead wrong.

No critic's taste can always be right. Indeed, it would be surprising if the critic were not wrong frequently and embarrassingly. There are also, alas, errors of fact—I once misspelled Robert Louis Stevenson's last name twice in an essay and in another wrote that Britain had mad cows instead of an outbreak of foot-and-mouth disease. Such mishaps are a chastening reminder of how easily those who love to be right go wrong.

A critic who can't force himself to believe that criticism is sacred should no doubt be hurled headfirst from the tower of criticism, even though criticism is just a minor art in thrall to a major one. (The critic who does believe in the sacredness of criticism should be sacrificing cats to Calliope.) That doesn't mean criticism can't have standards or bear them— Johnson's *Lives of the Poets* is worth a thousand poets, even if no sensible reader would save that book rather than *Paradise Lost* were the last library and the last copies in flames. I'm thinking, of course, of the rescue of Cotton Ms. Vitellius A XV when Sir Robert Cotton's library burned in 1731. The manuscript contained the only surviving copy of *Beowulf*.

The question often posed—or perhaps sneered—is "What is the point of criticism?" A good critic can detect what a poem is concealing, whether written four centuries ago with a goose quill or yesterday on a cell phone. A critic can make, at best, some judgment about how good a poet is. The history of literature is littered with misjudgments but probably fewer than is thought. Yet does poetry need critics so sour, so dyspeptic? Why allow so many grouches, bellyachers, and malcontents into the critics' guild? Why have critics at all if they can't see the magnificence for the mistakes, the flourishes for the flaws? Why can't the taste of the age be the taste of critics?

Because, says the better angel of our nature, the taste of the age is often blinkered as a fly-blown mule, sentimental as a spring rose, and full of notions that a decade or two later will be considered ridiculous. There's no particular right to criticism in the Constitution, apart from the tacked-on bit of romanticism called the First Amendment—but in many ways the whole document was drawn from profound criticism, and the armies of the Revolution were grumblers all. The critic has every right to kick, or grouch, or gripe, or even raise a hurrah or two. The surprising thing about poetry is that critics are felt to be bad for it. If we have no opinions about what we read, we're not readers at all—we're merely beasts gobbling up whatever's put before us and smiling contentedly. Even omnivores have taste. As Pound reminded us almost a century ago, the Greek *krino*, to choose, to pick out for oneself, gives us the critic as well as the criticism in him. It also means to separate, to prefer, and even to bring to trial.

Of course, to make this argument I'm clothing a few straw men in rags. Critics are no more than readers sometimes paid for their opinions. There are always a few readers who don't seem to mind hearing the critics' catcalls and Bronx cheers. All readers of poetry have opinions, often ferocious ones. However loud the cries that poetry criticism should—no, must!—go easy on poets, many poets have violent opinions they keep to themselves, more than a little afraid of what would happen to their careers if they didn't. In a century, most of those poets and probably all their critics will be cheerfully forgotten, and all that worry over the contagion of bad reviews will have been wasted.

Poetry is necessarily imbued with the past, not just the crisscrossing of influence along generations but the intimate survival and loss of language, both word and phrase. (Take "ungear," which once meant to unharness horse or mule, now employed by the day traders and investment houses in the farms along Wall Street.) Words and phrases are the beginning of poetry's DNA; but the past that rises into poetry is also the layering of allusion, the cold references to history, and the intimacies between one poet and another through form, structure, or meter. The past is everywhere in poetry, and the new is often the past reborn. Criticism is the enrichment of poetry by the archeology of the past. All poets—all critics, too—tread on borrowed ground. Wherever the past is present, it's the lot of critics to dig it out. Whatever critics say will be part of the ruined temples of the future.

At a time when scholarship has become so arcane that graduate students have to hire translators to understand what their professors are talking about, critics must be plainspoken. It's hard to imagine a world where it's necessary to write, as one scholar recently did, that "Oedipus' de-oculation concedes violability in the face of external impingements." The duty of critics is to reply, "When you're blind, you can't see the bastards coming for you." Critics must be honest so the future won't think our readers complete idiots.

If poetry aspires, to borrow a line from Pater, "towards the condition of music," criticism aspires to ballet—or, some would say, the bullet.

Dickinson's Nothings

When she died in 1886, Emily Dickinson left a large drawer of handwritten poems, poems soon plundered by relatives and only long decades later handed over to scholars. She had also squirreled away thousands of rough drafts of letters and poems on scraps of paper. These fragmentary remains, like the detritus of other authors not wise enough to pitch them into the fire, have become the heart of academic industry as well as academic fancy. Researchers now treat them with the reverence of biblical scholars piecing together the fugitive shreds of the genizah of Cairo. Reverence, and vigilance.

Dickinson is in many ways a tabula rasa. She was a cipher at death, a painfully, even pathologically shy woman who retired from society in her thirties and rarely emerged thereafter. She had once seemed a more-or-less conventional schoolgirl in the conventional village of Amherst, but her escape from family and village was short-lived. She left Mt. Holyoke (then Mount Holyoke Female Seminary) after two terms, possibly because of ill health or the proselytizing of her classmates. We know more about the Dickinson family—the ailing mother, the remote and some-times overbearing father, the adulterous brother, the sister and cousins and the rest—than about any other family in Amherst.

Emily remains a mystery. Almost no manuscript exists of any poem she wrote before she was twenty-seven. During the next eight years, until the end of the Civil War, she finished more than eleven hundred, better than one every three days. (Dickinson had perhaps begun some of them earlier—but not many.) Relatives and friends published a few of her poems anonymously, if not at her urging then with her tacit assent. She certainly felt curious about seeing her work collected in print. She was tempted more than once, and then withdrew, content to bind her handwritten pages into fascicles, in mimicry of books—the way a girl might care for dolls or pretend to cook. It was doll's house publication.

Dickinson had, after Coleridge, the deepest poetic mind of the nineteenth century. She thought in metaphor the way Amherst merchants thought in dollars and cents. Metaphor deciphers the world while seeming to encrypt it. No other poet after Shakespeare has made metaphor the basic currency of imagination—her range is not as broad, her experience not as comprehending; but to live in her poems is to live in a world of stifling privacies and shadowy longings and in a sensibility of extraordinary reach and demand. The woman is an enigma, her poems as revealingly unrevealing as Shakespeare's sonnets.

The Gorgeous Nothings examines a handful of scraps from the midden she left behind: specifically, the fifty-two scribbled on envelopes. Each is reproduced full size in color, front and back, on thick paper-stock. The striking photographs sit *en face* a diplomatic transcription in print about as large as a mouse could manage. This collaboration between a "visual artist" and a Dickinson scholar offers a peculiar array of analytical tools, including a "visual index" that sorts the scraps into shapes and a "directory" that serves up the information contained in what are normally called notes.

Gazing upon this extraordinary debris, I felt the delight of viewing the forbidden and the pang of conscience that comes from rummaging through a stranger's trash. Reduced to print, letters and drafts can't summon up the same sense of violation. (Auden felt differently, remarking in his introduction to Shakespeare's sonnets that much "scholarly research is an activity no different from that of reading somebody's private correspondence when he is out of the room, and it doesn't really make it morally any better if he is out of the room because he is in his grave.") These private thoughts give us access to Dickinson's naked imagination.

This edition, alas, refuses to let the drafts speak for themselves, offering instead the smoke-and-crystal-ball interpretations de rigueur among scholars now. The beauty of the objects as objects (who wouldn't want a ripped-open Western Union envelope, circa 1880?) and the *tendresse* due these fragments of poems- or letters-to-be are overwhelmed by the blowsy language of neo-Romantic criticism. Even the preface by the poet Susan Howe suffers the affections of affectation:

> Does form envelop everything? Can a thought hear itself see? These writings are suggestive, not static. How do you grasp force in its movement in a printed text? Is there any correct way to clear this entangled primal paper forest?

Primal paper forest! Though I admire the sidelong allusion to Darwin's tangled bank, the implicit opposition (handwriting, good; printed text, bad) is depressingly mawkish. Dickinson scholars are fiercely possessive. (Howe's book on the poet was titled, ambiguously, *My Emily Dickinson*.) The great virtue of feminist scholarship has been its rescue of voices long forgotten; its vice, indulging in ancestor worship, for the right sort of ancestor. Dickinson's art is more complicated than a simple quarrel between writing and print, one flowing, the other fixed.

Howe recalls her own enchantment with Dickinson, having first encountered her in the old Thomas H. Johnson edition: "That is how I first knew and loved this poet of poets. I believed I was reading exactly what she had written—I found the dashes and capitals both radical and formal." A lot of scholarly labor has been expended on Dickinson's dashes, about which there is little consensus except that they are, well, dashes. Attempts to interpret them as shorthand for various marks of punctuation have come to nothing, or the little that is nothing. Even as late as Dickinson's day, authors did not always care to govern their stops, which could be left to the drudges of the printing house, as had been done since before Shakespeare. Whitman's letters, as well as his poems, are liberal with dashes, and more dashes, and dashes in overplus. Dickinson's own letters, like her first to Thomas Wentworth Higginson, are sometimes dashed to pieces. It was a device common in nineteenth-century correspondence.

Even if she had an exacting hierarchy of punctuation in mind, Dickinson had no reason to prepare printer's copy. The interventions of her early and somewhat naive editors were—so far as punctuation went (their alteration of her words is inexcusable)—merely attempts to reduce manuscript to the demands of print. That Dickinson's poems now appear as they came from her hand, dashes treated like religious relics, reveals an unwillingness to make this author submit to print except on her own terms—if those *were* her terms—while serving as a just reminder that these poems are handwritten privacies broken by the reader's intrusion. In the poet's absence, it's the only fair way to give an accounting of the ambiguities the dashes create and the style of thought that often judders toward conclusion. The capitals seem "radical" to Howe because the old practice of capitalizing prominent words, especially nouns, fell out of use in publishing during the early part of Dickinson's century, though it lingered in manuscript. Whether she would have allowed either to be changed, we cannot know. She complained of revisions to her poem "The Snake," printed in the *Springfield Daily Republican* in 1866, but made no objection to an editor's meddling with the one poem she allowed to be published in a book, *A Masque of Poets* (1878).

Howe goes on to say that she found the meter radical, too, in some way she fails to explain. Perhaps to an ear tempered by the free-verse line, the formalities of common meter—the meter of hymns and ballads—seem revolutionary. She then reverses herself:

> In 1981, Ralph Franklin's facsimile edition of the *Manuscript Books* showed the same words, but with increasingly different line breaks, spread across the entire space of a page. . . . Franklin's updated variorum edition of *The Collected Poems* . . . continued to ignore the visual and acoustic aspects of the manuscripts that are particularly obvious in the late fragments and drafts. For almost twenty years few poets and fewer scholars, after seeing the originals, have dared to show us the ways in which what we thought we saw was not really what was there.

Continued to ignore? Dared? We have entered the world of Dan Brown novels. In her introduction, the artist Jen Bervin continues this theme of a poet still treated brutally by her modern editors: "Even in the most trusted scholarly editions, editors have restructured Dickinson's poems for print in opposition to the manuscripts, consistently overriding her line breaks." These "different line breaks" are merely where the poet, writing on narrow paper, turned one line to the next for lack of space—the run-overs, as typographers call them, have no effect on meter or form.

For a group of Dickinson scholars, these ruptured line-breaks have become an article of faith. The poet's lines have been chopped up like carrots in their transcriptions, simply because she wrote on paper too cramped for her longhand. The spaces between her words are now being measured no less precisely than once her dashes were. This takes whimsy too far. The attempt to find meaning where none exists has resulted in meaning where none is meant.

Of course no transcription can reflect the hurry or drag of handwriting, the ambiguity of malformed letters, the puckering of this word or the looping slouch of that—but then a writer's manuscript is usually raw matter for print, and only a madman would want his poems trapped in the idiosyncrasies of his hand. We are centuries past the date when a gentleman felt that no one but a commoner would let his scribbled manuscripts be reduced to common print—Ben Jonson (bricklayer, killer) became the model for poets after, proud of collecting his work in sturdy printed folios. Like so many scholars who have vested their interests in Dickinson, Bervin wants to find in accident some secret design, which is to raise the poet's mild pathology to art.

Dickinson's poems have been accorded special status because of the peculiarities of her character—and she *was* a peculiar character. She had originally written Colonel Higginson in 1862 because of an article in the *Atlantic* in which he offered advice to young authors seeking publication. What sort of supplicant, however, fails to sign a begging letter? Instead (shyly? coyly? frightened half to death?), Dickinson enclosed her name in a tiny separate envelope. She was not hostile to print per se; but, when Higginson later judged her poems unready for publication, she complacently accepted his counsel. (Two years after, she published five poems in various journals—but only two more the rest of her life.) By refusing to destroy her poems, by leaving fair copies bound in her imitation books, perhaps she prepared them for eventual publication—but, if so, she was hardly suggesting that the only way to read them was in her own script. For one thing, lithographic or copperplate facsimile would have been prohibitively expensive for a book of poems.

I love seeing Dickinson's poems in manuscript, love the sense of her rushed hand scratching out those remarkable lines; but I don't need three thousand facsimiles to love them—there's a point of diminishing returns. The beauty of her manuscripts is seductive, even too seductive, because however entranced we may be by our seeming closeness to the poet, we are no more intimate than the tourists tracking mud through her house, largely ignorant of her. We're tempted to believe that material remains bring us closer to the past, rather than to a comprehension that, as we seem to draw near, recedes before us.

The Gorgeous Nothings is based on a sentimental notion—that these envelopes Dickinson rescued and reused have some peculiar aura not available to the drafts found on the back of the guarantee from the German Student Lamp Company, say, or the invitation to a candy pulling. Had the editors merely presented these lush photographs of trash become manuscripts, and manuscripts that almost vanished back to trash (the photographs look as if someone tipped over a box of rubbish and carefully arranged the spillage), that might have been enough.

Why envelopes? Marta Werner, the coeditor, claims that "Dickinson's envelope poems seem charged with a special poignancy and hermeneutical burden." (Woe to things with a hermeneutical burden.) There's a beauty to old envelopes, to be sure, especially envelopes without their messages. As objects, they possess the same eloquence as the engraved tokens and bent thimbles left by mothers who abandoned their babies at the London Foundling Hospital, left so they might reclaim those children, though few ever did. Such things inhabit the privileges of loss— but an old envelope confers no touching feelings on whatever happens to be dashed down on it, at least none the same envelope wouldn't confer on a shopping list.

Dickinson left a lot of trash behind—thrifty trash, because, where some authors indulged only in sheets of foolscap or notebooks of laid paper, she on occasion used the corner of a magazine engraving; a memorandum from the Home Insurance Co.; fliers advertising a local drug store, or silks, or dry goods in Northampton, or a January sale somewhere or other; even a discarded leaf of stationery on which she had written and then scratched out the words "Ice Cream." The introduction mentions the single point that ought to puncture later fancies: at her birth, Dickinson's father presented her mother with *The Frugal House-wife* by Lydia Maria Child, a book that counseled wives to "preserve the backs of old letters to write upon."

The Dickinsons perhaps kept a basket of such waste paper. Indeed, the "wastepaper basket" was then used not for household garbage but for paper odds and ends that might be handy for kindling a fire or penciling down, as Dickinson did, a doughnut recipe. (The meaning is preserved in *Adam Bede*: "There was the waste-paper basket full of scraps.") At the time, unusable paper refuse was burned in the back yard if not in the fireplace, everything else buried in a corner of the property or hurled down the privy. Letter paper was four or five times more expensive than now, and even waste paper had value—if not reused, it could be sold, though at trivial prices. Yankees were known for penny-pinching economy and "cuteness," that is, acuteness.

The Frugal Housewife continued: "If you have children who are learning to write, buy coarse white paper by the quantity, and keep it locked up, ready to be made into writing books. It does not cost half as much as it does to buy them at the stationer's." Perhaps Dickinson's packets or fascicles found their origin here, in the "writing books" a mother might have stab-bound for her children. Family recipes were sometimes kept in just such a stitched-up book. The author on home economy speaks elsewhere of the virtue of saving wrapping paper: "Put away the paper and twine neatly, instead of throwing them in the fire, or tearing them to pieces." Dickinson wrote on such paper.

The poet usually slit or tore open the discarded envelopes to provide space for writing—on some occasions at the edges, at others along the glued seams. Sometimes she used just the top flap, or a squarish scrap cut from the whole. There's no sign that the shapes are in any way calculated. That does not stop the romance of old rubbish from infecting the tenor of criticism. One of the more curious drafts, dating to 1885, consists of two-thirds of the back of an envelope to which Dickinson has pinned a small triangular addition. She made notes going in three different directions.

Werner discovered this "sudden collage" by accident, "when it fell (rose?) out of an acid-free envelope." Because the "collage" has been folded, the scholar thinks it "resembles the hinged wings of the bird the holograph is becoming," conveniently because one of Dickinson's notes refers to the "Wheels of Birds." Werner goes on:

> On each wing, writing—inscribed by Velocity—rushes in opposite directions. To access the text(s), and to answer the question of where we have arrived, we must enter into a volitional relationship with the fragment, turning it point by point, like a compass or a pinwheel—like the *wheels of thought*. 360 degrees. As we rotate [it], orienting and disorienting it at once, day and night—each a whir of words—almost collide in the missing spaces just beyond the light seams showing the bifurcation in the envelope, and then fly apart in a synesthesia of sight and sound.

A volitional relationship? A synesthesia of sight and sound? ("Wheels of thought" is Werner, not Dickinson.) To such a reader, every gesture holds hidden meaning. It's useless to suggest that the pinning was practical, the common method of attaching papers before paper clips and staples (the old method persisted well into the twentieth century). Dickinson had pinned additions into her fascicles. I won't even go into the scholar's frivolous conceit that the poet "imped" the pinned fragment to the "wings," like feathers in falconry.

This *capriccio* of flight quickly leaves the poet's scrawled notes behind—were the fragment diamond shaped, no doubt Werner would see a kite there; if roundish, the moon. The cruelty of such imaginative witterings is that the genius of Dickinson is shouldered off the page—yet surely what is crucial about these drafts is their record of the rough beginnings of imagination. If you pin the phrases together, the passage runs,

> Afternoon and the West and the gorgeous nothings which compose the sunset keep their high Appointment Clogged only with Music like the Wheels of Birds.

This is related to other notes not included here, because they were written on snips from a paper bag, also pinned together:

It is very still in the world now—Thronged only with Music like the Decks of Birds and the Seasons take their hushed places like figures in a Dream—

Dickinson apparently composed letters from such scatterings of thought, nipping and tucking them as she might a poem. A later draft read,

That you glance at Japan as you breakfast, not in the least surprises me, thronged only with Music, like the Decks of Birds. . . . Sleigh Bells and Jays contend in my Matinee, and the North surrenders instead of the South, a reverse of Bugles.

The original "clogged" sounds too dire, where "thronged" suggests the heavenly flight of birds—or angels. The "Wheels of Birds" is a striking reminder of the aerial ballet of the flock. (By "Wheels," Dickinson means "wheelings," but the form of the word enlarges the metaphor. Longfellow wrote in *Evangeline*, "Merrily whirled the wheels of the dizzying dances.") "Decks" probably refers not to ships but to the carol appropriate to the season, "Deck the Hall with Boughs of Holly," first printed in 1862, in the second volume of John Thomas's *Welsh Melodies*— the lyrics were much later amended to "halls." (Her usage of "decks" is otherwise unknown, but Dickinson pressed her words hard.) By such adjustment of tone and scale, the poet approached her meaning—but she was penny wise and did not always waste on drafts the stationer's expensive letter-paper used for her fair copies. She pinned her fragmentary thoughts together as another woman might piece an unmade garment.

The calculation and recalculation of phrases reveal her slightly maddening nature—her improvements hardly seem worth the delay, at least for a letter meant to console a sick friend; but such yearning for exactness betrays the exaction to which she submitted. These lovely, wretched remains lose their trifling, their mishap, only if taken as less than artwork. (The collage does not enter the realm of high art until Picasso, though even he could not improve on the paper sculptures of a Mary Delany.)

The oddest addition to *The Gorgeous Nothings* is the "visual index," which sorts the makeshift envelopes into an ornithological or ento-mological taxonomy of "arrows," "pointless arrows," "flaps and seals," envelopes addressed by others, envelopes written in columns—or divided by pencil marks, or written diagonally, or every which way. There's little that cannot become a fetish—in Jen Bervin's own art, even the little crosses Dickinson used to mark possible variants. The fine-press edition of *The Gorgeous Nothings* was published last year, price $3,500.

We are used to thinking of the fragment as an artistic whole, because the fragment was the most intimate embodiment of Romantic form, inspired among younger Romantics in part by the shattered sculptures and incomplete ancient texts on show at the British Museum (think of the Elgin Marbles and the Rosetta Stone). Dickinson was not trying to write "Kubla Khan" or *The Giaour*—she was merely a working poet who left scraps behind. To treat her as a collage artist avant la lettre is gro-tesquely condescending.

> Pinned, unpinned, and repinned, the fragment's flights shatter the deep, one-point perspective of the letter and keep the texts/birds flying in a splintered mode of time, in the "terrifying tense" of pure transition.

Such critical language is toxically anesthetic—it deadens the roused feeling of the poet's words, providing only this artificial substitute more aggressive ("shatter," "splintered") and less insightful. A poet would never hammer away at that single dead metaphor of flight. "Look at it here," Marta Werner gushes, "flying on the page, vying with light."

The scholar wants to subordinate these scrappy works to the current fascination with an artist's late style—in this case, a rejection of regular-ity and form for something wildly abandoned.

> Her attitude of astonishing recklessness is reflected in her new prac-tice of writing on anything and everything near to hand: chocolate wrappers, the margins of books, scraps of paper.

Dickinson did use almost anything within reach: fragments of paper bags and wrapping paper, part of the program for an organ concert, a torn-up catalogue page, what may be a remnant of mourning stationery, as well as the back of a flyer advertising a book titled *The Children's Crusade*, and another touting the Standard Tubular Argand Lamp, and yet another advertising the services of a New York chiropodist. As for that pale yellow wrapper from baker's chocolate, the poet was a dedicated baker who at fifteen had won a prize for her rye and Indian bread.

Many of the surviving scraps come from after the Civil War, when Dickinson was composing far fewer poems. Such resourceful note taking might indicate a desperation to set down a thought immediately on whatever came to hand, or even a decline in imaginative faculty, when her finicky inkhorn drafts became just pinned-together forethoughts. Speculation starves for lack of evidence. These envelope studies could indicate an "astonishing recklessness" (or just ordinary recklessness), but to call this a "new practice" we would have to know what has vanished—we have few drafts from the period when she was making fair copies for the fascicles, no doubt because she destroyed them. We do not possess the scribbles of other members of the Dickinson family on the stock of waste paper. We have no idea what was lost in the bonfire of her correspondence after her death—a bonfire of the modesties.

There is trace evidence elsewhere of Dickinson's capricious, artistic side. On the folded leaf of notepaper that contains the manuscript of "Alone and in a Circumstance," someone has glued a stamp showing a locomotive. The uncanceled three-cent blue (Scott 114), issued the year the transcontinental railroad was completed, has been set sideways, with two narrow magazine-cuttings protruding like antennae aimed at the left-hand margin. One contains the name George Sand; the other, that of Mauprat, the eponymous protagonist of her novel of 1837. The snips came from a review in the May 1870 issue of *Harper's New Monthly Magazine*. While complimenting Sand's "power" and praising her introduction to an American audience, the critic worried over the novel's "moral tendency," fearing it perhaps a "dangerous book."

This Gothic tale takes place before the age of trains, so it's difficult to ferret out meaning from the collage, pasted to the middle of the page before Dickinson began work on the poem. Why waste a good three-penny stamp? A bit of print is visible below Mauprat's name, the words "of bandits a[nd]"; but these have been crossed through. The review says of the heroine, Edmée, who falls under Mauprat's power, that "by her noble nature he is subsequently transformed from a brute to a man, his sensual passion to a pure and holy love."

Some intention lay behind such attention. The draft is dated "about 1870" by R. W. Franklin, editor of Dickinson's poems and fascicles—the stamp provides a terminus post quem. The poet's withdrawal into resistant solitude had begun in her twenties; by her late thirties, she almost never met strangers, preferring to speak to people, if speaking at all, from the top of the stairs near her room or from behind a door left ajar. Exceptions were rare. When she finally met Colonel Higginson in 1870, she was almost forty. He wrote his wife that evening:

> A step like a pattering child's in entry & in glided a little plain woman with two smooth bands of reddish hair & a face a little like Belle Dove's; not plainer—with no good feature—in a very plain & exquisitely clean white pique & a blue net worsted shawl. She came to me with two day lilies which she put in a sort of childlike way into my hand & said "These are my introduction" in a soft frightened breathless childlike voice.

The colonel had an eye for fabrics. Locally Dickinson became known as the Myth.

The young poet had been charmed by the new mode of travel. In 1862, she had written a poem about the locomotive: "I like to see it lap the Miles— / And lick the Valleys up." Dickinson put trains into a number of poems—if she pasted down the stamp and clippings, was she thinking of the coming of the Amherst & Belchertown Rail Road in 1853? (Her father had promoted the venture and later became president of the company, which had gone bankrupt—after it was reorganized, a locomotive was named for him.)

At fifteen and twenty, Dickinson traveled to Boston in the cars. Was she remembering her only long journey, to Washington in 1855, when her father was a congressman? Almost certainly she went by rail. The station was two hundred yards from her home; Dickinson had taken the train even for the short trip to Springfield the year before; and there would have been no better way for a young woman of sometimes frail health to undertake such a journey, even had passenger stage lines not already been in steep decline.

On the return through Philadelphia, she met the preacher Charles Wadsworth, who was some fifteen years older. Though happily married, he became a sort of muse to her. Perhaps the snipped reference to Sand's novel provoked her. Was Wadsworth the Mauprat of her fancy, waiting to be civilized by a younger woman? Or was her own father the tyrannical Mauprat? Or even her flamboyant, intemperate, brooding, unhappily married brother? The reference in the poem to law books suggests that she is sitting in the family library at the Homestead or next door in her brother's library at the Evergreens.

The poem surrounding the stamp, "Alone and in a Circumstance," begins with a reverie interrupted by a spider, a spider more at home in the room than she. At the end, she thinks of the creature's "Larceny of time and mind." Had some old memory of railroads haunted her, or was the visit of the spider merely adventitious? Perhaps the stamp with its two "legs" is the spider, at the center of the web of words; or a frog in a puddle of speech; or perhaps it's just a stamp with words attached. There the matter remains. We have no evidence that the collage is even by Dickinson.

Had the editors of *The Gorgeous Nothings* mentioned this oddity among the poet's papers, they might have had stronger grounds for treating these envelopes as sacramental art—but it would not have been nearly enough. Another draft that excites ex tempore frenzy in Werner uses the Western Union envelope addressed to her sister Vinnie in care of Judge Otis Lord, perhaps delivered in 1880. The envelope had been roughly torn open, but Dickinson slit the sides and spread it out for the manuscripts of "Glass was the Street—in Tinsel Peril" and "It came his turn to beg."

Dickinson appears to be translating the electrical pulses of the original and unrecoverable bulletin into new messages associating swiftness with shock. The breakdown and cancelation [*sic*] of the final words and phrases of these dictations to Dickinson by someone or thing from the Outside appear as verification that the simultaneous communion between minds—or even between the mind that thinks and the hand that writes—is not achievable.

The loudest of P. T. Barnum's barkers would have been embarrassed to call this ragged envelope "one of the uncanniest documents in the constellation of Dickinson's writings on envelopes." *New messages associating swiftness with shock*? It's true that the first poem speaks of "Tinsel Peril," where "Shot the lithe Sleds like Shod vibrations / Emphacized and gone." However tempting it might be to make too much of those "Shod vibrations" (heavy footsteps, surely) on this old telegram envelope, the subject is merely the "merry venture" of boys sledding (the peril is icicles). The other poem has nothing to offer swiftness or shock.

As for "breakdown and cancel[l]ation," "Glass was the Street" has a single alternative for the last line, while the remaining poem straggles away in second thoughts, as happens when inspiration flags. To distort such variants into the failure of "simultaneous communion between minds" is far too farfetched. The poet would not have mistaken telegrams for instant communion—though much speedier than letters, they still required writing, transmitting, retransmitting (often numerous times), receiving, transcribing, and at last delivery. The reader's faith in the scholar's grasp of historical necessities is disturbed when she calls the envelope a "telegraph blank"—a blank was the form on which the customer wrote the message or the receiving operator transcribed it. (The book suffers from other unaccountable errors: Dickinson was thirty-four, not thirty-five, at the close of the Civil War; and she is unlikely to have written many poems with a fountain pen, which was not mass produced until the 1880s. Further, the Thomas H. Johnson edition of her poems was published in 1955, not 1951.)

Wish is the mother of invention and apparently the father of thought. The editor repeatedly bullies Dickinson's drafts for allegorical symbols. Calling the poems "dictations to Dickinson by someone or thing from the Outside" because they've been jotted on a Western Union envelope lets critical passion kill critical sense. (The envelope was not sent to Dickinson, and the message was not for her.) The deeper we go into the hagiography of criticism, the further we get from the sensible woman who wrote and the depth of the private dramas that gave rise to the poems. The envelopes are not allegories of communication. (Her poems have their own telegraphic style, of course—and what are telegraph messages but dots and dashes, a clever innovation in punctuation?) She would have been just as happy with a stack of chocolate-bar wrappers or a stock of paper bags. What would the scholar make of the drafts then?

It's impossible to see Dickinson plainly unless we understand the material conditions of her work. Marta Werner believes that the poet "lived and wrote at the very historical moment when the possibility of delivering through the modern postal system a private message to a specific addressee was first realized." This reveals a profound misunderstanding of postal history. The modern American post office began in 1792 and had no difficulty delivering private messages to specific addressees. Though home delivery was rare until the Civil War, the major innovation, in 1847, was the printing of prepaid stamps, which made posting and receiving a letter far easier. With the arrival of railroads, delivery became much faster. Telegrams were fiercely expensive, rarely used for messages of length. Ten words sent from New York to Chicago cost a dollar in 1873, twice that much to New Orleans. The average message during a given month was as little as six words. A half-ounce letter, by contrast, cost three cents.

A good number of the revenant envelopes have unstamped faces and merely the recipient's name. Such messages were delivered by hand, as was common within a village. The hand-carried notes leave no great mystery and hardly require the hyperkinetic argument that follows:

> Like Dickinson's untitled and undated poems, which circulated outside the conditions of print and the economy of technical reproduction, the original messages these envelopes presumably enclosed eluded the postal system's public circuits of exchange and were conveyed, if at all, by more intimate, now anonymous carriers.

Charming and evocative though empty envelopes can be, like one Dickinson addressed simply to "Little Maggie," it's hard to see how employing a trusted intermediary—a local Mercury like a pot boy or a domestic servant—for a private message is much different from using the "postal system's public circuits of exchange." (Walter Benjamin wanders through the prose of "technical reproduction" like Hamlet's ghost.) The post office carried messages just as private, by the same hand on the same paper in the same ink, delivered by carriers now equally anonymous.

Dickinson's handwritten poems, rarely seen by anyone not a close friend, could travel by either method with equal privacy.

This gorgeously photographed debris—a kind of bibliophile's soft porn—offers the visual attention usually reserved for a fashion shoot. The fragments are well known, their stray lines long published. Still, it is affecting to see exactly how Dickinson wrote lines like "It is the Past's supreme italic / Makes the Present mean" or "Society for me my misery." We would like to think that handwriting is revealing, but recall Lowell's childish printing or Thoreau's demonic scrawl—they allow no more than the illusion of the residues of personality, unless you believe in the science of graphology. These envelopes offer little as evidence, however much the editors believe in their "special poignancy." As Hemingway said, "Isn't it pretty to think so?"

Verse Chronicle: Song and Dance

ANNE CARSON

Anne Carson's new translation of *Antigone* is a real mess. She has taken one of the most moving plays of the classical world, charged with pathos despite its remoteness in custom and dramaturgy, and updated it like a new Honda. The Greek tragedies present a problem for modern readers; and translations often don't help, either mummifying the original, as if the ancients were best viewed in glass vitrines, or throwing the berobed actors into mufti and pretending that all the bloodletting occurred during the Jazz Age.

Carson wants to drag the drama into the page, an idea lovely in theory but loopy in practice. She has hand-lettered the translation herself, with a pen nib no doubt used to pry open beer bottles. The result possesses a neurotic energy, as if the very letters, all caps, squirmed with feeling. The stuttering punctuation is an afterthought, if it's a thought at all. Overlaying most of the text pages are translucent, slightly childish drawings by the illustrator Bianca Stone. The effect is like a graphic novel on crack.

Still, the interplay between drawing and veiled text is more striking than I would have imagined—if Blake had had no eye for art or ear for verse, he might have produced something like this. The play rises up through the sketches like the ghost of history, a palimpsest only teasingly visible. Sometimes the drawings take their prompts from the dialogue—mostly they're irrelevant. (Members of the chorus, one wearing a *Star Trek* uniform, have cement blocks for heads.) Setting the text at such a physical remove—like the material remains of the past—seems too clever by half, as well as dryly condescending.

Like many Greek tragedies, *Antigone* is as static as an insect trapped in amber. (The plays are full of family values, if your family is full of monsters, needing only a whisper of action for the pity and terror.) Two brothers have died in a struggle for the throne of Thebes. The new ruler arbitrarily decides to entomb one with the proper rites and leave the other to the vultures. Antigone buries the latter young man in secret. There's a lot of talk, then three suicides—the ending is half *Romeo and Juliet*, half *Lear*.

The main problem is Carson's translation. I'm all for renewing or renovating the classics (the king owns a powerboat), but modernist fracture must reveal something otherwise concealed or add more pleasure than it subtracts. Ezra Pound and Christopher Logue were masters of such radical corruption. Carson styles her verse like artificial jazz, chilly and soulless as a synthesizer—yet she can be mortally funny:

ANTIGONE: WE BEGIN IN THE DARK AND BIRTH IS THE DEATH OF US *ISMENE*: WHO SAID THAT *ANTIGONE*: HEGEL *ISMENE*: SOUNDS MORE LIKE BECKETT *ANTIGONE*: HE WAS PARAPHRASING HEGEL

It's hilarious that Hegel, so ripe with the classics, has been shanghaied by Sophocles—hilarious, at least, until in a later passage it becomes tiresome and preachy. There are moments when Carson's sharp tongue matches Antigone's, but the dialogue often has the frowzy odor of translations by Jurassic Period classics dons: "O ONE AND ONLY HEAD OF MY SISTER WHOSE BLOOD INTERSECTS WITH MY OWN IN TOO MANY WAYS," "AN UNBEARABLE FATE HAS LOADED ITSELF ONTO MY HEAD," "YOU GOAT'S ANUS, TELL ME WHO BURIED THAT BODY." The dead language has died a second time.

Carson has made a career of thinking obliquely about the classics. She's an all-or-nothing poet. *Nox* (2010), her family snapshot-album *cum* translation of Catullus, is one of the most original things in recent poetry, while *Autobiography of Red* (1998), her verse novel based on the myth of Geryon, is a self-indulgent disaster with a few splendid touches. Sometimes the classics are more effective played straight, if the reader is allowed to overcome his estrangement with raw imagination and if the translation can make the original fluent without trying to sound hip. ("WHAT'S UP," Kreon is unhappily allowed to say.)

The translation is titled *Antigonick* because Carson has invented a mute character named Nick, who is permanently onstage and who, she says, "measures things." (Why Nick? Nick of time, ho ho!) You're glad this insignificant noddy, this overdetermined dramatic idea—the male equivalent of Lachesis, the second of the three Fates—is never allowed to speak.

There are three or four roguishly droll moments. In her sole monologue, Eurydice compares herself to Mrs. Ramsay in *To the Lighthouse*, whose death was stuck inside a pair of brackets. Then there's the much put-upon guard:

GUARD: YOU LIKE NOUNS HERE'S SOME

DUST LIBATION   DONE DEAL

DEAD RECKONING
KREON: ACTUALLY I PREFER VERBS

Mostly, however, you get Hegelian blather, Carsonian blather, a dash of Sophocles as if rendered by Gilbert Murray, and some cartoons. Antigone's dilemma, to honor her brother and embrace death, grimly echoes the underlying theme of *Nox*—but a play that can still move an audience to tears, while dramatizing some fairly sophisticated ideas about kingship, won't work if the characters sound slightly stupid.

FREDERICK SEIDEL

Frederick Seidel started as an acolyte of Lowell, back when *Life Studies* was young. His first book, *Final Solutions* (1963), shows the manner of the master, every shred of cut and drape slavishly copied but with very little beneath, a kind of soulless knockoff of Dior for the racks at Macy's. Yet what a title! The title of *Life Studies* made modest reference to the apprenticeship of artists; the tastelessness of *Final Solutions* is like an incendiary bomb with Betty Grable painted on the casing. That shameless need to provoke created a brief, now forgotten cause célèbre when the manuscript was chosen for a first-book prize (Lowell was a judge), only for the sponsor and the publisher to grow nervous that the poems would be called libelous and anti-Semitic. The prize was withdrawn and publication canceled.

Seidel carefully developed the persona of a rich dilettante, a Harvard grad with a Ducati motorcycle, someone at the edge of the jet set who knew heads of state and a comtesse or two, but who was *literary*. His willingness to say that the rich aren't necessarily moral idiots, that even among the titled one finds philosophy entangled with tragedies of fate, tests a lot of the presumptions of late Romantic poetry (in some ways it's a reversion to the world of *Richard III*). Still, the shock tactics haven't gone away—Seidel wants to rub the reader's nose in class, in the trappings of wealth (that ever-present Ducati!), in his friendships with people in some galaxy of privilege out of reach of the gossip sheets. He's an equal-opportunity sadist.

You have to examine your prejudices on almost every page of *Nice Weather*—Lowell's brush with money seems by comparison almost accidental (his was a down-at-heels branch of the Lowells, though he was born on Beacon Hill and had a modest trust-fund). Seidel has sought out glamour with a vengeance. He loves to be obnoxious, an illiberal liberal who claims to like dictators. (The obsessions in his new book are Central Park, radical Islam, Harvard, and Obama. And sex. And death.) The poems of Seidel's maturity were often serious but excruciating—the music-hall, Archie Rice version of Anthony Hecht. Then something happened. Seidel started to rhyme like a maniac.

> Patent leather makes my shoes
> Easter eggs by Fabergé.
> The shoes say New York is still run by the Jews,
> Who glitter when they walk, and aren't going away.

His favorite philosopher must be the Duchess of Windsor. Or Isaac Asimov:

I ride the Cosmos on my poetry Ducati, Big Bang engine, einsteinium
forks.
Let me tell you about the extraterrestrial Beijings and New Yorks.
You are dear planet Earth, where my light-beam spaceship will land.
I'll land, after light-years of hovering, and take your hand.

Extraterrestrial Beijings! (Get it?) It's hard not to cringe when a poet lets
slip his inner Ogden Nash (just as it's worrying when a poet thinks that
light-years measure time, not distance). Rhyme with variable meter
requires a subtle ear few poets possess—the radical use of tradition is a
high-wire act that comes with every opportunity for disaster. You want
to throw *Nice Weather* against the wall when you read, "It was good to
be an ace in World War II, / And rather better than being a Jew" or "I see
the psalm and it's a woman's labia, / My pornographically all-mine
Arabia." I like the buried allusion to Donne's "To His Mistress Going
to Bed," but Seidel's a clod who has taken a correspondence course on
writing Cole Porter lyrics.

Once in a while, you find a vulnerability, a desperation to be liked,
that allows you to forget, or half forgive, all the posing and wheedling
of this narcissist who hates narcissists. Still, you'd like to crown him when
he says things like "Hauteur is the new hot" or, of McGeorge Bundy,
"His penis was a frosted cocktail shaker pouring out a cocktail, / / But
out came jellied napalm." The best poems here don't make every line a
tribute to nerve or a test of the limits of bad taste. A sequence about Harvard in the fifties is Lowell territory—there's some celebrity spotting
(Pound, MacLeish, Updike as a big-nosed geek) but also a tender open-
ness to a world of privilege now vanished, one that looks almost benign
compared to our new world of privilege. Alas, Seidel has become a poet
who will labor over a master drawing and then scrawl graffiti on it, just
to show he can.

There's still a poet here who admits all sorts of unlovely things about
himself—his casual racism, his delirious obsession with sex—a poet
who doesn't want to court your dislike, who doesn't always wear the
"Seidel sackcloth," who doesn't have to brag about having a girlfriend as
young as his daughter, if he had a daughter: "The mother of the woman

I currently / Like to spank, I'm not kidding, / Was my girlfriend at Harvard." It's hard to think of another American poet who could write that. Or who would.

JORIE GRAHAM

Jorie Graham's new book, *P L A C E*, is a feverish example of the arrogance of style. Some poets patiently develop style, while others leap about kangaroo-like before alighting on one. There comes a moment, however, when the poet believes that his style has been perfected and that everything after is just the pure expression of imagination. This fossilization usually occurs toward the middle of a poet's career, but it's all too common among poets who have scarcely begun. An Eliot or a Lowell, who reinvents himself brilliantly every book or two, is the rarest phenomenon in art, rarer even than genius.

Graham's poetry long ago became an obsessive-compulsive record of each breath, a moment-by-moment crawl along the stream of consciousness that composes her mental life—you can imagine how disturbing that would be if she were Coleridge, whose notebooks and marginalia form the most exacting idea of what genius, moment to moment, is. If you're not Coleridge, however, you write like this:

> it's stronger, the *yes* is taking over, your yes and my yes and our
> greed to overcome *what*, into this first-ever solstice
> with you in the born world,
> let no one dare pick this fruit I think
> as I cast the roundness of you up again now so high
> into a mouth of sky agape yet without wonder.

That's the poet playing with her baby daughter. There's little room in Jorie Graham poems now for anything but *The History of Seven Minutes of My Life in Twenty-Four Volumes*. Everything else has been crowded out, including most of the commas.

Graham can do a hundred lines on capillary action without breaking a sweat, but at the end you don't know much more than you did after the final in ninth-grade biology—all she gives you is run-on thinking and clumsy stop-motion photography, a technique better suited to Ray Harryhausen movies and Gumby cartoons:

> The vase of cut flowers with which the real is (before us on this
>   page) permeated—is it a page—look hard—(I try)—this bouquet
>   in its
> vase—tiger dahlias (red and white), orange freesia (three stalks)
>   (floating out).

Graham has become fixated on appearance, on the difficulty of conveying the breach between the real and the written; but this shows how badly poetry illuminates notions of ontology and epistemology. If you can't think as slant as Stevens, you're unlikely to produce something as charmingly devious as "Thirteen Ways of Looking at a Blackboard." There's more poetry simply in the name "tiger dahlias."

In Graham's new poems, every minute thing becomes a baggy monster, and every baggy monster has a lot of baggy fleas. However heartfelt her digressions on torture ("someone breaking someone's / fingers—just now—hear their laughter"), too many poems come down to a state of dotty exultation: "this world that / was, just minutes ago, the only one that / was—you're in it / now—say *yes* / out loud—say am I a / personal / wholeness? a congerie of chemical elements?" *A congerie of chemical elements*! (That should be "congeries," but no matter—she also believes that hawks hunt by night.) Graham patiently explains that the "wars, massacre, persecution, famine" that have killed some two hundred million in the past century were "all policy-induced." This is breathtakingly inadequate. You long for the days when disasters were caused by greed or hubris, the Oedipus complex or the death instinct, religious orthodoxy or the will to power. Or just bad weather.

Graham used to think in her poems, not pretend to think—she had an intoxicating way with metaphor, original if not always successful. Now a bird lands on the fire escape of her apartment, and it's like the day men landed on the moon. I'm not sure poetry needs a slow-motion account of a dog getting hit by a car or a fast-forward sci-fi apocalypse ("swirling floods tectonic plates like wide / bones shifting round me—elephants flow through, all gone, volcanoes emerging and / disappearing just like that, didn't even really get to see them")—or both in the same poem. Graham doesn't lack a sense of the tragic; but the tragic is treated the same as the injured dog. (She has a moral imagination both icy and sentimental.) Graham grabs at any contemporary issue—underwater mortgages, IEDs, unemployment—and makes mush of it. When she's not making mush, she writes portentous lines like "We must write the history of time." The actual title of the new book is *P L A C E*. (Get it? "Place" has little places inside!)

No reader over the age of seven needs to be reminded that a writer somewhere sets down the words ("I / entered the poem here, / on line 28, at 6:44 pm"—actually "here" is on line 27). In her desire to break down the fourth wall of the poem, in her fussy attempts to explore the mind's labyrinth (or make herself the point of Zeno's arrow), in her airless sanctimoniousness, a talent that for too long has fed on itself has begun to starve to death. The book ends with an alarming one-page manifesto—or perhaps minifesto. It reads like a press release from a particularly hip publicity department. This isn't publicity, however—it's the poet's declaration of intent cast as a diploma of accomplishment and pitched in a rather creepy third person.

> In *P L A C E*, Graham explores the ways in which our imagination, intuition, and experience—increasingly devalued by a culture that regards them as "mere" subjectivity—aid us in navigating a world moving blindly toward its own annihilation and a political reality where the human person and its dignity are increasingly disposable.

The human person! On and on it goes, long paragraphs of self-serving guff. I know what she's getting at, but it's hard to see through the murk of lit-crit buzzwords, the cant of English departments these days: *subjectivity, resistance, presence, unstable, margins,* accompanied by the inevitable scare quotes ("the day before the 'historical' events of June 6"). You wonder why someone hasn't invented Theory Bingo.

D. A. POWELL

D. A. Powell has a quirky, perverse style and a mind to match. He's a poet of untrustworthy romantic gestures and ironic deflation, with a taste for brute puns and plenty of foreplay. The poems in *Useless Landscape* find a surprising number of uses for romantic sublimity—he's not afraid to tease the reader with phrases like "pale plenitude," which sounds like hand-me-down Shelley.

> When the previously withheld faces grew tough as flax
> or softened into pliant pine in the umber wood, inclined
> together, numerous, when the cobble crushed underfoot,
> and pistachios cracked in their shells, grown heavy,
> grown consummate among the nibs of leaves, then curious
> seemed the stars, those nether eyes which scrutinized
> each shape that stirred against the unlit trunks of trees.

It's tough to say exactly where this lapses into gruesome artiness— probably about the time *consummate* hits the page. When we get to the Victorian inversion and the stars become "nether eyes," the poet is joking or has just lapsed into sentimental dementia.

The partial autobiography offered in this book reveals a poet long at war with himself and a style at war with almost everything else. Powell is drawn to the beauty of things and wary of what he's drawn to. There's hardly a gesture done well in one place that isn't done badly in others (it's not the mark of a visionary so much as of a champ of hits and misses). The preciousness of so many of these poems—their taste for words like *versicolor* and *pelotage*, like *planarity* and *asperous* and *mammillate* and *coombes*—is partly an Audenesque joy in the ruptures of language and partly a defense against the humdrum, an encoding of rage. You half expect things to start deliquescing.

Powell is a dandy who likes to slum in the demotic, and some of his best effects come when the disguise slips a bit:

> There's almost nothing to go back to.
> The wide flat palm of the prickly pear

outside Bent Prop Liquors. I kid you
not that the air's so red, day's end,
that it unlooses a fat ribbon of regret.
Yet the air does not move; it hangs
its squalid rags on the post; it poops
dirty bats out of the public
library's colonnade. I wasn't the first
kid you raped.

There's a lot to dislike in this squalid scene but a lot to admire, too—the
"wide flat palm" already vaguely threatening; the wry joke of Bent Prop
Liquors (referring to airplanes and, well, you know), the rough-handed
enjambment of "kid you / not" and the echo in "I wasn't the first / kid."
The little surprises are melodramatic, but they're also dramatic. Even the
self-conscious "poops" seems like a disgust to foreshadow disgust.

Powell's hyperbaric aestheticism is best in small doses. Where he lays
it on with a trowel, pretense often gets the better of him: "I am a soulless man. When I take you / into my mouth, it is not my mouth," says
the speaker in "The Fluffer Talks of Eternity," and you're sorry he does.
(That's one of the poet's many cheerful, mordant titles—if you don't
know what a fluffer is, look it up.) Powell, who loves to be risqué, can be
surprisingly awkward about sex:

Or to slip naked into the slough
with the wiry boy who peeled each apricot—
as if slightly uncertain how to partake of it—
and savored: dribbling it down his damp chest,
between his long clammy legs, and moistening
his whole delinquent body with pleasant juices.

This isn't a great distance from softcore porn, and the delightfully
pitched *delinquent* (so unexpected and, well, delinquent) doesn't make
things much better. Powell has learned a thing or two from Thom Gunn
("I long to know his vulgar tongue. To feel the cool verdigris / of his
shanks"); and his AIDS poems have been scoured of self-righteousness.
He's a sucker for the caustic one-liner: the darting phrase ("You only

have between now and o-dark-thirty," "their suck-me-off jeans"), the sexual brag ("I'd blow the devil if he offered. Apparently he did"), the shock turn ("Well suddenly the present arrives, and it's a[n] autopsy"). He's also fond of lectures, including a potted California history superficial when not simply mistaken—the Chinese did not "replace" the native Indians. To say that these immigrants were "used to build railroads" is true enough, but they had flocked in during the Gold Rush, years before. Mining and panning under grim conditions, the "Celestials" or "Mongolians" were hardworking, thrifty, thoroughly despised, and mistreated—many took on menial labors, like laundering, spurned by their betters.

If the poet's idiosyncrasies are sometimes far too mannered, if there are too many smirks per line, if the poems (as men are said to say in Texas) are often all hat and no pants, the gay life has rarely seemed so wicked or insouciant. Powell makes his Beau Brummell manner its own form of bravery.

NATASHA TRETHEWEY

Natasha Trethewey's bland, passionless verse comes hemmed in by expectation. Her mother was black, her father white; and she grew up in the penumbra of race, that shadow of larger arguments. However much we might wish to live in a postracial world, the postracial is often just racial by another name. *Thrall* looks warily at her father, their relation tainted by old guilt and labored suspicion, and at the long history of trying to capture in art the confusions of race.

Ekphrastic poetry has become a slightly addled and hidebound genre. There are few poems about paintings, for example, that don't make you wish you were standing in front of the painting instead, and fewer that, once you've seen the painting, make you want to go back to the poem. The new poet laureate makes the poet's task harder by choosing works that provide what might be called freeze-dried symbols: illustrations for the medieval tale of grafting a black's man's leg onto a white man; portraits displaying the bewildering variety of mixed-race children (mulattos, mestizos, castizos—you can find sixteen different taxonomic labels in Richard Twiss's *Travels Through Portugal and Spain, in 1772 and 1773*); and, beyond art, a lurid account of the dissection of a "white Negro."

The poems do what little they can, but the images are already like encyclopedias. Trethewey, who has a gift for elaborating the perfectly obvious (once you know the subject, you know almost exactly what she'll say), litters her poems with stale adjectives and battery-depleted language: "lovely dark hand," "flickering // lamplight," "the elegant sweep of her hair, / the graceful tilt of her head." She's fascinated by portrayals of two races merged into one, but the language is dull as a dirty mirror. Give her a clumsy genre painting of a mulatto girl holding a piece of fruit, and the poem is just choreography. The white father caresses his child's cheek:

> Then, the dominion
>
> of his touch: with one hand he holds
>   the long stem gingerly, pressing it
> against her face—his gesture at once
>   possessing both. Flanked by her parents,
>
> the child, in half-light, looks out as if
>   toward you, her left arm disappearing
> behind her mother's cloak.

This is a rather ham-handed way of describing things understood in a flash when seen—Trethewey spends so much effort on minutiae you lose sight of the visual architecture, and what she adds is merely PhD demonizing ("the dominion // of his touch," "his gesture . . . / possessing both"). She treats the reader like a brainless lout, but then didacticism is the last refuge of self-gratification.

When she confronts a painting like Velázquez's *Kitchen Maid with the Supper at Emmaus*, she browbeats the poor reader ("Bent over, she is the mortar / and the pestle. . . . / She's the stain on the wall") while missing the point—the artist has so transfigured this household domestic, has with such extraordinary skill rendered her quiet nobility amid the pots and plates, that Christ and his disciples shrink forgotten into the background. Trethewey can barely see beyond race and subjugation—she ignores the transcendence that would spoil her slightly privileged sense of injustice. The workmanlike prose of the poems too often succumbs to artsy poeticizing ("immanence, / the soul's bright anchor," "the heft / of lack," "the dark amendment of flesh"—if she can't think of a better adjective, she chooses "dark"). They're at once overexcited and dull, like caffeinated porridge.

You get most of the way through the book before you come to the inevitable poem (called, all too eagerly, "Enlightenment") about Thomas Jefferson and Sally Hemings. Such poems offer little sense of the complications of race (children of marriages between white and American Indian were said to be uncommonly beautiful) and almost none of Trethewey's own history. She mentions that strangers often mistook her mother for her maid, but goes no further. The most extraordinary poem in *Thrall* comes at the start, an elegy for a father not yet dead (a slightly frightening idea)—it recalls a day on a lake, a day ordinary in its ordinariness. Then:

> I can tell you now
>
> that I tried to take it all in, record it
>   for an elegy I'd write—one day—
>
> when the time came. Your daughter,
>   I was that ruthless.

It's a stunning moment, and one never repeated. The grudges here are long festering but secret. We never learn the father's sins, except that once he made a remark, seemingly in jest, about his "crossbreed child." The daughter seems so oversensitive, so quick to view the world through the narrow lens of race, that soon she loses the reader's sympathy. The slights she experienced may have been awful, but Trethewey has to work harder to make her father a fiend. *Thrall* is that most dispiriting thing, a book on a compelling subject about which the author has nothing to say.

AVERILL CURDY

I haven't read a first book as fresh and lively as *Song & Error* in a long time. Averill Curdy has come to mature poetry late in maturity—I gather she's fifty or so—but her new poems fizz with phrases, full of slant notes and weird angles that knock the reader off balance. She'll take on any subject, from Ovid in America to what might be called the negative capability of the sparrow:

Never the gods' favored glamour, never
The pelagic messenger bearing orchards
In its beak, never allegory, not wisdom
Or valor or cunning, much less hunger
Demanding vigilance, industry, invention,
Or the instinct to claim some small rise
Above the plain and from there to assert
The song of another day ending.

The style takes some getting used to—Curdy's sentences tend to be industrial-sized bulldozers, pushing aside everything in their path. Her efflorescent language refuses to acknowledge the contemporary fashion of dumbed-down subjects and dumbed-down sentences. You hear in her some of the balance and weight of Dickinson (Curdy's is a world where nature always contracts with morality), as well as the devil-may-care imagination, encyclopedic reference, and ramshackle lines of Amy Clampitt—indeed, the sparrow poem that opens the book is one long sentence in the patented Clampitt manner.

Curdy doesn't yet possess Clampitt's depth, the hard-won organization beneath the helter-skelter ideas (unpacking a Clampitt poem can be like picking a nine-tumbler lock with a hairpin). The younger poet, however, has a fearlessness rarely seen in new poets—her poems are breathless with their own discoveries.

Standing on this deck I have watched
Morning's first pale peach jeopardy
Of light flush alleys and rooftops,
Just touching my neighbors' gardens,
Until they seethed like the green smoke

Of a new world.

That stanza break has the quiet drama Keats gave to stout Cortez, silent before the majesty of the Pacific.

Curdy's weaker poems tend to be whimsical, or to straggle down the page like the plod of a weary traveler—and travelers there are, in an overlong poem on Ruskin, in a nearly endless sequence on the conquistador Álvar de Vaca (mistakenly called "da Vaca"). The long poems are earnest, full of good will toward their subjects, but tedious— Curdy is better in cramped corners, where you're not sure what she'll do, and not sure *she's* sure, either. Sometimes you can get so entranced by the local beauties, you can't remember at the end what the poem was about.

When the poems don't work, the poet has usually been carried away on a little cloud of excess, as if she had a secret addiction to Hèrmes scarves or Jimmy Choos:

>   potatoes the antique, mortal colors
> Of kilims, an orthodox minareted mix of shallots and onions,
> And a squash's dark, chiton-pleated lantern, winter-hardy
> Rind raked with yellow and tasseled by a dry, umbilical stem.

This is gorgeous but hollow—yet I love the wit of "orthodox minareted," the finicky eye of "chiton-pleated," and the visual thought and sassy music of "rind raked with yellow and tasseled." There's nothing to fault in such phrases but a beauty that does nothing and is nothing, even if they're meant to suggest how haunting a memory can be.

A preciousness hovers at the edge of these poems, or sometimes descends with the brute force of Athena—you hear it in lines like "the Kool-Aid–colored butterfly flaring / Across the tender, veined delta of your hand" or in the contrived wordplay of "neither miniature nor minaudière." When Curdy makes a joke like "another day, another dolor," you might laugh aloud if you hadn't already heard the same joke from William Gass, John Updike, Henry Roth, and Ogden Nash, each no doubt sure he'd invented it.

Yet if Curdy tends to pile up her phrases willy-nilly, if she gets lost in thickets of metaphor and loves too well an oddball X-of-Y phrasing (the "publicity of morning," the "secret ministry of satellites"), if occasionally she writes a line that even the elocution of angels couldn't save ("see its ire of surfaces sore with chairs"), these are faults she sometimes turns into virtues (unlike her need to thank thirty-nine people individually in her acknowledgments, as well as four arts foundations). There are a few poems I admire here that I can't make head or tail of; but Curdy does not shy from language dense with meaning, and her routines are not the routines of other poets. Any reader who loves poetry would be a fool not to read this book.

Verse Chronicle: Collateral Damage

PAUL MULDOON

If a poet sidles up to you and whispers that he's been writing song lyrics, drop what you're doing and run like hell! You might be fleeing the next Irving Berlin; but odds are the fellow's one more deluded soul who thinks lyrics and poetry have something to do with each other. Paul Muldoon is a man of many hats—Pulitzer Prize–winning poet; poetry editor of the *New Yorker*; president of the Poetry Society in Britain; professor at Princeton; and author of some of the quirkiest, most devious, crossword-puzzle-complicated, head-turningest poems of the past thirty years. He's clever in ways that almost give clever a good name. Still, a few years back, at about the time that middle-aged gents go nuts over Miatas and flock to high bridges where they tie themselves to bungee cords, he started a rock band and began scribbling lyrics. A small volume called *The Word on the Street* is the result, and his publishers have thought it wise to inflict it on the unwary.

Muldoon rarely does things by halves. He'll write twenty-one poems on old record albums or "90 Instant Messages for Tom Moore" and look as if he's just warming up. This isn't a poet's natural competitiveness gone awry; it's something darker, like a need to beat all comers in a dozen dif-ferent events in the *Guinness World Records*. That this book of lyrics is as skinny as a kid with rickets suggests that the poet feels he's trespassing on dangerous ground—if so, he should have obeyed his instincts.

Muldoon has perhaps the most capacious imagination of any poet liv-ing—he thrives on challenge, and his poems have secretive forms that spur him to great (if sometimes pointless) acts of invention. Yet he can't seem to write with the ease a song requires, to write as if the words had an emotional gravity that drew them together. At best they possess a mocking cynicism that compliments the reader who gets the point:

> Julius Caesar was a people person
> He knew how people felt
> He knew it took a little coercion
> When the people were the Celts.

This is simple, elegant, and savage. The anachronism of "people person" suggests all the ways the present tries to interpret the past, while concealing a judgment that irony isn't deep enough to cover. Auden would have been delighted. (If you like your highbrow references mixed with camp, Muldoon will give them to you in spades—*Blade Runner*, Elizabeth Bowen, Antabuse, Johnny Depp, the Big Bopper, *Oedipus at Colonus*, Botticelli, and Clint Eastwood don't even begin to exhaust them.)

The vivid or striking moments in these lyrics are so rare, however, it's almost useless to look for them. When he's not offering doggerel of a depressing sort ("The men who dreamed up the airplane / We know they were next of kin / Wilbur Wright rounded out Orville / They came through thick and thin") or bludgeoning rhymes ("We know behind the wolf bully / Is a sheep with a pulley / And its arguments get woolly"), Muldoon is noodling about like a man drunk on air guitar:

> I wish you'd lose at least one layer
> Of your obstinacy
> Even a mule's a team player
> Though its desk's a lot less laden
> Tonight Death Valley seems to run
> From Bleecker to Broadway
> You're hauling borax by the ton
> While I pay and display.

Its desk's a lot less laden! Tennyson would have wept. ("A mule's a team player" is a joke, but not a good joke.) The poet's Rubik's Cube–ingenuity is not the main problem here, but it's a problem—Muldoon simply can't help adding the filigrees and furbelows that in Cole Porter's hands would have been droller than droll. Instead we get "I flagged behind my flagon" and "it's kinda inconvenient / To meet in a convenience store" and "She put her horse / Before the cartel." Sidesplitting. These seem less those acts of genius in language the poet happens upon than simply muscling the words with a schoolboy smirk.

Song lyrics and poems work in such divergent ways, it's not surprising that a man might be prince of one and fool of the other. We don't expect that Ira Gershwin, Lorenz Hart, and Oscar Hammerstein could have written good poetry; and there's no reason to suppose that Wallace Stevens or Ezra Pound or Marianne Moore could have supplemented their incomes by dashing off Tin Pan Alley tunes. Miracles happen; but it's a lot more likely that a man will write a good poem than a good lyric, even if he has an infinite number of monkeys and an infinite number of typewriters behind him.

Song lyrics can be entirely artless or devilish artifice, composed by some magician of the word or just some putz; but whatever they are they need music to make them art, and without music they're just love without money. "Sha-na-na-na, sha-na-na-na-na" and "Do-wah-diddy-diddy-dum-diddy-do" and "Ob-la-di, ob-la-da" make perfectly wonderful lyrics, but on the page they look like gibberish. Cut out the tune, and lyrics are just words that look annoyed. With the exception of the blues—highly charged by image and wit, with a sprinkle of salaciousness added—I'd rather read the Des Moines phone book.

You'd like to think that Muldoon's lyrics could be redeemed by music; but I've listened to his old band, Rackett (which he puckishly calls a "three-car-garage band"), and Wayside Shrines, his newer one. Alas, on stage the songs are almost unsingable. It's no use telling Muldoon that he's tone deaf—what boy in the past fifty years hasn't wanted to pick up a guitar and join a rock band? Being good at it isn't the point.

MATTHEW DICKMAN

Matthew Dickman's poems go off like a bottle rocket. *Mayakovsky's Revolver* is stuffed with hyperactive lines, unrelenting trivia, and a devil-may-care manner that's better at the rueful absurdities of life than at the tragedy to which he's drawn. Dickman has become a master of Frank

O'Hara lite (he shares O'Hara's ADHD, and little else)—gorging on the detritus of modern culture, cheerful in their buffoonery, his poems are sweetly unserious and often out of their depth:

> only maybe the books are not
> what's saving me anymore. Maybe now
> it's reruns of *The Donna Reed Show*
> or the Marx Brothers
> or movies about people who are funny
> all the time. I keep watching the same rap
> video on YouTube.

Dickman has charm to spare and a teasing cheekiness hard to dislike—yet you wonder if life should be as dull as this. When I've read too much of such vacant mental stock-taking, I remember what Coleridge did one afternoon when *he* was bored—he wrote "This Lime-Tree Bower My Prison."

Even when Dickman stumbles upon an interesting idea—say, a man building an effigy of his absent lover out of her clothes—he tends to overwhelm it by jabbering on like O'Hara in his worst poems, and even some of his better. The title ("Weird Science") cheerfully refers to John Hughes's wet-dream movie of the eighties, and the ending ("I will hold you up and kiss you / where your mouth hurts because it's new and was only a handkerchief") almost redeems the junk it took to get there. Still, if all a poet wants is to be as good as Billy Collins, he has rather limited ambitions.

Dickman is capable of poems far more devastating, but he can't go at them without dropping some of his illusions. Occasionally there's a density of reference and invention, a little blizzard of off-beat observations; and suddenly the poem moves into a higher gear. Such passages reveal the poet he might be if he weren't in the grip of some hipster method of throwing lines together. (Has no one yet called this the Brooklyn School?) Dickman's a sophisticate who plays dumb, which is never very appealing—it's too much like slumming.

When he doesn't try so hard to come off as a feckless dope, Dickman can give a terrifying picture of modern life (modern love seems beyond him). The long elegy for his older brother is mostly a failure (dragging in Mayakovsky or his revolver doesn't help much), but one scene is worthy of Pinter. The boys' father

> talked about Costco the night of my brother's cremation and how
> pumpkiny the pumpkin pie was
> though he bought it in a frozen pack of twenty. Just like a real
>   bakery,
> he said, you just throw it in the oven,
> he kept saying that, you just throw it in the oven, you just throw it
>   in the oven.

I can't help but sympathize with the man in his need for chitchat, his beautiful use of the word "pumpkiny," his wish to deflect attention from the horror of his son's cremation, only to make it more horrible. His nervous remarks raise the ghosts of the Holocaust. These lines bear all the longing, the regret, the impossibility of communication in a family that has suffered.

Dickman is elsewhere never quite as confident, or confiding. He has a taste for freakish similes and mischief-making metaphors, and he's not at all bad at them: "the blue smoke / crawling out like a skinny ghost from between my lips," "She carried her hands around / like two terrible letters of introduction," "the way / blackberries will make the mouth / of an eight-year-old look like he's a ghost / that's been shot in the face." They're a showoff stunt, more often than not, and a license for the goofiness that doesn't serve the poet particularly well. I'd like to think that he's paying homage to the Auden of the thirties, but mostly these seem like half-price Raymond Chandler. Some are simply tasteless ("my tongue / like a monk in wartime, awash in orange silk and flames"), and one or two probably violate the law in some states ("Your ass is a shopping mall at Christmas, / a holy place. . . . / Your ass is a string quartet").

Dickman is happy taking a subject and simply riffing on it: Pavese, a dead goldfish, King George III, canopic jars. Then he slaps on a cutesy title. (He deserves a copy editor who would teach him the difference between "O" and "oh" and rap his knuckles when he writes "they have swam" or "shinning stars.") If you were kind, you'd say he pursues relevance through irrelevance—and perhaps he does, or perhaps he just doesn't give a damn.

JANE HIRSHFIELD

Jane Hirshfield's soft-hearted, soft-headed poems are just the thing for readers scared off by that grim, insensible thing, modern poetry. (That would mean most readers not of a flinty sort.) Hirshfield has her fans. I missed *Come, Thief* when it first appeared and am glad to catch up with the paperback. If the *New York Times* has called the book a "deep well full of strength and wisdom," heck, it must be some pumpkins.

Hirshfield writes as if all the world were an allegory waiting to happen. Take her thoughts on Sappho:

The poems we haven't read
must be her fiercest:
imperfect, extreme.
As it is with love, its nights, its days.
It stands on the top of the mountain
and looks for more mountain, steeper pitches.
Descent a thought impossible to imagine.

It's hard to see why Sappho's lost poems would be imperfect and extreme—or fiercer than the fragments we possess (some are a touch acidic). The comparison to love looks more inflated and ponderous the longer you linger, yet you can't say there's nothing to it—like mountain climbers, lovers take foolish risks, long for new passion out of reach, suffer desire meaningless when fulfilled ("enjoyed no sooner but despisèd straight," someone or other wrote). The first lines, then, are less a statement than the delusion of a lover never satisfied.

Hirshfield is clever to have packed so much into so little, to have such deft control of modest resources. Still, in its plain-clothed diction, its tidy summary, its high-flown thoughts on descent, the poem seems too pat. Hirshfield writes in shorthand, in sentence fragments that sometimes deliver more than they promise, in a soothing babble both heartfelt and irritating. She loves abstractions, but they're never blooded—they're just loose baggy monsters wetted down with tears.

> What some could not have escaped
> others will find by decision.

> Each we call fate. Which Forgetfulness—
> sister of Memory—will take back.
> Not distinguishing necessity from choice,
> not weighing courage against betrayal or luck.

I like her flowchart of fate, her invocation of the Greek notion of Anangke (Necessity), her recognition of the occasional inconsequence of courage (it's a notion out of Montaigne); but the argument is as subtle as a dump truck. Hirshfield tries to sound profound without bothering to work for it. You might say her mind is more discriminating than her poems.

Come, Thief comes larded with Zen wisdom hardly worth queuing for ("Call one thing another's name long enough, / it will answer," "A window is only a window when stepped away from"), often with a lethal coat of sappiness: "Your ordinary loneliness I recognize too as my own," "I don't know what time is. // You can't ever find it. / But you can lose it." The inner gimbals of Hirshfield's poems have been heavily influenced by the balance and weight, the Balanchine choreography, of haiku; yet, like so much haiku in English, her imitations sound precious: "On the dark road, only the weight of the rope. / Yet the horse is there." (Hirshfield has more animals under contract than Aesop—in the opening poems, there are squirrels, jays, a hummingbird, an ant, a donkey, a horse, a dog, a billy goat—then I lost track.)

You sense her affinity with Sharon Olds and Louise Glück, poets who have carved out fiefdoms in that great realm of the damaged, the one a scenery-chewing diva and the other a poster child for wounded souls—but where Olds's poems are brazen as billboard advertisements, Glück's are tough-minded and darkly narcissistic. Hirshfield is, by contrast, just a mild, touchy-feely poet with an occasional gift for genteel humor:

> In the nursing home, my friend has fallen.
> Chased, he said, from the freckled woods
> by angry Thoreau, Coleridge, and Beaumarchais.
> Delusion too, it seems, can be well-read.

Perhaps this friend also appears in the poem about Alzheimer's that follows. ("'How are you,' I asked, / not knowing what to expect. / 'Contrary to Keatsian joy,' he replied.") The guy should do stand-up.

Hirshfield takes seriously the minor business of life; but she wants to browbeat the poor reader, reminding him that torture is very, very bad and the Holocaust positively wicked ("anything becomes familiar, / though the Yiddish jokes of Auschwitz / stumbled and failed outside the barbed wire"). Whenever she starts talking like an adjunct lecturer in semiotics, you feel sorry for all the cats and dogs and billy goats that have to listen. Someone somewhere is always getting injured by philosophy. The animals are just collateral damage.

JOHN ASHBERY

John Ashbery celebrated his eighty-fifth birthday last year, but he's still cranking out poems like a combine harvester that turns, not straw into gold, but wheat into Wheaties, or wimples, or whales. Few poets have possessed such facile invention or bizarre imagination—either Ashbery is extraordinary (as in some ways he is), or he's hit upon a magic formula that will let him toss off poems long into his dotage. Hardy would have been jealous.

> The drive down was smooth
> but after we arrived things started to go haywire,
> first one thing and then another. The days
> scudded past like tumbleweed, slow then fast,
> then slow again. The sky was sweet and plain.
> You remember how still it was then,

a season putting its arms into a coat and staying unwrapped
for a long, a little time.

You have to love a poem that starts like this, with its diligent jostlings of
language, its pinball-carom images, its humble-jumble diction. Ashbery
loves American English as much as Whitman did, and his lines shift from
Goths to Gothic in a flash. The first sentence might be his *ars poetica*.

The poems in *Quick Question* look lazy—the sentences are alert but
arthritic, often ending with a flat-footed turn. Yet there's almost always
more going on beneath the surface—I suppose tumbleweeds can scud,
but what's important is the unstated alliance between the tumbleweeds
present and the clouds absent (tumbleweeds are far more comical). Ashbery is rewriting Romantic puffery for the depressive modern. The half-
overdressed season might be Keats's Autumn, now a woman who has
changed her mind and stands there, unable to stay or go.

Ashbery is cleverer than he seems; but his critics are too clever by half,
or three-quarters. He has attracted more willful and perverse scholarship
than almost any modern, while readers—those who don't simply throw
brickbats—remain delighted by a language that doesn't behave as it
should. (The trouble with most other avant-garde poets is that they have
no sense of humor—or, worse, that they think they're funny.) Ashbery's
poems often suffer from a rare neurological disorder, able to recall the
sentence just written but not the one before that. They live on, almost
making sense; and readers return for the promise of meaning infinitely
delayed.

I love the abstract platonic Ashbery more than the real thing. His last
dozen books have been more or less the same—he could write this stuff
till doomsday, much of it guff, but some pinched with the sorrows
of age:

Invariably the fabric is chafed,
the wood aisles feathery to the touch
as though autumn had fallen off the truck again.
Are these animals to be prized for their musk
or will the kids imbibe us, recognizing each
toy as a distinction, something to be shelved

and consulted when distracted, at some kind of grand
occasion or event no one recognizes anymore?

Is this about a holiday no longer much celebrated or the writing of
poems? Perhaps it's a little of both. (Ashbery's most memorable poetry
has often been about poetry.) His poems are now infused with an *ubi
sunt* melancholia made no more comforting by the wry little touches.
He's a poet the way Frank Gehry is an architect—he prefers that poems
look like twisted wreckage, twisted but beautiful. Ashbery has always
been an aesthete (therefore suspicious to an avant-garde that thinks aesthetics toxic), but of a peculiar kind. His poems live on ruin, busted
memory, and the vague sense of an apocalypse soon to arrive, or perhaps
already here—it's not surprising that Auden chose his first book for the
Yale Series of Younger Poets.

There's nothing in these poems that Ashbery readers haven't seen a
dozen times over. He's an old stager, taking one more turn—reading
Quick Question is like seeing Sarah Bernhardt in *her* great age, a ghost of
herself and yet still Bernhardt. His patter has become a bit leaden ("In
my mature moments I was robotic like you"), his turns of phrase creaky
("Because if it's boring / in a different way, that'll be interesting too"),
and his titles have as usual been tacked on apparently at random. Still, he
makes me laugh when he refers to the Rake's Progress Administration or
claims that something has been "stepfathered in." "Is it all doggerel and
folderol?" he asks. The question confesses nothing and confesses all.

A lot of young poets write as if they didn't want to think very hard—
Ashbery has made not thinking an art. (A minor poet is a major poet
with something major missing.) The new poems have a subdued moral
edge, half joked away; but some of his valedictory remarks now sound
like valedictions, not just whistling in the dark. In an alternate universe,
subject to a different physics, Ashbery might make perfect sense, his every
lacuna a rift of ore (literary critics there would scratch their heads over
the unaccountable nonsense of Lowell and Bishop). Few American poets
have rendered American life so richly or done it more ridiculously. Ashbery ought to be declared a national treasure, like baseball cards, or
Edsels, or Oreos.

ADAM FITZGERALD

Adam Fitzgerald's messy first collection is full of flash turns, a few extraordinary phrases, and a lot of blather. A poet who titles his book *The Late Parade* labels himself a Johnny Come Lately, while mocking his tardiness a little.

> To write about one thing, you must first write about another.
> To speak of the death of King Charles V,
> you must first speak of the HòChí Minh Dynasty.
> To understand the rotund ministries of, say, moonlight,
> you must first be blind, and understand fencing.

You must know about fencing, presumably, because you'll be stumbling around in the permanent dark. Any poet who can write a phrase like the "rotund ministries of . . . moonlight," however off the point his poems, is worth watching. There are phrases elsewhere that display this complicated imagination to advantage, whenever he stops trying to be John Ashbery Jr.

Fitzgerald has a devilish way of throwing a poem together, modulating from the colloquial to the preciously poetic and tossing in Victorian poeticisms along the way ("o'er," "fore'er," "'tis"—metrical makeweights rescued from the grave). I'm not sure how much irony is attached. Fitzgerald is a magpie, as Lowell often was, willing to take his influences broadly; yet something is lost as well as gained—the poems have a fatal lack of character and a strangely manic style.

> It was a shock. A shock for everyone. Not exactly a killing
>   to be had, but from a zoneless dust, a millioned doodads
> of pinkish/beige crumbcakes built in stuccoed stone, you
>
> could almost taste the ageless warrens; baronial hodgepodge
>   shroomed on hill-jammed streets; the bay's smoky pines
> wrestling for the stiff swim trunks of ancient summertime.

That's a fair portrait of Naples, but the frivolities of "zoneless" and "millioned" and "shroomed" and much else overwhelm the rest. I like "shroomed," a reminder that American towns sprouting up overnight along the transcontinental railroad were called mushroom towns—I like it, but it's distracting. The stiff swim trunks are harder to parse; but I suspect he's slipping the drying trunks of modern summers (stiff from salt water) onto the Naples of two millennia ago, a playground for the Roman rich— Pliny the Elder had a villa nearby and died in the eruption of Vesuvius.

If Fitzgerald never learns to underplay his effects, the reader will starve to death chewing wood pulp. The poet is full of phenomenological doubt inherited, or thieved, from Ashbery, and infatuated by what sound like offcuts from *The Bridge*—"the pedal-steel graves covered in nosegays and eelskin," "those dental waters / oft-ringing." It's not that you can't make sense of such lines; it's that the labor is scarcely worth the reward.

The reader has to work his way through the occasional nod to the *OED* ("hypethral") and a lot of language too hip for its own good ("a tad ghetto," "goof magentas," "bake-a-thon," "mojo," "gulag-y years," "can-opened night"). Still, I love a "flossy shiv of sea-holly," am glad to know "tombstress" (a cemetery sculpture of an angel or goddess), and pledge to use "über-mundanity" with only a trace of embarrassment. I'm grateful to Fitzgerald for the National Museum of Vastness, for "remorse code," for "a boy in jockstraps is a joy forever" (though why is he wearing more than one?). For the rest—the sentences that outstay their welcome, the lines easy to write and impossible to speak ("like a gilt slit / on bodily macadam where cockscombs spill. // The sun pronates to my left, akimbo")—I hope he doesn't get praised too highly, because it's easy to be seduced into repeating your flaws. The best poems arrive early in the book; once the poet is infected by Ashbery, it's Ashbery all the way down.

Fitzgerald with a dose of tranks is better—there's a touching pantoum that begins all ajumble but comes to a confident and compelling close. When he's not shooting off flare guns, he gets to the business of writing without so much mannerism.

Some peaches were gathered in your name,
and that was enough beneath panels of

trick moonlight, parsing out phrases from
      clouds, asleep like a Subaru in the suburbs.

The poem is cheerfully titled "Vowels and Continents." The Fitzgerald
lurking in the shadows, more conventional but not shy of feeling, giddy
but not bouncing off the walls, doesn't grandstand so furiously, or
wearyingly.

This turbocharged book is full of arrogant charm, but it's disappointing that the poet has done so little with so much—it's easy to
quote his bad lines, there are so many of them, and tough to find his
good ones. He's already been compared to Hart Crane by that dashing
old blowhard Harold Bloom, who will compare anyone to Crane at
the drop of a hat. If Adam Fitzgerald now seems like another Ashbery
clone or Crane wannabe, that's no mean accomplishment, but it's hardly
enough.

ANNE CARSON

Anne Carson has revisited the characters in her most idiosyncratic
book, *Autobiography of Red* (1998), a portrait of the boyhood of Geryon,
a red-winged monster with issues. Though the monster appears briefly
in the *Inferno* as a puddle-jumper ferrying Dante and Virgil downward
to the Circle of Fraud, he has little role in postclassical literature. In *Red
Doc>*, Geryon is simply called G. His sometime lover Herakles, recently
discharged from the army and suffering a bad case of PTSD, is now
known as Sad But Great, or simply Sad.

The poem begins dizzily with dialogue in medias res:

Goodlooking boy wasn't he / yes / blond /
            yes / I do vaguely
            / you never liked
            him / bit of a
            rebel / so you
            said / he's the

one wore lizard
pants and

pearls to graduation / which at the time you admired /
            they were good pearls

This description of the young Sad has the right-angled turns and deadpan humor of Beckett. Carson is a take-no-prisoners kind of poet. The
breaches in the classics let her imagine worlds that are a mash-up of ancient
Greece and the present day.

The Herakles of myth stole the cattle of Geryon as one of his labors,
in the version of Apollodorus going as far west as the Straits of Gibral-
tar. Carson's poem is cast mostly in long narrow columns—if these are
meant to remind us of the Pillars of Herakles (as the arms guarding the
straits are still known), it's a fairly dopey idea; but some of Carson's best
ideas sound dopey. The slightly disjointed narrative is occasionally interrupted by passages labeled "Wife of Brain," seemingly by the author's
alter ego. The poem judders along in fits and starts, its flat-bottomed
prose helter-skelter, studded with far too many references to Proust and
the Russian surrealist poet Daniil Kharms. The minor characters include
Ida (part of an odd threesome with G and Sad), Io, Lt. M'hek, CMO (a
chief medical officer), and 4NO (Air Force code for medic), with high-
minded dross thrown in, like a play titled "Prometheus Rebound."

Carson's poems rarely seem calculated or designed—they're slapped
together by whim, or what passes for whim. About halfway through *Red
Doc>* you realize that, like *Autobiography of Red*, the poem will be much
less than the sum of its parts—but then the parts aren't much to begin
with. *Autobiography* was suggestive in exploring the adolescence of an
outsider—it was hard not to see Geryon as the late embodiment of a long
list of teenage loners, a Holden Caulfield for the age of video games. *Red
Doc>* (the computer designation for her text file) has much less reason to
exist.

The trouble with sequels is that they're sequels. The *Purgatorio* and the
Paradiso are brilliant poems, but no more than Dante's versions of *Die
Hard 2* and *3* (same hero, different adventures). Who has ever fallen in
love with *Paradise Regained*, when Milton has killed off everything

appealing about his antihero, Satan? When Carson gives way to her inner lecturer, the poem takes a little nap:

> You
> know the Carthaginians
> liked to use oxen for night
> fighting. I'm talking about
> Hannibal I'm talking about
> the battle of Ager Falernus
> 217 BC. Like tanks but
> more frightening. They'd
> tie lit torches to the horns
> and stampede them toward
> the enemy.

This is riveting enough, but her disquisition on the mechanics of Geryon's flight would have stopped the Trojan War cold. At one point we get six pages on rations—an interminable list of things followed by more than you need to know on the subject. Too much of the poem is just Carsonian stratigraphy, grinding down through private musings too often dull as dirt. There's no subject so interesting she can't make you sorry you asked.

Where *Autobiography of Red* used a volcano as its centerpiece, *Red Doc>* meanders toward a glacier (later there's a volcano, too) where Carson finds her inner Pynchon—there's a colony of ice bats as well as an ice garage called Batcatraz. This homage half to Batman, half to Superman's Fortress of Solitude (she must also have read a few issues of *Hellboy*) is the most exhilarating and inventive in an otherwise leaden book. Eventually the poem comes to the hospital where G's mother is dying. *Red Doc>* might have been titled *The Hardy Boys and the Secret of the Glacier.*

This sequel is not so much a tale as a series of blackout sketches. English poetry has probably not had since Pope—and certainly not since Eliot—a poet so drenched in the classics or so capable of breathing the musty air of ancient texts as if it were the pure serene. Unfortunately, Carson is full of dippy, adolescent notions that probably go down better from the podium, where being inert with your own fancy is not a disadvantage. Her characters have all the emotional range of department-store mannequins, and not intelligent mannequins at that.

I read this poet, with her original and disconcerting mind, in the same unease as I read late Geoffrey Hill or minor T. S. Eliot. But just as it's possible to underrate poets working in an out-of-date style, it's the lot of readers to overrate what seems brand spanking new. Perhaps Carson is a poet whose idiosyncrasies can be forgiven—and whose weaknesses will one day be thought strengths. Still, in the middle of *Red Doc>*, when she apparently doesn't have a clue where the poem is going, Carson is a poet standing in the desert without a map.

The Iliad, *Reloaded (Alice Oswald)*

The *Iliad* is the goriest of ancient poems. Homer never sugarcoats the death of a hero or even that of some insignificant myrmidon. He's an anatomist of death, a forensic pathologist of the bronze spear and the bronze sword. The Greek and Trojan warriors meet their fates in ways violent, bloody, and graphic—had Greek battlefield surgeons existed, they could have used the *Iliad* for a textbook. Hollywood's violence is merely a weak modern imitation of what the Greeks heard for centuries.

The British poet Alice Oswald has had the provocative idea of boiling down the poem to two of its most striking features, the gruesome deaths and the heroic similes that often lie in pastoral counterpoint to the action. Her version shifts the moral center of the poem from the anger of Achilles and the death of Hector to an oral history of the dead (in her fine phrase, an "oral cemetery"). The subtle portrayals of emotion, the strikingly modern psychology, the ancient tactics, the fate-haunted warriors— all that life almost three millennia old has been reduced to little more than a bureaucracy of death.

Despite the crippling losses, Oswald's *Iliad* has a strange, luminous quality. With the narrative stripped away, what's left is obituary—and the domestic similes that draw in the workaday ancient world: winnowers cleaning their chickpeas, a woman weighing out her weaving, fish trying to escape a ravaging dolphin. Oswald brings the poem closer to the begats of Genesis, meant to carry fact through the fog of time, than to the tales of Beowulf and Roland, which may have begun in history but ended in legend.

Homer was writing some four centuries after the events of the Trojan War, if there ever was such a war—the excavations at Hissarlik, the site of what is probably ancient Troy, have revealed little of the history from which the *Iliad* emerged. The poet probably knew less about his Bronze Age Greeks than Shakespeare about the world of Macbeth. Imagine a modern author trying to recreate the Age of Elizabeth using nothing but hand-me-down stories. Homer composed his poem toward the end of what we assume were centuries of oral tradition—the *Iliad*, like the *Odyssey* and other oral poems, had a genetic ability to reproduce itself, changing with each recital, picking up new details even as old ones were discarded, but always remaining recognizable. Almost nothing material in the poem can be traced with certainty to the Mycenaean Greeks (the scholar G. S. Kirk thought the remnants of Mycenae amounted to no more than a wheeled work-basket, Nestor's cup, and a few pieces of armor). Indeed, Homer had only the sketchiest idea of Bronze Age arms and battle tactics. He treated the war chariots as if they were hackney carriages, ferrying the warriors to battle and then dumping them like so many fare-paying bankers.

Oswald's condensed version of the poem is rudely partial, an *Iliad* after centuries of further loss and the accretion of a few modern artifacts like parachutes and motorbikes. She doesn't go as far as the late Christopher Logue, whose take-no-prisoners translation equipped the warriors with helicopter and Uzi (and the similes with fighter plane and A-bomb). Oswald, whose work has often been striking but verbose, has found a quiet way of facing death, a way as moving as the bulletin boards of the missing after 9/11. The warriors are marked less by who they were than by how they died—that is part of the ethos of war, where a heroic life can be marred by a cowardly death.

MNESIUS rolled in sand THRASIUS lost in silt
AINIOS turning somersaults in a black pool
Upside down among the licking fishes
And OPHELESTES his last breath silvering the surface
All that beautiful armour underwater
All those white bones sunk in mud
And instead of a burial a wagtail
Sipping the desecration unaware.

This is Homeric with very little Homer in it—the *Iliad* simply lists the dead here. Oswald does not pretend that her version is more than a cheeky strip-mining of the ancient poem—the subtitle of the British edition was "An Excavation of the *Iliad*."

Leaving out the boring bits, the long arguments and interminable speeches, forces us to see the *Iliad* through the lens of its fatalities, to recognize how extraordinarily violent a poem it is. Oswald's annotated casualty-list places the deaths within the same Bronze Age bureaucracy revealed when the Linear B tablets were deciphered—there was not a scrap of poetry, just inventories of sheep, goats, and weapons. We shall be lucky if what remains of our culture is more than a pile of credit cards.

The poet claims that she has paraphrased the lives of Homer's warriors but translated his similes—in fact she plays fast and loose with both. In book 12, the Greeks (in Richmond Lattimore's translation) defend themselves like bees who "make their homes at the side of the rocky way, and will not abandon the hollow house they have made, but stand up to / men who come to destroy them, and fight for the sake of their children." In Oswald this becomes

> Like tribes of summer bees
> Coming up from the underworld out of a crack in a rock
> A billion factory women flying to their flower work
> Being born and reborn and shimmering over fields.

"Factory women" is wryly ingenious, but this is far from translation. A deeper and more disturbing problem is her Frankenstein-like transplant of similes from the original. When Menelaos and Meriones, bearing away the body of Patroclus in book 17, are compared to mules dragging a roof beam or a ship timber, the king and his companion are reduced to draft animals by their labor—we see what a dead weight the dead are. By grafting the simile onto the deaths of a Trojan and his chariot driver, Oswald denies us its unsettling contrast:

> He was a great captain but Menelaus killed him
> And his driver MYDON in the act of turning his horses
> Was killed by Antilochus

Like two mules on a shaly path in the mountains
Carrying a huge roof truss or the beam of a boat
Go on mile after mile.

The lines are very hard to follow. The Greeks do nothing with the bodies here, and the mules come out of a syntactical nowhere—it's not clear if these absurd mules refer to the dead men or the living horses. Too often this rough-and-ready recycling destroys the *Iliad*'s force, and its cunning.

Oswald's rendering is often more vivid than the Greek, but the lack of punctuation makes the syntactical relation of her similes obscure or impossible. Worse, her insistent use of "like" for "as" turns her narrator into a gum-chewing Valley girl ("Like suddenly it thunders," "Like when a ditch-maker takes a mattock"). The similes are printed twice in succession, as if the reader were too dim to get them. Such an homage to the oral origins of the poem probably works well at a poetry reading—on the page the choral effect is merely tedious. Worse, Oswald at times seems to misunderstand Homer—Pandarus's difficulty isn't that his arrows were "flying off at angles" but that they hit his enemies without killing them (she thinks the arrows were flint-tipped, as if the Trojans were Sioux braves). Her description of his death makes nonsense of the original—a spear that hits him "between the eyes" cannot somehow emerge through his chin.

The life of the *Iliad* has vanished here—life often petty, grumpy, ridiculous, but always aware of mortality. Yet reducing the brute struggle of epic to bottom-column obits, focusing on the minor kings and hapless grunts, underlines the shocking waste of these deaths. Oswald's war memorial has taken the forgotten names and chiseled them in marble. She has made a poem that blooms out of slaughter.

The Beasts and the Bees (Carol Ann Duffy)

C arol Ann Duffy, the British poet laureate, is almost unknown in this country, which makes her no worse off than blood pudding, haggis, or Marmite. Britain and America are no longer divided by a common tongue—for fifty years or more, we have been listening to British music, watching British television, and welcoming British writers as warmly as once we welcomed Dickens. Still, most poets don't travel well; apart from an oddity like Seamus Heaney or Derek Walcott, poets are rarely known outside their home countries (worse, they're rarely known outside their hometowns).

Rapture is a book of love poems first published in Britain in 2005, when it won the T. S. Eliot Prize. Any reader not a complete misanthrope will give a lovestruck poet a good deal of leeway, since in the grip of love we're liable to say all sorts of silly things, making promises that should never be considered binding contracts. ("'I will love You forever,' swears the poet . . . ," wrote Auden. "*I will love You at 4:15 P.M. next Tuesday*: is that still as easy?") Duffy is a peculiar variety of *Homo amans*, gassing on about the ups and downs of love without ever giving a convincing picture, or any picture at all, of her beloved. There's a forest, see:

> I followed you in,
> under the sighing, restless trees and my whole life vanished.

> The moon tossed down its shimmering cloth. We undressed,
> then dressed again in the gowns of the moon. We knelt in the leaves,
> kissed, kissed; new words rustled nearby and we swooned.

We swooned! (When was the last time a poet swooned? The autumn of 1878?) Duffy is particularly susceptible to this fairy tale of love, the trees ever sighing, the moon whipping up more gowns than Givenchy.

The laureate needs the full-blown LSD Technicolor version of love, where "I part the leaves and they toss me a blessing of rain," where "love spins gold, gold, gold from straw," where the "birds stitching the dawn with their song / have patterned your name" (isn't that *Cinderella*, the Disney version?). A little of this goes a long way, and a lot goes nowhere at all. Between the dogged rhymes and doggerel sentiments, the stuttering repetitions ("your name / rhyming, rhyming, / rhyming with everything," "Take this . . . / and this . . . and this . . . and this . . . and this."), the poems punch-drunk on monosyllables, and the frequent helium ascent into Victorian diction, the poor reader isn't sure just which century he's in: "I want to say / thee, I adore, I adore thee, / and to know in my lips / the syntax of love resides, / and to gaze in thine eyes." Anyone trying to channel Elizabeth Barrett Browning at this late date is asking for trouble. When the love affair is eventually smashed to pieces, the reader feels not schadenfreude but relief.

Duffy's new book, *The Bees*, has most of the tics of her love poems; but they don't have the excuse of coming from someone intoxicated by a long swig of Love Potion No. 9. The poems are made no better by giddy lists of images ("the moon a diet of light, sliver of pear, / wedge of lemon, slice of melon, half an orange, / silver onion"—they're phases, get it?) and the mindless natter of Old English alliteration ("No folk fled the flood, / no flags furled or spirits failed— / one brave soul felled. // Fouled fortune followed"). It's one thing to be drunk on sound (or love, for that matter), another to let your style be nothing but its twitches.

The poems take their sources from myth, ancient literature, and modern war (as well as bees, bees, bees). Yet why should Scheherazade's tales be reduced to childish jingles ("Forty thieves in a crowd, / bearded and bold. / A lamp rubbed by a lad / turning to gold") or the death of the falling soldier in Robert Capa's terrifying Spanish Civil War photograph be commemorated by an Irish jig?

A breakdance to amuse your mates,
    give them a laugh,

a rock'n'roll mime, Elvis time,
pretending the rifle's
just a guitar?
Worse by far.

Duffy's jollification may be a satirical counter to Horace's *"dulce et deco-rum est,"* but she's far too heavy-handed.

There are few glimpses of the cold, wounded observations that marked the poet's first books, a quarter-century ago—the canny social malaise, the slightly bitter tone, the whiff of misery, the suspicion of what the world offers, all reminiscent of Larkin without being slavishly indebted. These have been replaced by knee-jerk politics, third-rate knock-offs of folk tales, and a vision of England where Sunday cricketers still gather on village greens and bell ringers yank the ropes in the local church. Duffy is pure Labour in her politics (old Labour, that is) but cheerfully Tory in her postcard views.

A poet laureate used to be able to console himself with a butt of sack, his by ancient right; but for the occasional dram he was obliged to compose poems on stock occasions. The laureate is still a royal lackey, though it's never put that way—the hundredth birthday of the Queen Mother and Princess Diana's funeral were duly and dully noted, laureates beavering away at poems with an industry that would have done honor to their predecessors Alfred Austin and Colley Cibber.

There hasn't been a laureate of much depth and substance since Tennyson, though long before he was laureate Ted Hughes seemed to many a young god. The official duties have rarely drawn good poems even from good poets, and the poet's private poems usually get worse. As the first woman to receive the honor, Duffy might have brought fresh air to the stuffy hallways of the laureateship; but the robes of tradition are heavy. Her recent ode to the Olympics outdid in mediocrity anything by her predecessor, Andrew Motion:

We are Mo Farah lifting the 10,000 metres gold.
We want new running-tracks in his name.
For Jessica Ennis, the same; for the Brownlee brothers,

Rutherford, Ohuruogu, Whitlock, Tweddle,
for every medal earned,
we want school playing-fields returned.

The sentiments are earnest, but earnestness has its price.

Two Gents *(August Kleinzahler and William Stafford)*

AUGUST KLEINZAHLER

August Kleinzahler is a romantic bad boy, a Shelley with a chip on his shoulder. Such a hipster's hipster has probably memorized long passages from *On the Road* and made pilgrimage to the Mexican railroad track where Neal Cassady fell into his fatal coma. In *The Hotel Oneira*, Kleinzahler's slouchy, doomed demeanor infects a lot of poems about travel as he bangs up in the odd hotel with a volume of Kafka by his side.

> That was heavy freight moved through last night,
> and has been moving through since I'm back,
> settled in again by the Hudson at the Hotel Oneira:
> maps on the walls, shelves of blue and white Pelicans,
> multiple editions of the one epistolary novel by K.,
> the curios—my sediment, you mighty [*sic*] say, my *spattle trail*.
>
> Look at them down there by the ferry slip,
> the bridal party, organza, chiffon and lace, beside themselves,
> being wonderful, desperately wonderful, a pastel foam.
> Behind them a tug pushes a rusted barge upriver.
> Helicopters, small planes, passenger jets above.
> They behave, these girls, as if this is their last chance to be thus.

There's much to admire in these stanzas: the slow tracking through the room's waifs and strays ("spattle" is a nonce word, presumably the things life has spat forth), the little touch of the "blue and white Pelicans" (paperbacks, of course, but with the dreamlike suggestion of impossibly exotic

plumage), even the bullying symbol of the "heavy freight," and only then
the closely managed scene of the bridal party, the girls—banally overdressed, silly in their silliness, yet revealing a profound loss. O tempora!

In his angsty self-regard, Kleinzahler often sounds like the narrator
of a bad Chandler novel. This sort of thing plays well into your forties,
but by the time you're ready to draw Social Security it's a bit much. If
the opening is straight from the chapel of rawboned romantic gestures
(patron saint, Tom Waits), the lines about the girls are full of rueful sympathy. You can tell the speaker doesn't like such frippery (he juxtaposes
the bridal party with that pushy barge, that empty busyness of air traffic), but he's taken with them despite himself.

The moment might have dripped with sentiment, but Kleinzahler's
best poems risk overegging the emotion without quite making you
cringe. Every page is a dangerous balancing act—the poems ramble from
idea to idea, less an argument than a drunk man's walk, incorporating
humdrum details on the fly, as if that were a sign of being cool in the
midst of romantic agony:

> They follow you around the store, these power ballads,
> you and the women with their shopping carts filled with eggs,
> cookies, 90 fl. oz. containers of anti-bacterial dishwashing liquid,
> buffeting you sideways like a punishing wind.

The poem is about Whitney Houston. Though poems about pop stars
are usually a disaster (we're lucky Lowell didn't write about the Beatles),
Kleinzahler almost makes a case for the emotion pop songs embody. (The
antibacterial dishwashing soap is just right for housewives a little too
prim about dirt.) And yet. And yet. By the time he gets to the song that's
not being played in the supermarket aisle, the poem has collapsed into a
crying jag. He manages not to mention Houston's sordid death in a Bev-
erly Hills hotel bathtub, he's so busy comparing such songs to neuro-
toxin ("it wouldn't be just you dying in aisle #5. / All the girls would be
dropping like it was sarin gas").

That's the trouble with Kleinzahler. He has about all the talents the
god of poetry could have bestowed upon him: a fine ear, the ability to
launch into poems with deceptive suavity, oddly shaped perceptions, a
surprising eye—and a heart of mush. He's never afraid to let the poems

unfold in unexpected ways, yet on page after page there's cloying sentiment or an eye-rolling and affected delivery that makes even the best
poems suspect in their touches of feeling. Such a poet suffers from mixed
blessings—as well as mixed curses.

Too many of Kleinzahler's poems embrace their slack winsomeness
and slacker wooziness, which would be fine if you liked your poems winsome or woozy. (The poet seems to moan, "Pity the poet! Pity the poor
poet!") Worse, the archness often dissolves into weary, jacked-up humor.
There's a poem about macaques that starts in what I take to be an
Amos 'n' Andy voice ("thass me, your jibber-jabbering Sulawesi booted
macaque") and quickly descends into the music-hall turn few but Eliot
could pull off:

> *A-monk-a-monk-a-mee, a-monk-a-monk-a-yoo*
> *I once knew a lady wot lived in a shoe*
> *Had so many laces she didn't know wot to do*
> *So many laces, faces, places . . . Wot's a girl to do?*

Perhaps Kleinzahler has been reading "Fragment of an Agon" like Scrip-
ture. As the younger poet says, "I jibber-jabber'd, jibber-jibber-jabber'd
myself to a proper lather."

These new poems sometimes toy with history, if a little fast and loosely.
German exiles (Brecht, Mann, Oscar Homolka) live out World War II
in California, but suddenly among them there's the long-dead Nietzsche
playing golf at Bel Air. In another poem, Francis Ponge obsessively
watches Looney Tunes. Throwing dead philosophers into our cartoonish culture doesn't seem very fair to philosophers, though perhaps with
the phenomenologist Kleinzahler is making a backdoor joke on the character known in France as Bob l'éponge.

The most curious of these historical turns, seemingly cast in the
baroque eighteenth-century style Pynchon pastiched in *Mason and Dixon*,
in fact consists of passages from the 1703 weather diaries of Thomas
Appletree:

> And thus did the Atmospherical Theatre play out,
> with its transmutations & shifting of vapours,
> whether the rain-bearing clouds of January

riding over our heades like vast Carracks
or Bulging, dull-swelling Bas-Relieve clouds
bloated & pendulous, *ubera caeli fecunda.*

"Milk-dripping breasts of the sky," more or less. Ah, those wild Oxbridgians of the Stuart age, always dropping into Latin for the salacious bits. The poem is a giddy romp and giddily inane.

Kleinzahler is a man at ease in these poems, letting them fill up with the dreck of the day; but then he labors to make a point; or invents elaborate setups for clumsy jokes; or writes something as unbearably twee as "To My Cat William," which is not a patch on Christopher Smart, or a long, gadabout study of Vachel Lindsay, whose naive, tom-tomming poems Kleinzahler does nothing to rescue. There are poems that seem mere jottings—like a writer's summer journal, feisty scrappy but also scrapbook scrappy—and poems that live like remittance men on unearned pathos. You can have only so many apocalyptic visions about the Age of Trash. Yet when he juxtaposes Hitler's invasion of Russia with Napoleon's disastrous retreat, this fitful, posturing poet seems to harbor something greater inside him. He lets the details of war do the work, as Anthony Hecht did. The obvious message is that dictators never learn from history (not that anyone else does, either).

You never know quite what Kleinzahler will do next. Too many poems in this lively ragbag of a book are less than the sum of their parts, too many a train wreck; but in half-a-dozen places he finds access to feeling nervous in its despair. The reader has to put up with a lot of sketchy thought, hipper-than-thou gestures, and gushing romanticism (Hotel Oneira? Give me a break) to get to the deeply rendered meditations of place, full of Melvillean glamour and sadness. It's no use asking Kleinzahler to leave out the gruesome sentiment, it's so mired in his manner, his conception of what it is to be a poet. (He's always ordering a handkerchief with sniffles to go.) The poet should never take credit for being a poet.

WILLIAM STAFFORD

William Stafford was a minor figure in American poetry thirty or forty years ago, neither famous nor infamous, just a hardworking poet who wrote too much and had a poem in most anthologies—almost always "Traveling Through the Dark," which most readers remember as the dead-deer poem. Stafford was like a lot of poets who never rise to the heights of the local Parnassus, an honest journeyman whose work rarely drifted beyond his forty acres. There's never much room at the top—fame is not a zero-sum game, but it's close.

Stafford was modest enough, and sensible enough, not to mind. He was unassuming in person; and the poems were the model of the man, written in bark-plain prose, accidental, unpretentious—like Hardy's without the shape of genius. He fared better than many poets: there was a National Book Award early on and later the appointment as poet laureate (at that time, the Consultant in Poetry to the Library of Congress). If there's a case to be made for his poems, it's that plain American is hard-wearing. Many poets of the postwar are almost unreadable now—they chose a literary language dripping with artifice or a vernacular dull as boiled cod. The difference between a Lowell and, say, a Nemerov or an Eberhart is the difference between a cheetah and a housecat.

The poems in *Ask Me: 100 Essential Poems* are drily written, conversational, without shape or tension—they just start, and just end, sometimes without much in between. Occasionally Stafford has an intriguing thought and just keeps pushing. A woman he knew named Lorene goes missing:

> Usually, it wouldn't happen, but sometimes
> the neighbors notice your car is gone, the
> patch of oil in the driveway, and it fades.
> They forget.
>
> In the Bible it happened—fishermen, Levites.
> They just went away and kept going. Thomas,
> away off in India, never came back.
>
> But Lorene—it was a stranger maybe, and he
> said, "Your life, I need it." And nobody else did.

The idea might have gone nowhere; but then he recalls the apostles, torn from their lives. And chillingly, almost an afterthought, a murderer, perhaps—though he doesn't say murderer (Christ was a stranger, too). Stafford's poems are never a tour de force; they're a tour de réticence, their strengths in what he doesn't say. Kim Stafford, the poet's son, who edited this volume, recalls that at a reading a stranger in the audience remarked, after his father finished a poem, "I could have written that." Stafford replied, "But you didn't." A different poet might have left it there, yet after a pause he added, "But you could write your own." Stafford was one of nature's democrats.

That kindness and humility (there's a brief flare of pride as well) was essential to the poetry; the better poems go a little further than you expect, and they take you unawares. In "Traveling Through the Dark," the speaker stops his car after finding a dead deer along a narrow river-road. He says at the outset that to prevent an accident travelers normally rolled a carcass into the canyon. There's a hitch, however. The deer was pregnant.

> Her side was warm; her fawn lay there waiting,
> alive, still, never to be born.
> Beside that mountain road I hesitated.
>
> The car aimed ahead its lowered parking lights;
> under the hood purred the steady engine.
> I stood in the glare of the warm exhaust turning red;
> around our group I could hear the wilderness listen.
>
> I thought hard for us all—my only swerving—,
> then pushed her over the edge into the river.

The poet never quite admits he could have saved the fawn, but his actions make clear he thought so. "My only swerving" is a touch of Frost; but Frost would have made the poem darker, morally tougher, perhaps less haunting. Some of the impact of Stafford's poems comes from their very quietness. It's a pity that he felt it necessary to make the wilderness listen— surely the point of the poem is that in nature the death would have gone unnoticed.

Stafford's best poems were often little parables or fables whose meaning remained undefined. He loved his moments of prairie wisdom, or mountain wisdom, or river wisdom—he *was* the sort of man who listened to what a place was trying to say. It was half crazy, but half touching, too.

Stafford possessed a sentimental streak broader than a barn door, and it spoiled a lot of poems. "Why I Am a Poet" starts ruefully ("My father's gravestone said, 'I knew it was time'"), then breaks into cheerful absurdity: "The singers back home / all stood in rows along the railroad line. // When the wind came along the track / every neighbor sang." That beats anything in *Oklahoma*! If you write about your life in such a highly stylized manner, the way WPA painters portrayed America in post-office murals, the style conceals all the suffering. The poem ends weakly, miserably:

> I looked back where the sky came down.
> Some days no train would come.
>
> Some birds didn't have a song.

That's a Just So story for poets, and sappy at that.

On the other hand, Stafford may have written the only poems of the Vietnam War that can still be read without embarrassment. His political poems learned something from Auden, adding dashes of whimsy that made the politics more bearable—and more unbearable, too:

> Remember that leader with the funny mustache?—
> liked flags and marching?—gave loyalty
> a bad name? Didn't drink, they say,
> but liked music, and was jolly, sometimes.
>
> And then the one with the big mustache
> and the wrinkled uniform, always jovial
> for the camera but eliminated malcontents
> by the millions. He was our friend, I think.

The reader thinks, plus ça change.

Stafford was born in 1914, the same year as Berryman and Jarrell and Dylan Thomas. His parents were not wealthy—like a lot of small timers before and during the Depression, they moved around trying to find work. Stafford hoed weeds in sugar-beet fields, delivered newspapers, jobbed as an electrician's mate. He was lucky to go to college, but while finishing his master's he was drafted. He became a conscientious objector, like Lowell, and spent the war in work camps in California and Arkansas, where he wrote poetry. His first book was not published until he was forty-six.

There was something hardscrabble about the life and hardscrabble about the career. To say Stafford wrote too much might seem a critic's exaggeration, but by his son's count he wrote twenty thousand poems. This isn't a record (Lowell's psychiatrist, Merrill Moore, wrote at least 25,000 sonnets, probably more); but it's far over the border of graphomania, that peculiar country of the damned. "Scribble, scribble, scribble!" doesn't begin to cover it. By comparison, Eliot wrote about seventy poems, Bishop one hundred, Larkin 120, Moore 250, Pound and Frost three hundred or so, Auden somewhat more, if you count the tiny ones. A poet who writes too much almost always has too little to say, and very few ways of saying it; but beyond the limitations of talent there's something darkly psychological in Stafford, some desperate need that could be assuaged only temporarily by writing.

Stafford was so reserved (humility can be heroic, but also other things), it's difficult to guess from the poems what that need was. He found his style early and stuck to it. When you read the poems, you feel you know the man (there were worse men to know—worse poets, too), but really you know only the voice. You can read all of Frost without getting more than a glimpse of the rage and desire lying below. If you published the poems Stafford left behind, a book a year and a hundred poems a book, you'd finish about the year 2200; but you probably wouldn't find them much different from the poems we have.

It's not clear what editorial principle his son used to gather these poems or organize them—he likes the political poems well enough and the sentimental ones even better. You could probably get a selection almost as good by putting your hand in a grab bag of the throwaways. Out of the common sorrows of common life, Stafford made poems with modest ends, and modest means.

In scenery I like flat country.
In life I don't like much to happen,

In personalities I like mild colorless people.
And in colors I prefer gray and brown.

There was something a touch sad about the poems—yet Stafford manages to seem a member of life's Optimists Club. He was one of the rare poets, in an art that favors the monk and the monster, whose salt-of-the-earth gentleness did not count against him. Poets often get by on personality—an authentic voice is more appealing than verbal pyrotechnics—but a poet of slender gifts could write a poem every day of his life and never write a great one. Writing poetry is not like standing in traffic until you get hit by a truck; it's like standing in hell waiting to get knocked down by a snowball.

Kipling Old and New

R udyard Kipling was a conundrum even to himself. One of the first modern writers to live in the fraught intersections of empire, he wrote between two worlds. Born in Bombay, named after the picturesque Staffordshire lake where his parents had courted, he enjoyed a pampered childhood among the Anglo-Indians, as they called themselves, with a native *ayah* and loads of Indian servants. At five, he was banished from this paradise and sent back to the mother country to be raised by a placid English couple. The husband had the bad manners to die, leaving the boy in the charge of the wife, who was secretly a monster. Kipling suffered, as did Dickens, a Dickensian childhood whose cruelties could never be erased.

Kipling was a poet first, if not last, with a knack for the catchy phrase—admen have cheerfully pilfered the "white man's burden" for soap, and for perfume "the female of the species is more deadly than the male." When we read Kipling now, it's through the darkness of the collapse of the British Empire and with a sense of embarrassment that anyone could ever have taken "The White Man's Burden" seriously. *100 Poems Old and New*, this new selection of his work, attempts to change the way we think about a poet whose poetry we scarcely think about at all.

From the start, Kipling had such an array of identities, it's a wonder he could keep them straight (he published many early poems under pseudonyms). He wrote some of the most merciless, unsettling, unsentimental short stories in English, tales about life in India among the servants or in the barracks, then tales no less exotic about life in England. (The only thing you can say about his stories is, read them.) He composed the great novel of the English occupation of India, *Kim*. In between, he scribbled poems the way other men scribble editorials, and it can be hard to tell them apart—Kipling loved the soapbox, and on hearing news that provoked him he often dashed off a poem. He also, of course, wrote the *First* and *Second Jungle Book* and the *Just So Stories*. If a child knows Kipling now, it's usually the Disney version. If an adult knows him, it's probably with fading memory of the few poems still clinging to the anthologies or with the recollection that one day he must finish *Kim*.

Though Kipling's politics could be hidebound and retrograde, he loved the common soldier and, despite his own brass-button patriotism, often detested officers and the government. Even so, Auden was premature when he wrote, "Time that with this strange excuse / Pardoned Kipling and his views." The trouble with Kipling is deeper than politics. The sympathetic eye and rough grace of his stories cannot distract from the vulgarity of the poems or his now mortifying views of empire.

Thomas Penney, who edited the massive three-volume edition of Kipling's poems published last spring, wants this selection to knock readers from their slumbers. He has picked twenty-six "familiar" poems, presumably those once known by heart by that mythical creature, the common reader—"Danny Deever," "Tommy," "Gunga Din," "The Law of the Jungle," "The White Man's Burden," "If—," and "The Female of the Species" among them. The remainder consists of poems almost no one will know—and many no one will want to know. These dreary second-raters have been swept out of Kipling's closets and plundered from his bottom drawers, poems long forgotten or never published at all, most with good reason.

There are a few comic turns worth the cost of salvage. Only a man serious about Lewis Carroll could have written "The Turkey and the Algebra":

> The Chalk was sciffling on the board
>   Squirfling with all his might
> And though he made the figures wrong
>   The Sum would not come right
> Which wasn't odd because you know
>   His clothes were much too tight.

A ballad on a ship of the P & O Line has been happily infected by "The Rime of the Ancient Mariner," and some droll nonsense where Cupid heads a department in the Raj suggests that the gods might have flourished in bureaucracy. The book might have included the sardonic attack on the press (present in the larger edition but omitted here), showing just what Kipling would have thought of our celebrity culture:

What's your last religion?
    Have you got a creed?
Do you dress in Jaeger-wool
    Sackcloth, silk or tweed?
Name the books that helped you
    On the path you've trod.
Do you use a little g
    When you write of God?

The others are meager compensation, however, for the mass of minor verse the editor has shoveled forth under the name of Kipling. The reader must endure a poem where apples natter on like sixteenth-century rustics, a lot of lifeless lines about a lifeboat, and parlor verse even worse.

For a good poet, Kipling was surprisingly coarse in his tastes, and for a bad one far too canny and intelligent. (One might say he had an ear too easily seduced.) Lardy abstractions, clichés in abundance, sentiment iced over with treacle, endlessly cantering fourteeners, Victorianisms galore, and the deadening overuse of what might be called Kipling Cockney are not the least of his defects—if not all were considered vices at the time, in poetry today's virtue is often tomorrow's vice. Kipling had gifts not uncommon in a popular writer, but the more fluently he wrote the more he became the victim of his gifts. He was just housebroken enough to have made a wonderful poet laureate, though it's not clear that he was ever asked.

To read Kipling now requires not just adjusting our ears to the language of another day but suspending judgment to enjoy, where we can, poems that jar our sensibilities. Yet how fine he was when appreciating the condition of the soldier, poor Tommy Atkins who served in India and South Africa and on the battlefields of France. Kipling thought as soldiers thought, just as Stephen Crane did. "Tommy" is scathing about the hypocrisies of the citizen who loves the soldier in war and loathes him in peace, while "Danny Deever" captures the sharp end of military justice:

"What's that so black agin' the sun?" said Files-on-Parade.
"It's Danny fightin' 'ard for life," the Colour-Sergeant said.

Orwell's report of a hanging is superior, but not much.

Many of Kipling's old standards seem badly careworn now: "If—" ("If you can keep your head when all about you / Are losing theirs . . ."), for example, sounds like advice from a Victorian Polonius. Even so, however cheap the sentiments of "Gunga Din" and "The Law of the Jungle," "The Female of the Species" and "The Ballad of East and West" (oddly not included here), they are still crudely effective—"Gunga Din" is a *Boy's Own* tale reduced to verse, one of the few poems ever made into a movie. If I were seven again, I'd fall in love with it.

The problems of *100 Poems* are not just those of taste or misguided principle. Other poems missing include the Browningesque "The *Mary Gloster*," "The Widow at Windsor" (a soldier's cynical view of the queen), and "Epitaphs of the War," the most devastating poem Kipling wrote. Few men have written a better war poem than the epitaph for a coward: "I could not look on Death, which being known, / Men led me to him, blindfold and alone." A modern ear may find most of Kipling's poems more fit for the music hall, which may explain why T. S. Eliot liked him, though he hedged his liking quite a bit. Kipling did have an influence on other poets, though it can be hard to trace—Auden was indebted to the ballads; and Frost wrote the best Kipling poem not by Kipling, "The Bearer of Evil Tidings."

This edition eliminates just those historical notes that could explain occasions long buried in rotting newspaper files. Who now recalls the alleged conspiracy of Irish soldiers serving in India or the grumbles of the bishop of Bombay over the "sinful game of 'Tommy Dodd'"? Hasn't the Draft Theatre Bill of the London County Council passed from living memory? And what of the accusation that Lord Dufferin's staff hated kissing? The reader might have been reminded that the village that voted that the earth was flat did not exist—it was the subject of a Kipling story.

Sometimes when an editor lives so long with his subject he forgets just how ignorant everyone else is. What should they know of Kipling who only Kipling know? The reader who does not have a copy of *Hobson-Jobson* lying about will badly need a glossary if he doesn't recall what a *punkah*, or a *barasingh*, or a *chirag* is. The editor's insistence on keeping Kipling's rough-and-ready punctuation, his failure to explain the presence of two poems incestuous in their similarities, and his inclusion of so much wastage make all the more difficult the rescue of a poet who has almost disappeared into the shadows. Even if you turn to the judicious selection Eliot made in 1941, you are unlikely to think Kipling more than a major minor poet.

Kipling's poems show the lack of introspection of a man seemingly without an inner life. He had an inner life, often a movingly sad one (his son was killed on the battlefield at Loos); but the poems have the emotional range of a schoolboy. They were written, unlike most poetry now, for purposes other than the display of private disappointments and despairs. Even when the subject was love, the poems are derivative or wearyingly sentimental, as if written by committee—but then, in a way, Kipling was a committee. The world that adored his poems is not our world, it's prejudices no longer our prejudices. That world is gone and not likely to return.

Frost at Letters

In the early fall of 1912, a blandly handsome, tousle-headed American schoolteacher arrived in London. Nearing forty, coming without introduction or much of a plan—except, as he later confessed, "to write and be poor"—he was making a last attempt to write himself into poetry. It would have taken mad willfulness to drag his wife and four children out of their settled New Hampshire life in a quixotic assault on the London literary scene. Still, he was soon spending a candlelit evening with Yeats in the poet's heavily curtained rooms, having come to the attention of that "stormy petrel" Ezra Pound, who would boom him in reviews back home. Little more than two years later, the schoolteacher sailed back, having published his first two books, *A Boy's Will* (1913) and *North of Boston* (1914). He had become Robert Frost.

The modernists remade American poetry in less than a decade, but like the Romantics they were less a group than a scatter of ill-favored and sometimes ill-tempered individuals. Frost was in most ways the odd man out: he despised free verse, had only a patchy college education, and wrote about country life. He knew the dark and sometimes terrible loneliness that descended upon stone-walled farms and meager villages. Looking back on his work, this throwback to Chaucer and Virgil plaintively asked one of his correspondents, "Doesnt [*sic*] the wonder grow that I have never written anything or as you say never published anything except about New England farms?" *North of Boston* was originally titled *Farm Servants and Other People*.

Though Frost had come from Yankee farming stock, his father was a hard-drinking San Francisco newspaper editor who died young of tuberculosis. (He was also a Harvard-educated race-walker.) The boy was eleven before he saw the East Coast, where he spent his adolescence in mill town and village, working, while not at school, as shoe nailer, hotel handyman, and mill assistant-gatekeeper. Even when he later came to live on a farm, he never knew "shovel-slavery." Indeed, until middle age he spent only half-a-dozen years or so on a farm, mostly raising chickens.

He had heard, however, the "real language of men," as Wordsworth called it—in Frost's words, sounds "caught fresh from the mouths of people." Frost brought the ebb and flux of plain American back into poetry. He disliked fancy metaphor or decoration (his poems are litera- ture's answer to Shaker furniture); but more than any poet since Whit- man he devoted himself to the American tongue. You get snatches of conversation in the hilarious pub scene of *The Waste Land*, in dribs and drabs through *The Cantos*, and in the anodyne drabness of William Carlos Williams. More than any poet since Whitman, Frost devoted him- self to the real gimcrackery and moody flamboyance of the American tongue. "My conscious interest in people," he once admitted, "was at first no more than an almost technical interest in their speech."

This opening volume of a complete edition of Frost's letters meanders from a schoolboy's love notes ("I have got read a composition after recess and I hate to offaly") to the dashed valedictions of the poet at forty-five, fleeing a cushy job at Amherst. Generously annotated, it replaces the selected letters edited by Lawrance Thompson half a century ago. As he grew older, Frost acquired those two enemies of the letter writer, a telephone and a secretary, so the edition will require only three or four volumes more—Eliot, that man of letters who lived in letters, will need at least twenty.

Frost was a stolid correspondent, apart from the whims of fancy with which he indulged close friends. He doesn't have the nervy wit or deeply nuanced intelligence of Eliot, the panache and bulldozer man- ner of Pound, or even the finicky authority of Marianne Moore. Frost's pronouncements on the "sound of sense" and "vocal reality" may have proved crucial in explaining himself to himself, but they add little to the poetics of the last century. Machiavellian calculation, or deeper-seated insecurity, may explain why he found solace, or something like solace, in the fawning letters to literary politicians like Amy Lowell and Louis Untermeyer. The latter was one of the few correspondents to receive something like the poet's devotion. Frost praised many another minor poet to his face, only to slip a knife between his ribs when his back was turned.

The most attractive letters record Frost's adventures as he made his way into the rough trade of poetry—a man proud, prickly, grateful for favors soon resented. He fell out with Pound, "that great intellect abloom in hair," but elsewhere in England found sympathetic spirits among the duller if not the dullest versifiers around. Frost had a gift for the attentions of amiable second-raters; and his letters were directed largely to minor littérateurs like Lascelles Abercrombie, F. S. Flint, and Wilfrid Gibson (he thought Gibson a better poet than Pound), as well as, when he returned to America, a group of long-forgotten and inoffensive academics. He was fortunate to find abroad the man who became his closest friend, Edward Thomas, a poet of greater subtlety and depth than all the other English poets Frost came to know. Their correspondence was cut short when Thomas was killed at the Battle of Arras in 1917.

In his letters, Frost habitually indulged in literary snits and little bouts of bragging. Not long after his grimly conventional first book, he wrote, apparently without a smile, "I am one of the most notable craftsmen of my time." Yet he could rouse himself to charm, and when he was struck by something—the sort of farmer, for instance, who leaves his horse mired in mud for a week—the reader is struck, too. Frost had a poet's eye for country things and paid equal attention to a fossil taken from a chalk cliff or the way a hoe was made.

For Frost's life, the reader must still turn to Thompson's three-volume biography, completed posthumously in 1976 by his research assistant. Thompson has long been a bête noire among Frost scholars. Though he was the authorized biographer and spent decades winkling information out of the poet, his portrait of an American grotesque riven by vanity is a caricature of a man far more complicated. Though the preface to this new edition bristles every time Thompson's biography is mentioned, he cannot be entirely ignored. Frost was an imperfect father and imperfect husband, a man who had in his blood the "cuteness" and longheadedness of a Yankee trader. "I am but a timid calculating soul always intent on the main chance," he wrote. There's no reason to think he wasn't in earnest.

Frost didn't much like England, where he found no American news, no cellars, no sun—and, in the lunch rooms, never a glass of water. The most appealing Frost is the self-mocking man who wanted to go back to New England "and get Yankier and Yankier," or the poet who says fiercely that a "poem is never a put up job." The meaner-minded Frost makes snippy comments about the "festering free verseters" and refers cruelly to "some single-bed she professor." Worse, he could remark, "I will tell you what I think of niggers" and "to the German all Americans seem niggers and Indians," as well as call a black literary critic a "duodecaroon." There's also an odd cri de coeur in the voice of some late-nineteenth-century Democrats who, in Frost's words, believed that America should have done a better job of "disfranchising the nigger." I'd be inclined to discount this use, since Frost—whose political notions were quite jumbled—was no friend to the Democrats, past or present (later he despised Roosevelt and the New Deal). However, he wrote that he hoped to have this rant "cut on my tombstone as a surprise to my enemies and critics." That's no doubt more bumptious jocularity, but his language is uncomfortably close to the remarks elsewhere. (It would not have been the only time Frost used a false flag to smuggle in a disturbing thought of his own.) The best one can say is that even his humor was tainted. The poet was no more wretched than many—such slurs are broadcast through the letters of other modernists—but I wish Frost were better than his time.

In almost every way, this new edition is a triumph of scholarly care. It suffers few of the problems that afflicted the disastrous edition of Frost's *Notebooks* (2008), whose editor, Robert Faggen, is one of the editors here. My own entanglement with the notebooks required two very critical reviews; and it is no credit to the publisher of Frost's works, Harvard University Press, that the book was secretly revised and printed in paperback with almost as many errors as in the hardcover. Comparing the manuscripts of two dozen letters to the transcripts in this edition, I discovered numerous trivial errors, half-a-dozen more substantive, and the missing page of a letter declared incomplete. The standard is high but falls short of the "carefully verified transcripts" promised by the editors.

The notes are as thorough as most readers could wish, though frequently all too repetitive: minor figures are reintroduced for those who don't like to use an index. It's surprising that the editors don't know the nineteenth-century American phrase "and found," as in Frost's remark that a man "earns from five to six dollars a week and found," meaning that he received room and board in addition. They might have explained why the poet mentioned "hot times" in August 1914 (the Great War had begun) or why there were bombs in Bloomsbury in 1915 (they were dropped by Zeppelin); and they should not have made such a hash of Frost's reference to Blue Hill (his correspondent probably wrote from East Blue Hill, Maine, where she had a home). They might have pointed out that Frost's injunction *"Cave Poetam"* is a play on *"Cave Canem"* (Beware of the Dog) or noticed that the source of Frost's *"aestus se ab alto excitavit"* lies in Caesar's *"cum ex alto se aestus incitavisset"*—Frost's roguish rewriting, if that's what it was, might better be translated "The passion roused itself from the deep" (he was in the grip of fierce emotions), not "The fire drew itself down from on high." Frost knew Latin well enough to pass the entrance exam at Harvard.

In a book so keen to detect Frost's allusions, it's odd that the editors miss those to "Ode to a Nightingale" and *Hamlet*—and fail to note that, when Frost speaks of "outer darkness," he's referring to the book of Matthew, probably the Parable of the Talents. Most readers will probably wish to be told, when Frost wrote "brown day," he meant it was gloomy; that by a man's "bays," he meant laurels; and, when he said that "poetry is a drug here now," he meant it was unsellable. Such small derelictions little distract from the immense labor toward clarity the editors have performed. If Hercules had merely twelve labors, he was lucky—editors have thousands.

Letters require that the writer—unless he's an acid-veined narcissist who spills gossip in all directions—know someone distant only too happy to hear about the unhappy accidents of daily life. The recipients must be the sort who don't throw letters straight into the bin or on New Year's Eve make a bonfire of the year's correspondence, at least if later readers are to enjoy, somewhat illicitly, these privacies made public. Even then, time and circumstance wreak their havoc.

The editors hope that this new edition, which has provided hundreds of letters previously unpublished, will reveal a Frost radically different from the man in Thompson's biography—a kinder, gentler Frost, perhaps. That revised portrait may have to wait for later volumes. Only a handful of letters exists from the years before the poet left for England; and in the later years covered here there are few to family, few that reveal much about the inner Frost. Though his oldest son had died of cholera as a boy, most of Frost's sorrows lay ahead—the death of his wife in her sixties, the suicide of his other son, the death of a daughter after childbirth.

Randall Jarrell long ago recognized the terrifying landscape in which Frost set his poems and the uncompromising bleakness of the poet's imagination, at least before age and self-satisfaction settled in. Even his drollery had a cold edge: of New Hampshire, he once wrote, "I mean to get back there in time to freeze to death this winter." Haggling with editors over the price of his verse; worried to distraction by his London publisher's punitive contract; enraged by his daughter's Latin teacher at Wellesley, Frost was a man others feared to arouse. Yet he risked his job at Amherst by attacking a popular fellow professor bent on seducing male students. For all his private flaws, American literature—and the language itself—owes a profound debt to that dark, demonic, beguiling figure, Robert Frost.

Verse Chronicle: Seeing the Elephant

WILL SCHUTT

Will Schutt's debut, *Westerly*, is a young man's book, full of pizzazz, and panache, and a lot of trans fat. The thing about young poets' books, the best of them, is how fearless they seem—they take in a lot of territory, and chew a lot of scenery, and ask for more.

> Two doors down lived a descendent of de Sade.
>   He rode a vintage Trek in a gingham shirt.
> A blue Hamsa strung around his neck
>   waved when he waved. The name meant
> nearly nil to us, cluelessly humming the catalog
>   of history in "We Didn't Start the Fire"—
> *Harry Truman, Ho Chi Minh, Rockefeller, Roy Cohn.*
>   Hunting arrowheads, we made off with a haul
> of tangled wires, nickeled tubs. Some inheritance.
>   *Children of thalidomide, hypodermics on the shore.*

The references go every which way at once, from the marquis to a popular bike to a Middle Eastern amulet to a fading Boomer pop star. (It's a wall of words reminiscent of Phil Spector's Wall of Sound—that is, partly a horror vacui.) Billy Joel's potted postwar history was itself a blizzard of 120 references, and Boomers should recognize every one. Schutt was born decades too late: the search for history is the search for a once familiar world now mysterious. The children chant names and phrases that have no meaning for them—such ignorance is the beginning of poetry.

If that were all, Schutt would be no better than Joel, tossing out names for their frisson, just to see if there's any juice left in the capacitor. It's like giving white rats Pavlovian shocks. But that's not all—those arrowheads suggest a past still to be exhumed, even if the only thing the young Indiana Jones turns up is industrial rubbish. Some inheritance.

A young poet—and young in poetry now means halfway to Social Security—sometimes begins with *Bildungsgedichte*. (*The Prelude* became an old man's book because Wordsworth never got round to what it was prelude to.) Much as I like Schutt's catch-as-catch-can vision of daily life, his store-bought allusions to childhood, I'm more interested in the poet who sees in Velázquez's *Las Meninas* the "narrow / face of a rousing mastiff / whose dark narrow eyes betray / knowing, which is to say restraint." Or who uses the funeral of Napoleon to make a sinuous point about human nature:

a young foot soldier tried fitting on
the emperor's hat, hoping to spring to life
for the lachrymose officers and ladies
gathered in cool St. Helena. Having homage
and well-meaning mime in mind.
They were, after all, shutting Napoleon
inside four coffins as if he'd breathe like a potato.
It had that solemn air of the ridiculous,
you know, the soldier not getting his hat on square.

There's something deeper masked in gesture, in the eyes of that dog or in the comic farce of the foot soldier (the old-clothes version of "The Emperor's New Clothes").

A poet who can do such things so offhandedly is wasting his time on *Kulturdreck*. If Schutt were a less canny poet, such cavils would be pointless; but he loves his vices more than his virtues. "Put everything into it," his father says—and the son does, the kitchen sink last of all. Schutt himself says, "I'm off on allusions / again" and, after too long a detour, "I am coming around / to my own subject." He can't help himself—that's the epitaph of many young poets.

Westerly is a book of sensibility, where sensibility too often substitutes for argument.

> Brilliant lemon morning. Tania outside
> dumping mulch. Two doorstop snowshoe
> hares by the door: winter morphs with ferruginous
> scuff on their ears. Set on dishcloths,
> they're a mix of iron sconce and birch bark.
> Honey bunch in the garden. On the sill
> a Ziploc bag of permanently wet radicchio
> we bought at the farmer's market
> from kids in Carhartts who return each year
> to tend the horse-powered farm.

It takes a painter's eye to see the "mix of iron sconce and birch bark" in the winter coats of those rabbits, but the product placement (surely there's now an agency to arrange such things) derives from the same campy frivolity that drives pop songs. Even enduring brands like Ziploc and Carhartt may all too soon need a footnote, as Cummings's Cluett shirt does. The raddichio tells the reader much more about middle-class pretension— and salad trends, too.

As an homage to "Skunk Hour" (remember, for brand names, Lowell's "Tudor Ford"), Schutt's bunny poem doesn't go far or deep. The rabbits are just grace notes, and the poem later fritters away its purchase on the past. Still, Lowell's half-mad heiress bought up eyesores that fell to follies; Schutt's children each year return to the "horse-powered farm" where they can't make a living—it's a museum of lost hopes. The kids have probably moved to the city, like everyone else.

Much as I love Schutt's addiction to the curiosa and extranea of modern life, the weaker poems collapse into mere arrangements of detail— recall that Walker Evans spent his last years photographing pop-top tabs picked up in gutters and arranged in his sink. A culture at war with itself needs an eye sensitive not just to effects but to aftereffects. (When Schutt, however, defines "seeing the elephant" as to "see from a high perspective," he's mistaken. It meant to see the attraction, the wonder you'd come for—and was used by Forty-Niners, for example, when they'd been to the mines, or even just to San Francisco, and headed home.) Critics accuse the overambitious of aiming too high, without remembering that bullets and shells have a trajectory—if you don't aim high, you miss the target completely. *Westerly* is a tour de force that spends far too much energy on flotsam and jetsam, only hinting at the darkness below. The difference between Schutt and a lot of young poets is that there *is* a darkness below.

VICTORIA CHANG

Victoria Chang has a thing for bosses, but then who doesn't? The poems in *The Boss* have just one Scrooge-like subject—there's a good boss, a very bad boss, a child boss, and the poet herself, who can be bossy, too. In devil-may-care style, sans punctuation, sans much by way of organization, the poems have been thrown down on the page like a cry from the heart, or from the executive washroom.

> The boss is sitting at the desk the boss doesn't look
> at her the boss is waiting for the black telephone
> to ring she also waits for a ring from the boss he is
> waiting for the files from her
>
> her blue dress like a reused file folder around
> her body her hands tight around the files
> the filing cabinet might eat her might take her hand off
> the boss might eat her

There's a whiff of socialist realism to these arbitrary quatrains, of the up-from-below anger that stokes revolutions; but the poems offer not an argument but a relentless whine, the causes shallow and almost unexamined ("The boss rises up the boss keeps her job / the boss is safe the workers are not / the boss smiles the boss files the boss / throws pennies at the workers"). It's complaint with all the thinking left out.

America has long suffered a fixation on business—the Age of Jackson was the first Age of American Commerce. (Napoleon said, "The English are a nation of shopkeepers"; had he lived long enough, he might have added, "The Americans are a nation of ad men.") Given how much of business is office work, it's surprising how difficult it is to bring the modern office into fiction, much less poetry. The nineteenth century did better—Dickens was half in love with clerks and lawyers; Trollope let loose his great monster, the financier Melmotte; and Melville found something narrow but punishing in Bartleby. What are *Moby-Dick* and *The Confidence-Man* but fictions about a place of business? By comparison, Joseph Heller's *Something Happened* and David Foster Wallace's *The Pale King* have been neutered and evacuated by their subject. (Heller's *Catch-22* is a brilliant comic novel about business, but the business is war.)

The manual work that once straggled into poetry honored the dignity of labor—from "The Leech Gatherer" to "The Village Blacksmith," drudgery was ennobling. Has any poem overcome the stink of ennui that permeates offices? Roethke made a fine attempt in "Dolor," but he's no Baudelaire. The drama of the office has passed to movies and television, hungry for plot, not meditation. If Chang finds no apotheosis in office work, she's hardly alone; but poems about offices are scarcely better than poems about kitchens—too much suppressed anger leaks into both.

Though Chang knows how little poetry lies in her grievances ("The boss is not poetic writing about the boss is not poetic"), she hammers on like a miner against a coalface. Only rarely does she allow a stray *capriccio* to sneak in:

> I could stand on the pier
> the whole day and peer at the pelicans that fall
> from the sky with their briefcases of fish in their
> oily grey suits and shined black shoes.

There she catches the freedom denied the worker, with the insubordinate defiance the poems for the most part lack. For brief moments, the personal breaks through—there's mention of a child, and a father who has suffered a stroke. Chang's grumbler otherwise remains as faceless and soulless and anonymous as Everyman, an Everyman wearing sensible heels.

Many poems visit and revisit Edward Hopper's paintings (among them, *Office at Night*, *New York Office*, and *Office in a Small City*). Hopper was the Michelangelo of anomie, but his office paintings are clumsy and peevishly symbolic—and none has even the casual depth of *Nighthawks*. Chang interprets them in the same maddening run-on, nattering stream of consciousness, all too reminiscent of a one-sided cell-phone conversation. Few poets can riff in a straitjacketed style without becoming tedious—even *The Dream Songs* and *Notebook* have their terrible longueurs.

The poor reader wandering through Chang's office hell, accompanied by her banal observations ("how much I hate computers with their / gaudy square teeth that hurt people") and nagging wordplay ("Maybe the letter isn't from a lover the letter is a layoff letter / a lay-aside letter a lay-into letter"), her imaginative paralysis and convenient embrace of victim culture, begins to wonder if a modern version of Job might not have cut deeper. The boss of bosses, after all, isn't the snake in the garden but the Old Testament God.

VIJAY SESHADRI

Vijay Seshadri's aw-shucks demeanor and kindergarten metaphysics threaten to turn him into the John Ashbery app of the cell-phone age. *3 Sections*, his first book in almost a decade, comes upon its subjects seemingly by chance, and it serves them up with a big dollop of pretentious inanity.

> The mountain that remains when the universe is destroyed
> is not big and is not small.
> Big and small are
>
> comparative categories, and to what
> could the mountain that remains when the universe is destroyed
> be compared?

Pound said that poetry must be at least as well written as science fiction—well, he didn't, but I'm always a bit suspicious of a poem that would make a fanboy roll his eyes. (And even more suspicious of a poem fanboys would love.) Such lightweight philosophical musing is hard to do well, however easy it seems. "Thirteen Ways of Looking at a Blackbird" is the poem that launched a thousand shipwrecks.

Seshadri's poems have a hard time settling into a style. He has a talent for rhetorical densities unfashionable now ("I recognized the scowl on his face, / the retrospective, maskless rage of inception") and once or twice manages to make his linsey-woolsy prose darkly effective ("They lived in a boat upside down on the strand, / but he was of the kind who couldn't understand / that land was not just land / or ocean ocean"). Alas, too often his taste for confession comes with bragging rights attached:

> The real story of a life is the story of its humiliations.
> If I wrote that story now—
> radioactive to the end of time—
> people, I swear, your eyes would fall out, you couldn't peel
> the gloves fast enough
> from your hands scorched by the firestorms of that shame.

Exaggeration can be funny, except when you're not funny.

Seshadri's likes oddball ideas, and many are no worse than a Billy Collins idea: an updated vision of Paradise, a man who awakens on an autopsy table, a world in which every other person is you. They're decent notions, or decent enough; but there's too much sweat equity in the poems. You see the hard work that went into them, not the ease that should conceal the fabrication. It's curious that a poet so obviously sensitive to language writes as if he had just been introduced to a thesaurus ("The simulacra are marching everywhere, / and deep in the caves the chimeras are breathing") or had taken whatever drug academics take before they write their papers ("Unexpected useful combinations between cognitive psychology and neuroscience have fostered new observational protocols"). Some of the time he's kidding, but it's hard to tell the kidding from the bad writing—his irony is easy to mistake for incompetence.

I'm sure Lord Chesterfield would be delighted if the eighteenth century came back into fashion, but a poem that in a few lines goes from

How such a one, so circumstanced by parentage—
the mother crippled by disappointment; the father by rotgut and
    Percodan—
as to blight his prospects, and blacken with untimely frost the buds
of those ambitions justly excited
by manifest powers, graces, and propensities

to "in and out of juvy, jacking cars at fifteen, / snorting lines of Adderal,"
tries too hard for its tomfoolery. You could make a poem out of either
manner, perhaps—they're just pastiches—but it's hard to make one of
both. I know, I know, Seshadri is imitating Samuel Johnson (the poem
is "Life of Savage")—but that's not enough when so many poems sound
like bad translations, especially the translations from Urdu: "The very
cosmos is thwarted because / in none of the ways you could be mine are
you mine"; "How many of my glittering memories of the feast of love /
were warehoused in oblivion."

The publicity makes heavy weather (a "confounding of such expectations," a "deliberate challenge") out of the lack of sections in a book
called *3 Sections*, but it's hardly a mystery—there's a pile of poems, a great
tedious wodge of prose, then more poems. Lowell famously padded out
Life Studies with a disturbing memoir, but all Seshadri can offer is a
long-winded recollection of commercial fishing off Alaska more than
thirty years ago. He begins with a potted history of the seventies
("Large sections of society were experimenting. Cults multiplied, with
some bad consequences. Therapies multiplied. Flying saucers carried
people away") and ends with the sort of strained revelation that gives
"life writing" a bad name, quoting along the way the wisdom of Joni
Mitchell and Glen Campbell. There's no experience so dull he can't
make a duller lecture of it. His poems, addicted to the gaseous metaphysical, are reminiscent of Stevens—without the panache, the vocabulary, the metaphors, or the genius.

CLIVE JAMES

Clive James arrived in England half a century ago, part of a small Australian diaspora of artsy young intellectuals that included Germaine

Greer, Robert Hughes, and Bruce Beresford. London, no less then than in the first Elizabeth Age, offered many opportunities to the enfant terrible. Even a chancer like Shakespeare once muscled his way out of acting and into playwriting—upstart crow though he was called. The trade of artist and intellectual has always been more knockabout in Europe than in America, where a man who doesn't stick to his last threatens the country's Calvinist roots and Puritan stock. America is suspicious of the man who wears more than one hat.

Over the years James has been novelist, songwriter, literary critic, travel writer, translator of Dante, and British television's cheeky gadfly, hosting a chat show and fronting everything from pop music to Formula 1. If an American set out to create such a Frankenstein's monster, he'd have to use spare parts from Johnny Cash, David Letterman, Edmund Wilson, Dick Clark, John Updike, and perhaps Mario Andretti. James was such a dabbler, the most charming of growlers, that most people eventually forgot that he began as a writer of mock-heroic satirical verse. In the past decade, defiantly old and then defiantly ill with leukemia, he has returned to poetry.

Nefertiti in the Flak Tower is stuffed with lavish descriptions, contrived similes, and tortured metaphors, the lines usually cast in a garage mechanic's idea of iambic pentameter. All James's professional polish can't conceal the lifelessness at heart. Two lovers sit on a terrace in Taormina, Etna quietly erupting in the background:

> The spill of neon cream will cool,
> The crater waiting years for the next spark
> Of inspiration, since the only rule
>
> Governing history is that it goes on:
> There is no rhythm of events, they just
> Succeed each other. Soon, we will be gone,
> And that volcano, if and when it must,
>
> Will flood the slope with lip-gloss brought to boil
> For other lovers who come here to spend
> One last, late, slap-up week in sun-tan oil.

It's a symbol, reader! And not a bad one, either, for the mortality that eventually overwhelms all lovers. (Not bad for ejaculation, too.) James can't resist, however, the garish metaphors of "neon cream" and "lip-gloss" or the weird shifts in tone elsewhere, from "one romantic setting, am I right?" to "you, my star" in a heartbeat, from wide boy straight to Keats.

James has the curiosity of a polymath (he's his own *Wunderkammer* of oddments)—he'll write about typewriters, Rococo paintings at the Wallace Collection, reading Hakluyt on a plane, or about a wild array of figures from Subrius Falvus to Suu Kyi, from Samuel Johnson in King George III's library to Jean Arthur in *Shane*. He'll turn a review of his wife's edition of Dante's *Monarchia* into a sappy love poem. (The couple recently separated after the revelation that for most of a decade he'd been carrying on with an Australian model.) There are so many poems about his love life that he might fight Derek Walcott to a draw for the title of Most Priapic Modern Poet.

The poems leaning on anecdote have the best chance of escaping the afflictions of James's personality. He recalls the visitors who threw pennies at a shark in a Sydney aquarium, pennies that on occasion stuck and became at least in memory "flush or even countersunk like screws." His own complicity is a wrong he cannot redress:

> I tossed half-hearted pennies from the rail
> Suspecting that she might be sick of things,
> That shark, in slow pursuit of her own tail,
> Pock-marked with pictures of the British kings.

That's all that needs be said about empire. Other anecdotes, like one about the aged Whitman and a moth, offer similar possibilities; but too often the poet bullies them into submission until everything is *symbol, symbol, symbol*! James never met an insight he wasn't eager to repeat.

For all his television wit and autodidact authority, James suffers from two maladies difficult to overcome. One is a slightly coarse and peremptory imagination that never does a subject by halves when he can do it time and a half plus overtime. The other is what Thomas Pynchon once called Bad Ear, which in a poet makes every waltz a clog dance of prose:

> The guns sent up eight thousand shells a minute, some of them big enough to turn a whole B-17 into a falling junk-yard, but the mass concussion, spread through so much concrete, was just a rumbling tremble. In each tower at least ten thousand quaking people sheltered, their papers having proved them Aryan.

It's unfair to have removed the line breaks, but the reader would have to have Chopin's hearing to detect that this is iambic pentameter. To the poet the lines may resound with the sonorities of Yeats, but counting iambs on your fingers can't save prose from being prose.

James's similes often preen in their own artifice—didn't he even hesitate before writing that yellowfin tuna tear at a school of sardines "until it comes apart / Like Poland, with survivors in single figures"? A few metaphors manage to repay their ingenuity—a "lobster fortified with jutting eaves / Of glazed tile, like the castle at Nagoya" would have amused Pound—and here and there a passage suggests that, had the Muse given James a dash of reticence, the poems might have been different. A beauty queen lies on the beach:

> With a loving hand
> She strokes her thigh as one by one they fall,
>
> Those high walls in the water. Look at her,
> But shade your sad glance carefully, old man—
> For she will never see you as you were,
> A long way out, before the end began.

The waves for this Helen are perhaps the walls of Troy, but the stanza break slyly makes them her male conquests, too. Though the tone's too roguish and self-gratifying, the pathos in that final glance at mortality is as good as in a poet much better, Anthony Hecht, whose rueful ironies are more deeply laid and more cunningly felt. James, of course, can't let the girl be some local knockout—she has to be Miss Australia. He's too much where he should be too little and too little where he could be much more. James has a poetic sensibility the way a cobra has a soul.

There are worse things for poetry than a few gadflies, even if they produce poems as stilted as Beaux Arts architecture or Roman statuary. James is like someone's Dutch uncle, with an opinion about everything, an acquaintance with royalty, *Titanic*-sized self-confidence (the publisher's marketing flack wrote, presumably by mistake, that he's an "internally celebrated poet"), and the belief above all that he's a witty raconteur. In other words, a Polonius half the time hypnotic and the rest a total bore.

ANGE MLINKO

Ange Mlinko has gods on the brain. *Marvelous Things Overheard* has a cast list drawn from the Greek pantheon—they're still invading the modern world, still mystifying the hell out of ordinary things.

> Three ciabbatini for breakfast
> where demand for persnickety bread
> is small, hence its expense, hence my steadfast
> recalculation of my overhead,
>
> which soars, and as you might expect
> the ciabbatini stand in for my fantasy
> of myself in a sea-limned prospect,
> on a terrace, with a lemon tree . . .
>
> Not: Assessed a fee for rent sent a day late.
> Not: Fines accrued for a lost library book.

Poetry has always had its element of wish fulfillment. Though we can't know if Shakespeare identified with Hotspur and Hamlet, or Homer with Achilles and Hector, the idea isn't ridiculous—besides, every poet becomes the fiction of his own voice. Mlinko lingers on scenes of disrupted longing, the lines hurtling ahead, almost concealing their rhymes, the language so aware, even raw detail whispers of allegory—should that lost book remind us of the Library of Alexandria or the burnt scrolls in the Villa of the Papyri?

The poem ends in a vision of that "sea-limned prospect" such routine has denied her:

> I think of a great "rock-eating bird"
> grinding out a sandy beach,
> the foam said to be particulate matter
> of minute crustaceans, each
>
> brilliantly spooning up Aphrodite
> to Greek porticoes, and our potatoes,
> and plain living which might be
> shaken by infinitesimal tattoos.

The poet makes a lot of these figments of daily life (the influence of O'Hara is all too palpable), partly by remaining vulnerable to those forgotten gods—the old gods, due not even a whisper of faith. The tattoos might be tiny designs indited or clawed out in Tyrian purple, the dye the ancients derived from the snail they called the *murex*—but Mlinko is unlikely to have mistaken an arthropod for a crustacean. Those tattoos must be the faint beat of waves upon the shore. The "rock-eating bird" turns rock to sand, and the "particulate matter / of minute crustaceans" eventually forms limestone and at last marble, like the Pentelic marble long ago carved into Aphrodite on the frieze of the Parthenon.

Mlinko's ordinary hours hurtle downward into densely layered imagery—it's no surprise to find Aphrodite jostled by those potatoes and plain living. That's the very argument of the poem, reduced to a syntax wrenched to ambiguity between "spooning up . . . potatoes" and "I think of . . . our potatoes." Daily living is the drudgery, the grind—our lives are unlikely to be spooned into Greek sculpture, or be contemplated by the goddess of beauty. I can't think of another contemporary poet who inhabits metaphor so deeply, or so devilishly. (I'm sorry the poet felt it necessary to title the poem "The Grind"—there's also a hand mill and "life ground down to recurrence," in case we didn't get the point.)

At times these poems seem a throwback to that faddish motif of the fifties and sixties, in which Apollo and Aphrodite enjoyed a second coming, or Odysseus and Orpheus straggled back from the underworld. Mlinko may be the last survivor of some cult of Mithras, yet condemned like everyone else to chop carrots or wash dishes. The ancients knew a book called *Marvelous Things Heard* (*De mirabilibus auscultationibus*), a bunch of old wives' tales stuffed with nature lore, written by Pseudo-Aristotle but ascribed to the great man himself. (I'm not sure why Mlinko's note pretends otherwise.) It's a wry title for a book of poems not fooled by past or present but keeping one eye on each, just in case.

Mlinko's high-school crush on gods can be wearisome. An overlong poem beginning with an incident near the end of World War II straggles through Leto and Hera and Arcadia and the wandering island Asteria and much else—yet, in the final lines, we're given Apollo, Leto's son,

> a god
> in whose presence it is forbidden to cry.
> Did you know? Apollo! Arrester of tears.
> A god in whose presence it is impossible to grieve.
> Application of the tender to the elemental:
> my thumb stops the knife's turn through a carrot.
> A dog roughs his tongue lapping rain on cement.
> A callus rises. But words? Words are the reverse of pain.
> Where pain is, no words are. Apollo loves words.

The poet sees through the scrim of ordinary life to that thumb calloused until it can take the edge of the blade. The peripeteia of those last lines, like some formula out of first-order logic, looks simple until you try to solve it. Apollo, born of great pain, becomes the god of poetry. Words and grief are antithetical, like words and pain—this quietly rejects the idea that poetry can be wrought in throes of passion, recognizing the virtue of Wordsworth's "emotion recollected in tranquillity" and Dickinson's "After great pain, a formal feeling comes." "Where pain is, no words are"—but not, note, where words are, no pain is.

The endless hopscotching through worlds long estranged, the relish for *discordia concors*, the Audenesque love of *OED* words like *rhododactyl*,

disperpling, fundus, desquamate, penillions, parasangs, chatoyance, addorsed—
all these might have been mere affectation if the poet weren't so cheerfully enthusiastic. For such a knowing writer, Mlinko strikes notes of
charming naiveté, reminiscent of Marianne Moore—and there's a
Moore-ish poem on Lonesome George, the last Pinta Island tortoise.
Mlinko will try almost anything—a long poem, for instance, requiring
a glossary of Anglo-Saxon, that merges the traditions of Arabic literature and *Beowulf* while hinging on the use of *ana*, which means "alone"
in Old English and "I" in Arabic. Or a clutch of eight villanelles that, ravaging the repeating lines and suppressing rhyme, refashions the tired
form into something half conversation, half choral.

Some of Mlinko's wordplay is irritating—"putty, not putti," say, or
"cucucurrucued curriculum" (*cucucurrucú* is the Spanish for cock-a-
doodle-do or just the cooing of doves). Lost in the thickets of her own
inventions, she writes lines as knotted as "the grasses kept / rebearding
where hosanna-ing thalassas / massacred oysters to pure nacre"; but you
have to forgive the indulgence if you're going to be grateful for everything else. The meaning breaks through the archness: the grasses keep
growing and seeding, while the sea (Greek, *thalassa*) scours away at the
sands, reducing oyster shells to their mother of pearl (nacre). Those
incoming waves sound the hosannas of the Bible.

It's hard not to fall in love with a poet who can turn the lost colony of
Roanoke and the Dutch tulipomania bubble of the 1630s into forgotten
fairy tales. Or who can write, perhaps inspired by Rutger Hauer's death
scene in *Blade Runner*,

> If you'd seen
> the Gaillardots' mullein in the cedars of Al-Shouf;
> if you'd seen the Aleppo dock, russet with iron,
> in Bsharre where the Adonis River's said to run as red
>
> with what was
> thought his blood . . .

Even an excess of charm can't diminish the ravishing intelligence of this
fervent, loose-limbed, sprightly book.

Verse Chronicle: Civil Power

CHARLES WRIGHT

Charles Wright is an old, old hand now, still hammering out, as he has for decades, meditations on life, liberty, and the pursuit of angels. He doesn't deal in country wisdom—only wisdom countrified, the way every suburb south of Canada and north of Mexico has a bar with a roaring trade in cowboy hats and cowboy boots. At worst Wright's poems offer wisdom shtick that at the upper end competes with W. S. Merwin's free-floating ramblings and at the lower Mary Oliver's doggy pastoral:

> No darkness steps out of the woods,
>
> no angel appears.
> I listen, no word, I look, no thing.
> Eternity must be hiding back there, it's done so before.
>
> I can wait, or I can climb,
> Like Orpheus, through the slick organs of my body.

"Slick organs" is a wonderful touch that almost rescues the sentiment of the rest. Such musings never sound all that deep, and they're never as deep as they sound—the tone is rarely raised or lowered, the lines droning on like an electric substation.

Wright turns seventy-nine this year, and it's a pity that he's lost the capacity not just to surprise the reader but to surprise himself. How much you'd give for a little glee, or for the smack of rage! (Think of Pound's fury even into his eighties.) The anger that muscled into Wright's early poems is a dead memory now. He has pared away the rough-hewn past to live in the eternal present of these lovely, lazy, comprehending lines.

The older you get, and the more the end looms up, the more diction falls into valediction—it's not just that the end is ever closer but that thoughts of the past come with more regret. Wright's recent poems seem insulated from feeling, even when he's musing on mortality. The only thing he responds to is landscape, and he's borrowed from Pound the precisely cut description that lingers long after whatever provoked it.

> Like time, the meadow narrows
> up to its creek-scraped end.
> At sundown, trees light-tipped, mountains half-slipped into night.

He can do this sort of thing all day—limpid visions with a few dabs of paint that Constable or Crome would have adored; but a poem can't make background always the foreground (if it could, a poet like Walcott would be Milton). Wright fills the gaps with metaphysical putty.

This poet was once in thrall to Pound's patented rhythms as well as his landscapes. The rhythms have softened, but the language still lives for moments of splendor, moments when words seem more gorgeous than the world itself: toadstools that "glow in the twilight like rooted will-o'-the-wisps," or "honeysuckle in deep distress along the snow-slugged hedgerow," or "twilight papier-mâché in the crimped pine trees." (Wright loves his twilight, but he makes me love it, too.) He's also capable of such silliness you wonder if he's only half listening to himself: "Unless the late-evening armada of clouds / Spanished along the horizon are part of it" (the grammar is the least of the problems). Or, even worse, "The dog gets sick. The dog runs away. / You've got your mind on transubstantiation." Too many poems move from shadow to light or light to shadow as if he were a set dresser with one idea.

Wright has become a poet of extraordinary skill with nothing much to write about. With his rangy, Marlboro Man looks, he came from a Tennessee that never leaves you. He compensates by hard-peddling the verities:

> There is a heaviness inside the body
> that leans down, but does not touch us.
> There is a lassitude that licks itself, but brings no relief.

There is a self-destructiveness no memory can repeal.
Such breath in the unstopped ear,
>   such sweet breath, O, along the tongue.

Do you hear the catch in the throat or register the slight tremor of lip, things young actors learn in Emoting 101? The reference to a dog licking itself is cheerfully sly—I wish Wright were stealthy more often—but the allusion to "Hugh Selwyn Mauberly" only emphasizes the gulf between Pound and Wright, the difference between having emotion and converting it to retail rapture.

Wright has won nearly every prize a poet can—the Pulitzer and the National Book Award, the NBCC and the Bollingen—but American poets are too often rewarded for an aw-shucks vision of immensities, warmed-over Will Rogers with a dash of Barnum. A lot of Wright these days boils down to: (1) We're not here long, (2) We're all going to die, and (3) Angels, wow! The new poems barely have subjects, they're so sodden with theme and symbol, paralyzed meditations that vanish from memory almost as soon as you've read them. They're folksy in some of the good ways and all of the bad. When Wright stops the moony philosophizing for half-a-dozen lines, stops being the Leeuwenhoek of dailiness, I perk up again—but he never stops for long. In the rare stanzas written as if he means them, you remember how good he can be:

>   What's needed is something under the pond's skin,
> Something we can't see that controls all the things that we do see.
> Something long and slithery,
> >   something we can't begin to comprehend,
> A future we're all engendered for, sharp teeth, Lord, such sharp
> >   teeth.
> Heaven's eel.

Donne would have been jealous of that.

James Franco

It's good to have ambitions. James Franco is a charming, callow actor with a lopsided grin, specializing in jaded innocence and sleepy-eyed California soulfulness. His A-list parts—Harry Osborn in *Spider-Man*, Scott Smith in *Milk*, the wizard in *Oz the Great and Powerful*—all seem vague around the edges, characters with no there there. He has also played James Dean and Allen Ginsberg and Hart Crane, no mean feat when you don't have much personality or an ounce of charisma.

Almost a decade ago, Franco decided to return to school, and since then he has become a degree junkie. Having finished his BA at UCLA in record time, he entered various graduate programs, some of them simultaneously. I'm not sure even Franco can keep track. They include an MFA in film, at least three others in fiction or poetry, and a PhD in literature at Yale, not forgetting classes at the Rhode Island School of Design.

If *Directing Herbert White* is the result of too many MFA programs, poetry must be in trouble. A modestly intelligent young man ought to be able to write a few lines that aren't embarrassing, like any West Pointer a century and a half ago. With Franco, you get this:

Viewers are too used

To polished performances from which
The editor has taken away all the messiness.
Bring in

The seams when possible: a shot that goes
Out of focus, an actor stumbling on
A line.

This might earn a C+ in Introduction to Film, but adolescent insight and lumpish prose don't make the grade in free verse.

Franco writes like a man who has vaguely heard about poems and received some rude instruction from a passing stranger. He writes what he knows, and what he knows is acting. When composing their memoirs, most actors don't make the mistake of waxing eloquent on the art itself, because acting is a mystery even to them. If Franco is dull about his life, he's duller about acting—he runs through his approach to various roles ("I'm still surprised / By the response / To that character. / The secret there: / Minimalism"), which proves that, however shallow an actor seems on screen, he's always shallower in life. It's no surprise that he's been out-acted by a number of boulders and a ceiling or two.

If actors stick to anecdotes and have a flair for gossip, they do all right. For a famous actor who knows other famous actors, Franco is short on the goods. There's a hilarious moment when he's stalked through the Chateau Marmont by Lindsay Lohan in heat, but other-wise names are dropped like cinderblocks: John Belushi, Natalie Wood, Robert De Niro, Sean Penn, Sal Mineo, Sam Shepard, Catherine Deneuve, Monica Vitti, Brad Pitt—and, I'm tempted to say, a cast of thousands. There's a dreadful poem in the voice of River Phoenix ("It's me, River, calling you / From the underworld") and one even worse in the voice of Lohan:

> But that fame raped me.
> And I raped it, if you know what I'm saying.
> How many young things selling movies and wares
> And music and tabloids fucked the kind of men I fucked?

Movies and wares? The other poems are generally cast in the relentless me-me-me of late-stage narcissism. The book might better have been titled *James Franco*, written and directed by James Franco, based on the life of James Franco, and starring James Franco.

Like too many third-generation confessional poets, Franco assumes that tales of elementary school have Lowellesque depth:

> Mrs. D. was Mrs. Donnelly and I
> Know that means nothing to you
> But to me it is a round woman
> With a white bob and sharp nose
> Like poultry parts.
> And she was strict.

That's second grade—I was afraid it was his MFA at Columbia. "Poultry parts" would have tickled Flannery O'Connor, but the rest is as crude as a child's drawing taped to the fridge. Franco loves baroque writers like Ginsberg and Crane and Faulkner, but even plain speakers—Hemingway, for instance—must write as if a sentence were composed of gunpowder, freshly lit. If you want deep thoughts, Franco will give them to you:

> Life was like moving through something
> Thick and gray that had no purpose.
> And now I see that everything has had as much purpose
>
> As I give it, or at least it can all make its way
> Into my poem and become something else.

That might become the mission statement for the poetry-as-therapy movement.

There's an earnest sweetness, an abashedness, that steals into the poems now and again; but the poets who encouraged Franco have done him no favors. He writes, at best, in PR slogans and tabloid headlines: Brando "has the strength of all that America / Has to offer from its art, / He is the bull and the ballerina" and "The movie palaces were built with the bones of ten million actresses." The ludicrous similes ("My father's spirit was released, / As a green light releases an SUV") and witless wordplay ("Stabbed near his heart, / In the heart of Hollywood") are just an added attraction. A series of "sonnets" on classic films proves only that film criticism is beyond him, too.

Franco's great flaw as an actor is his ingratiating manner, which reads not as vulnerability but as tiresome neediness. He's best in roles that don't permit weakness—his ruthless Gator Bodine in *Homefront*, an otherwise undistinguished Jason Statham vehicle, was an excellent example of the tensions available to the actor cast against type.

Directing Herbert White comes with a clutch of fawning blurbs by poets who should know better—the poems are "fearless yet disarming," "distinctive and powerful," "brave and whip-like," while the author is a "contemporary Renaissance kind of guy." Better, "Franco knows it like Melville knows whaling." "It" is Hollywood. You feel sorry for the poets he studied with, the MFA programs that spawned him, his publisher, and, hell, poetry itself.

SPENCER REECE

When Spencer Reece published *The Clerk's Tale* a decade ago, his life seemed made for Hollywood. You could hear the elevator pitch. Miami mall salesman (Brooks Brothers suits) writes poetry on the down low. Discovered at Schwab's. Showered with awards. Who could star but Joaquin Phoenix? James Franco, alas, has already made the title poem into a short with Charles Dance; and, as luck would have it, he's a better director than actor. *The Road to Emmaus* is the sequel. Suit salesman turns priest. *Pretty Woman* (the Rodeo Drive scene, Bubbala!) meets *Seven Years in Tibet*! Boffo!

Reece is another late-generation confessional poet with a life that stumbles toward art. His poems are often straggling narratives, jury-rigged constructions slapped together out of scrap lumber and recycled nails. He has a deft sense of place, with landscapes that suddenly sharpen into focus.

> His was an Irish body,
> inherited from parents whose bodies were punished
> by the tin-colored rains around Croagh Patrick—
> no food and poverty, a relative said:
> "County Mayo is pretty all right, but you can't eat scenery."

This has the masochistic glamour of Heaney, who might have made clearer that the line means "they had no food and were poor" and likely would have thrown a comma after "pretty" so the phrase didn't become low-rent American slang. (Reece has a slipshod sense of punctuation that makes you wonder if his copy editor quit in a huff.)

The devotions here live through hints and whispers—you're never sure how much Reece is revealing. You learn a lot about the edges of the life—the dysfunctional family, the spate of early deaths, the grandfather who may have been a Jew—but the poet is as parsimonious with facts as a good press-secretary (and at any moment ready to walk back every statement he's made). The most striking poem in the book is a modern *Gilgamesh*. The title "Gilgamesh" is a mordant joke, since instead of epic battles and a quest for immortality we get Scrabble, and the gay community center, and a dog with a Xanax habit.

It's one thing to want to make an epic out of fragments, another for the reader to endure the tedious prosiness apparently required. Two men meet in midlife, one a decade older. They have a strained romance that eventually falls apart. The poem is self-consciously autobiographical, and like the cuneiform texts its parts don't entirely match up. As for the poem's notion that Gilgamesh and Enkidu were lovers, it's tough to crack the sexual codes of a culture four thousand years in the dust, and tougher when any translation must be speculation. More important than truth is the longing to find hope trapped in myth or religion, a mirror in myth to the facts of life, like a Christ who is a "childless, bachelor Jew, slightly feminine." This is no different, and a good deal more agreeable, than the centuries of art that turned a Nazarene into a Norwegian.

For a poet so modest, Reece suffers fevers of grandiosity. He defines himself by place; but the reader hardly needs fifteen pages that limp around Hartford (Wallace Stevens and the circus fire of 1944 make inevitable appearances), or seven on Miami, especially when the lines sink toward sludge:

> I have a dinner engagement in Coral Gables at Books & Books
> where I will see the poet Richard Blanco.
> I hope he will tell me stories of his beloved, broken Cuba.
> Nearly five o'clock now, and I am late.
> When I arrive, Richard Blanco speaks of Cuba
> as I had wished, and the city quiets all around him.

This is the Twitter feed of a life, and it's like Chinese water torture.

Reece is capable of all sorts of romantic gassiness. If a poet writes, "while the moon's neck wobbled on the Charles / like a giraffe's, or the ghost of a giraffe's neck," or "bees are sticky with tourism inside the motel rooms of the rose," or "the clock is a wheelchair disappearing down the corridor of time," you wish he'd never been introduced to metaphor.

Worse, when the poet finds a prisoner's expression "reminiscent of Sitting Bull after he won the Battle of Little Bighorn and had entered those rodeo shows with Wild Bill to tour Europe," you suspect the local fact-checkers have keeled over. Sitting Bull was a medicine man probably some distance from the thick of battle, not a Lakota war chief like Gall or Rain-in-the-Face. A decade later, he rode briefly in Buffalo Bill's Wild West but never toured Europe. That's Buffalo Bill's, not Wild Bill's—Bill Hickok never ran a pony show and was long dead by then.

The road to Emmaus is the road to grace, where two disciples met Christ after the crucifixion. This book is haunted by suffering, but the suffering often showcases the poet's humility as he walks among the poor and wretched ("two sisters had been left at a street corner on a sheet of cardboard; / their mother told them to wait, then never came back"). However moving such snapshots, the poems, though they stop short of pride, also stop short of epiphany.

Like Frederick Seidel, Reece's has a canny eye for fancy gear (Stubbs and Wootton slippers, Verdura eardrops), the corruption of morals, and the ridiculous excesses of the rich—as well as creatures of society too grotesque even for Proust. He reports seeing an aged baroness "inserting another biscotto behind her lips / which were puffed up and shaped not unlike luggage handles." Reece can write lines as winning as "the night cross-dressed into dawn," or "palm fronds shook as wildly as pornography," or, even better, "my grandmother resembled George Washington with lipstick." The forced austerity and soulful, plodding reportage elsewhere are in violent opposition to his gifts. This Lazarus was dead in a Miami mall until poetry woke him up.

LINDA BIERDS

Linda Bierds writes poems the way Cordon Bleu chefs make wedding cakes—you can hardly imagine a poem with more layers of icing or empty calories. Every poem is approached like a feat of engineering, and the results are hollow as puff pastry:

> Albrecht Dürer, first
> having purchased spectacles, shoes, and an ivory button,

rode a wheel-etched swath of longitude
from Antwerp toward Zeeland, where a whale—
one hundred fathoms long—pulsed on the dark sand.
First having purchased snuffers and furnace-brown,
and coated the pages of his silverpoint sketchbook,
where his scratch lines—like pears, or tarnish, or thought—
would gradually ripen, he circled Zeeland's seven shores,
past Goes and Wolfersdyk and *the sunken place*
where rooftops stood up from the water.

The whale shows up eventually. Note the delicate touch, just a fillip of
fashion, in that ivory button after the plainness of the spectacles and shoes
(no spectacle, those spectacles). Note too the alpha-to-omega journey
from Antwerp to Zeeland, the beautiful sealike verb "pulsed," the long
intoxicating clause (all straight lines) driving toward "he circled" (the sentence lives for its own complication), and not least the arcane texture of
the silverpoint sketchbook and "furnace-brown." The last is less mysterious than it seems—it's merely the translation of *Kesselbraun*, the plant
known as prickly glasswort, burned for the soda ash used by glassmak-
ers. (Dürer didn't pass by the town of Goes—he stayed long enough to
draw a girl in the local costume—and "seven shores" would have been
clearer as the "seven islands" of the original.)

A poet who can write a phrase as Pynchonesque as the "wheel-etched
swath of longitude," a metaphor more Byzantine the longer you unpack
it, has every right to be proud of her craft. Yet as the poem uncoils its
tightly wound springs of verbal felicity, something goes missing—the
result seems a mere jumble of watch parts, and all that facility falls a good
deal short of art.

The poems in *Roget's Illusion* are entranced by the famous dead. We
get Roget, that wordy master of words—and Dürer, Michael Faraday,
Virginia Woolf, Henry James, Darwin, Pasteur, most of them more than
once. There's scarcely an underachiever in the lot. These refugees from
art and science have much to say, and they go on and on saying it. The
whole strain of the persona poem perhaps comes from Shakespeare's
pitched monologues, if not Chaucer's tales—after hearing those, no wonder Browning spent his career giving his characters the business and

letting them spout that business at preposterous length. Pound in his apprenticeship loved dramatic masks (his short poems were collected in *Personae*), and in recent decades Richard Howard has shown how sly and corrosive the persona can still be.

Bierds's period pieces, with or without personae, are showy without much to show. It's one thing to pay homage to the dead, another to decide how to populate our private cemetery of great dinner guests. I'm happier spending time with Faraday than with Virginia Woolf, but our taste for the dead tells us little about them and much about ourselves. Bierds has such fun with her minor invented worlds, having done the library research necessary to the consequence (for Dürer she used his journal, its accounting so meticulous a CPA would swoon), that she forgets to give them much purpose. Fabergé eggs had a purpose, but one so frivolous it's best while admiring the craftsmanship not to consider that they were made to distract rich people so privileged that eventually they were forced to pay in blood.

> Before lanterns
> re-cast human hands, or a dye-drop
> of beetle first fluttered across
> a flicker book of papyrus leaves,
> someone sketched a creature along the contours
> of a cave, its stippled, monochromatic shape
> tracing the vaults and hollows,
> shivers of flank and shoulder
> already drawing absence nearer,
> as torchlight set the motion
> and shadow set the rest.

The views are as gorgeous as a coffee-table book, and meant to be; but it's easy to overlook the shrewd gestures concealed in phrases like "drawing absence nearer"—and I'm tempted by the flicker of foreshadowing in the shadows, as it were. The torchlight is man, in whose presence extinction looms for those beasts painted on cave walls. I like these moments in Bierds, but there aren't nearly enough of them. (I have my doubts about the ancient papyrus flicker-book, but no doubt she's joking.) It's curious that a style with so much to offer the surface seems so played out, as if all its force had gone into good looks, leaving nothing for animation beneath.

Such poems, in love with their own beauty, could be spun out endlessly, because they have no place to go. When they make a turn, often about three lines from the end, it's just a tired flourish to bring matters to a close. Preciousness has a double burden—beyond the empty beauty of the extraordinary, there's no room for the pathos of the ordinary.

GEOFFREY HILL

Volumes of collected poems are rarely large enough, when dropped from a height, to destroy a small city or at least a herd of cows. (Our language has long forgotten the explosive origins of "blockbuster" as well as "bikini.") Had Geoffrey Hill stopped writing at fifty, he would have left a handful of thin books from *For the Unfallen* (1959) to *The Mystery of the Charity of Charles Péguy* (1983), less than two hundred pages of muscular, jostling phrases that make him the major English poet since Auden. In the three decades since, he has written five times as much, a late flowering—or, as he might say, anthesis, not antithesis. *Broken Hierarchies: Poems, 1952–2012* will stop many a door.

Hill's recent work forms what he calls *The Daybooks*, half-a-dozen sequences here wittily preceded by "epigraphs and colophons," though they feel more like outtakes and in-jokes—or just fragments that didn't fit. Each of the daybooks (half of them unpublished until now) finds its form—ABBA or ABAB quatrains, long stanzas of dizzyingly intricate rhyme—and packs in the rough matter of Hill's musing. Those familiar with the poet's recent efflorescence will know what to expect: the crabbed, ludic shorthand, like telegraph messages across damaged wire; the bodybuilder's steroidal posing; gestures toward meaning like clues to an unsolvable acrostic; and sudden passages of achieved beauty and clarity.

The seraphs chime their wings of florid stance.
Things are as strange as need be, never rise

Up from this blur and cleave of centuries;
Grace condescending to things framed in chance.

Humility can afford the brutal
Splendiferousness of those Medici tombs.
Let the brain empty its own catacombs.
For love only one might hazard souls immortal.

There is the nod to a faith that has demanded Hill's doubt (his wife, a converted Jew, is an Anglican priest), there the long tumble of centuries, the glories of art sometimes commissioned by scoundrels and murderers, and the quiet rust and peril of love.

At the cost of mild labor, it's on occasion possible to take the measure of Hill (which is close to the verse taking measure of you), all that hard-won thought, rattling around like marbles in a coffee can, made lucid by a phrase. As in his early poems, Hill often finds his charities—as Pound did—in snapshots of landscape, rarely more than a line or two: "Fresh snow crimples the ground / with thin wires of frail sound," "wet coal and gritstone setts, / Spackled and wintry with hoary moonspill," or

Across fields where the rye's been whirried down
The horizon's rim stands threatening, abrupt,
Streaked with red as a reaper's skin's raw-striped,
Such consanguinity impels the dawn.

These moments where the muck of thinking is cleared, where landscape offers a distracted purity or at least a realm nearly free of bafflement, have become increasingly rare. Hill seems drawn willy-nilly to such visions yet repelled by what they might signify. They stand in opposition—again, as often in Pound—to the gabble of high talk and the phrases crying out for footnotes:

Gone from radar claim it by what you know.
Little blame to show how brand leader outshone.
Grand time for imagination only.

Nation-image draped fondly for certain bidder.
Gravely display—pull curtain—marge ration,
Dives-bar-Lazar bravely having it away.
Fix lame propeller for game gospeller;
powered by new buzzword bearings run hot.

A reader can make a few test borings in such a passage, but without more context even the Hill acolyte might be tempted to call it quits. It's not certain what has vanished from radar (are we mired in the real or the figurative?) or where exactly the little blame falls. There's something about England's lost glory, the kowtowing of nation to capital, heritage sold off cheap. That margarine ration, which ended only in 1955, is within reach, part of the legend of British grit; but "Dives-bar-Lazar" defeats me. (In the parable from Luke 16, *dives* meant rich man and the leper was named Lazarus, so this might mean Dives, son of Lazarus—but to what end?) And "Fix lame propeller for game gospeller"? Acrostics, once more. By the time a few lines later Hill gets to "Steer enclichéd pierrot towards peer riot," even the CIA would be puzzled.

I have searched in vain upon my shelves for that famously rare book, *The Wit of Geoffrey Hill*, yet there are moments enough to remind us how droll the old dog can be, even if the jokes smell of the lamp (as was said of Demosthenes, to whom Hill bears more than slight resemblance). We have "Hypocrisies bertbrechted and kurtweillt" and "Jacob wrestling with the angel one thing; / With a ladder another." These are scholar's jokes, to be sure. Is his copyright citation for the King James Version a quiet joke or just one of many examples of over-nicety?

Hill has long taken pleasure in obscurity, but there comes a moment when obscurity bears too harshly upon the reader. Much of the poet's later work would benefit from a council of scholars, or just a dedicated wiki. Hill has admitted a disgust at being understood, or at least being understood too effortlessly. Modernist poetry often took that path, a path close to what the avant-garde has taken ever since. The good reasons—the liberties intricate wordplay allows, the disdain for readers who want poetry to yield slobber and tears—are sometimes overwhelmed by the bad: the willfulness, the contrivance, the narcissism.

Michael Ventris needed far less labor deciphering Linear B—at least he knew that cities were probably mentioned, and kings, and that the main point of the script was to convey meaning across distance. Hill's late poems are so often unforgiving, few readers will pass muster—and perhaps those few will soon quarrel among themselves and form violent sects. Art speaks only to art at the risk of becoming a closed circuit, sealed off from whatever pushed the original out of the roil—the shadowy eye, the languor of meditation, desire.

These new sequences are inflections of age, with all the regret and manner of age. The mists of childhood rise up, each daybook possessing a company of scolding, untempered ghosts as tutelary spirits—Machiavelli, Donatello, William Lawes, Nye Bevin. The nearly incomprehensible out-weighs the nearly comprehensible like a bucket of lead a bucket of feathers. Hill has pursued, with cunning and ham-fisted garrulity, the maverick strain in himself. Yet the early poems remain ravishing, fraught and stunned by language, the result of a wrestling with speech few modern poets have managed. Young poets are now so intent on telling everything and saying nothing, on a brand that never burns, that they write in meager prose, all for show.

A *Collected Poems* allows the poet to look back, sometimes at a younger self now a stranger. If the early books are most likely to keep Hill's reputation intact, scattered among the later a few have the mark of wintry flourish: *Canaan* (1996), *The Triumph of Love* (1998), and *A Treatise of Civil Power* (2007). The last was thoroughly reworked after its first appearance from a private press, and throughout the collected poems Hill has not stayed his hand when it comes to revision—more than one poem has been deep-sixed, and many lines have received the flicker of second thought, usually for the better. The poet has expanded *Hymns to Our Lady of Chartres* and *Pindarics*. This elephantine book is testimony to a career newly ungoverned, newly confounding, occasionally magnificent.

Seven Types of Ambivalence: On Donald Justice

Si je mets bleues après pierres, c'est que bleues
est le mot juste, croyez-moi.
—Gustave Flaubert

We commonly use the word *aesthetics* in two ways knotted like snakes on a Celtic ornament. It's helpful to unpick that snarl at the start. When we speak of a poet's aesthetics (such aesthetics as he has, I'm tempted to say), we mean the program or philosophy to which he's declared allegiance (Vorticism, perhaps, or LANGUAGE poetry), else the little sum of twitches and habits that go into the writing of poems. These get tangled when, as is often the case, a poet's leanings or fancies become the tenets of a manifesto. Pound's "A Few Don'ts by an Imagiste" responded to some hint of private preference toward which he had long been tending. A manifesto does not have to be published or nailed to a door. There have been movements enough—the Movement, Confessional Poetry, the Cockney School—where some critic christened a group by noticing affiliations unrecognized by the poets themselves.

I make the distinction because Donald Justice was never a joiner, never entered a school or founded one. There was a principled reserve, but also a reserve according to inclination. Most art, good or great, is selfish—that is, made for the artist alone. As soon as you lead a movement other artists can join, you're engaged in the will to power. That doesn't mean the loner is necessarily uncompetitive. Art is not just selfish but sovereign in creation (and therefore, to the degree it does not recognize the past, narcissistic), even if the art itself is generous, even if the artist himself is generous.

That generosity includes, but is not limited to, the training of other artists different in character. Though it is not the subject here, when the history of poetry in the last century comes to be written, the two teachers of greatest influence may be Donald Justice and Richard Howard. Yvor Winters, John Crowe Ransom, Robert Lowell, and many another were teachers of great virtue; but the intelligence of far more poets was formed and structured in the workshops of Justice and Howard, both of whom had long careers in large writing programs. I mention this only as far as it bears on aesthetics, because the peculiar thing about good teachers is how varied, even how opposed and antithetical, their students become. Not unaffected, of course—Howard's students sometimes favor monologues and alliteration, and Lowell's often wrote appalling imitations of *Life Studies*—but the best students have drawn something beyond the surface features of a taste, have drawn some bearing toward language itself.

My consideration of Donald Justice's aesthetics is partly affected, even circumscribed, by my memory of him as a teacher. He parried his way into a poem, fending off false meanings where he could and calling attention to them when he couldn't. He inched toward meaning by niggling shrugs—I'm reminded of that phrase Eliot lifted from Webster for an epigraph, "two religious caterpillars." Justice was a religious caterpillar; and the formula or rite by which he explored his observations, even his objections, was forensic: "On the one hand," he'd say. Then, reconsidering, "On the other hand." At last, if you were lucky, he'd add, "But on the other hand." Each reading had its point, and the impaction and scatter—even reversal—of readings their point as well.

This fine discrimination and rueful suspension of judgment were, I think, characteristics deeply veined in the poetry. His poems seemed written line by line, their means in view but not their end, and toward the satisfaction of the line rather than the intention or design of the whole—yet, in the end, the design had a whole. Until each line had had its say, the poems often withheld their meaning. Justice was never an obscure poet, though I'd like to say that obscurely; but his gorgeous plainness, not always plain, was never entirely revealing and may be considered a form of discretion.

In "On the Porch," from the sequence "My South," the theme is the passage of time, but the subject, perhaps, the passing of the Old South.

There used to be a way the sunlight caught
The cocoons of caterpillars in the pecans.

A boy's shadow would lengthen to a man's
Across the yard then, slowly. And if you thought
Some sleepy god had dreamed it all up—well,
There stood my grandfather, Lincoln-tall and solemn,
Tapping his pipe out on a white-flaked column,
Carefully, carefully, as though it were his job.
(And we would watch the pipe-stars as they fell.)
As for the quiet, the same train always broke it.
Then the great silver watch rose from his pocket
For us to check the hour, the dark fob
Dangling the watch between us like a moon.
It would be evening soon then, very soon.

Justice was born in Georgia in 1925, when many Civil War veterans were
still alive; his grandfather had been born at the outbreak of the war. The
dreamlike cast of the land, as if the caterpillars and pecans and white-
flaked column were eternal as sunlight, is a stasis slowly, gradually,
being lost. From the small boy's view ("And if you thought / Some
sleepy god had dreamed it all up—well, / There stood my grandfather,
Lincoln-tall and solemn"), the grandfather must seem immensely old, old
as a god. When the train passes in the distance, he may simply be a man
who every afternoon checks his watch against the train (or the train
against his watch, depending on which he trusts, if either—habit may
always be empty) or a god making sure his whole creation is running on
time. Or seeing, perhaps, if time has stopped.

The association with Lincoln goes beyond height to the depth of a
vanished age, an age not just when gods were tall but when great men
seemed gods. Mention of the man who presided over the destruction of
the Old South may suggest that the manners of the South were changing (though not, when Justice was a boy, the ancestral racism). The line
may mean only that the defeated Confederacy had at least one rival for
Honest Abe's magnificent bearing. Readers can go too far down that
path—it's unlikely that the falling pipe-stars, the glowing embers, are an
allusion to the Night the Stars Fell, the great Leonid meteor shower of
1833, which survived more than a century in the memory of slaves and
their descendants. Perhaps in that white-flaked column, though, there's

some trace recollection of the poverty of the postbellum South—but perhaps, only perhaps. The South always had hardscrabble farmers.

All that is fairly straightforward, but look how Justice has prepared the end as far back as the third line ("A boy's shadow would lengthen to a man's / Across the yard then, slowly"). Does the boy see his shadow in boyish pleasure, or with some dawning apprehension of the movements of Earth and Sun? The reader can't parse such a line until the poem has run its course; only then can he look back and see not only the small signs of decay and vastation (the caterpillars, the flaking column) but the foreshadowed future where the boy's shadow will *be* that of a man and, at last, perhaps, of a man as old as his grandfather. This mortal contingency within a poem that looks fondly back to childhood is darkened further at the end ("It would be evening soon then, very soon"). The boy himself will die—soon, very soon, by the measure of seasons, however slowly the watch ticks out a life. Notice, as a grace note, how the watch rises like a moon from the grandfather's pocket.

No matter how beautifully and carefully rendered the description, you learn very little about Justice in Justice, though you learn a great deal about the manners of language. "On the Porch," for instance, probably recalls one of the summers Justice visited his grandparents in southern Georgia. Many poets write in a kind of sentimentality or fugue of form— they love the forms more than what form contains. In Justice you feel the form's identity as vehicle or medium, but the content fits the form without much overflowing. (This may be less a vice than a transforming virtue.) There's nothing in the verse loud or declamatory (if anything, you wish that sometimes Justice would overreach); but there remains what is otherwise difficult to obtain, an exactness of expression and purchase that takes the part for the part and the whole for the whole—in sum, a kind of antisynecdoche.

Justice's strongest, most architectural work was not accomplished until late, only after he had wrestled through a number of styles and at last stopped resisting the subject always before him—his complicated, driving relation to memory, the memory he may always have feared would sink into nostalgia. The language grew richer and more implicating after *Departures* (1973), offering much greater range for the forms of ambivalence. His early books were tentative, half-grown, curious, but never quite his—reviewers sometimes sensed the poet's failure to commit himself to the terms of the work but could not see how firm the sense of purpose, how tortured the ambition beneath. Indeed, Justice spent much imagination on surface, as if to deny the depths he could not yet embody.

It is in his exactness, his casting among alternatives for the most suggestive, the most philosophically or psychologically balanced (weighing possibilities for their moral as well as aesthetic densities), for the purest and most moderate of words that Justice defined and defended a middle style for American verse. Such a style was drawn, like hot wire, from two artists of antithetical densities—Wallace Stevens for the aesthetic, the superfluous, the ornamental, the woolly and philosophical, and William Carlos Williams for the domestic, the demotic and humdrum, no ideas but in things, things, things. Without this tension, an artist like Justice might have been held back by his delicacy, his modesty, his withdrawal; but instead the terms of his personality as an artist (the personality of the man may be different, just as his impersonality may be different) were engaged by the exactness required and the alternatives judged. This might have ended simply, if such things are ever simple, in the fetish of the Flaubertian mot juste.

The mot juste is sometimes strangely mistaken for the bon mot, a word that ends words, a snide remark by Oscar Wilde, the showstopper that poets of a gaudier tendency than Justice employ. What Flaubert meant, in the lesson of his style, is a word that fulfills its labor as no other word could have done, not a word that calls attention to itself (either by its triumph or in its latency)—rather, a word content to let the sentence move toward its undefined and unforeseen end, taking modest satisfaction in its contribution. Such words must possess, must embody, a complex tension in their origin suppressed in the moment of action. Words, like poems, mean not because but in spite of their ambivalence—that is, both in their local actions and in their action at a distance. The tremor of their meanings must be felt as we pass through them—their valences facing two ways, like Janus, Roman god of doorways. Within such ambivalence, invited into the origin if suppressed in the action, I would isolate the chief characteristic of Justice's style.

What are the manners and contradictions, then, of this instability, these gathered tensions that might be called an aesthetics of ambivalence?

(1) That the poetry make no apology for addressing the literate, that it revel or roil in allusion, figures of speech, the modernist digestion of foreign and classical poetry (if not to the extent of Pound or Eliot), the desires and delights of form while employing a voice indirect, guarded, more or less plainspoken—if not homespun, certainly never tailored or bespoke. However much the art lies in the knowledge, the referential frame, of such poems, the only artifice is at times the seeming lack of artifice. Consider a poem that begins with a statue, or a man no longer one.

A Man of 1794

And like a discarded statue, propped up in a cart,
He is borne along toward the page allotted to him in history.

To open his heavy-lidded eyes now would be merely
To familiarize himself with the banal and destined route.

He is aware of the mockery of the streets,
But does not understand it. It hardly occurs to him

That what they fear is that he might yet address them
And call them back to their inflamed duty.

But this he cannot do; the broken jaw prevents speech.
Today he will not accuse the accusers; it is perhaps all that saves
    them.

Meanwhile his head rocks back and forth loosely on his chest
With each new jolt and lurch of the endless-seeming street:

Impossible to resist this idiot shaking.
—But it is hard after all to sympathize

With a man formerly so immaculate,
Who, after a single night of ambiguous confinement,

Lets go all pride of appearance. Nevertheless,
Under the soiled jabot, beneath the stained blue coat,

Are the principles nothing has shaken. Rousseau was right,
Of that he is still convinced: *Man is naturally good!*

And in the moment before the blade eases his pain
He thinks perhaps of his dog or of the woods at Choissy,

Some thought in any case of a perfectly trivial nature,
As though already he were possessed of a sweet, indefinite leisure.

The language of the beginning is almost prosaic—everyday language, more or less, suited to the everyday event. The simplicity ignores where the cart is heading—and even the alert reader may at first miss the real destination, since the poem is mildly, resistantly titled "A Man of 1794." The poem has identified the when, not the where; if the reader is no student of history, the date and the "soiled jabot" will do nothing. Only much later have further clues been dropped like scraps of worthless assignats: the man is a speaker of note, has suffered a broken jaw, has accusers, and though once immaculate has abandoned "all pride of appearance." The "idiot shaking" ("With each new jolt and lurch of the endless-seeming street: // Impossible to resist this idiot shaking") is the cart's, not the man's; yet his shaking might be read by onlookers as fear. The narrator in these lines disappears into the victim.

Even given all that, given even the passing reference to Rousseau, a reader might be surprised, three lines from the end, when "in the moment before the blade eases his pain / He thinks perhaps of his dog or of the woods at Choissy." The reader might imagine that blade as a surgeon's blade—which in a dry way it is, for this is revolutionary France, and the man is Robespierre on his way to the guillotine. A reader without the benefit of reading might miss how much the poem perhaps owes, how two or three times it seems to tip its hat to, Auden's "Musée des Beaux Arts." The great man is at last just a man thinking of his dog. Justice might have made high-flown drama here, but as so often he plays in a minor key. That key gives more scope to irony.

"Appearance" is an ambivalent word. Drawn deep into the word, ambivalence is not, not just, ambiguity (a shudder in the meaning) but also a shudder in the aim and condition of feeling, the writer's toward the word, even the poem's toward the word. This is a speaker used to appearing, now about to disappear—and part of the poet's ambivalence is his wish not to have a stake in feeling, not to express any disillusion about a man merciless during the Terror he helped create.

The suspension of resolution, that wish to leave the reader in a state of unknowing as long as possible rather than giving him genial—or blaring—updates along the way, is what makes art of the rubbish of the past. Though the borrowing is from that magnificent artist, History itself, Justice makes each turn of the cartwheel nothing but ordinary until we realize that the business is the ordinary business of death. Ah, and isn't Death that renowned physician, that sweet easer of pain, that charitable dispenser of analgesics?

At the end, before the blade falls, the man has "Some thought in any case of a perfectly trivial nature, / As though already he were possessed of a sweet, indefinite leisure." "Indefinite" does furtive work here, indefinite because no man knows how long in retirement his lease will run—and isn't the grave also a place of indefinite leisure, whatever his religious belief? "Trivial," however, is the ambivalent word, the poet's judgment on a thought he has no access or right to—or is "trivial" Robespierre's own judgment?

The wretchedness of life may be made bearable through mild irony—and yet that fallen condition, that death shortly to arrive on the falling blade, has been there from the start, evident and yet concealed by the opening line, for the cart is a tumbrel. What does history make of discarded heroes but discarded statues? The language has little interest in something as emollient as style—if there is a whisper of the literary, it lies in the borrowing as well as in the syntax winding through the "mockery of the streets." (But is he mocked by the gathered crowds or by the very streets of his own Paris?) The lines seem like free verse; but there is a rough, reliable accentual meter—between four and seven accents per line, between ten and nineteen syllables, never lapsing into prose, because entirely funded by iambs and anapests. That is the indefinite leisure of the form trundling along the path to the Place de la Revolution (now the Place de la Concorde). The tension rises from the very capture of the colloquial, the literary colloquial, in the hard service of fate.

(2) That the poetry at times be about poetry—and may speak to the reader, may lament the failure of earlier poems or the lost favors of the muse. The poet may even title a poem about a poem—what else?— "Poem," but one written in such a deliberate craftsman's way, with the delicacies and pleasures of a task well done, that the idea of the mot juste is refracted by the lens of the artist's quiet, absorbed pleasure. Thus an art about art never seems an art for the sake of art.

Justice's use of other poets was as much provocation as imitation or homage. In his essay "Tradition and an Individual Talent," Dana Gioia calculates that more than a quarter of Justice's poems subsist on literary borrowing, which should remind us again how close the poet lived to the precepts of the moderns. Like many of his generation, Justice was a modernist decades after the event; but he continued into a time when that became radically retrograde.

Recall a section from the sequence "American Scenes (1904–1905)," which draws on Henry James's sadly tinged return to the country of his youth, his half-forgotten and largely still unseen America. Justice's sequence consists of three sections of paired quatrains, followed by a sonnet. These quatrains seem little fragments of James's thought as he made the rounds of Cambridge, where his brother William lived, then turned south for the journey that forms the end of his melancholy memoir *The American Scene* (1907). They seem fragments because they are taken partly from James's own words.

ST. MICHAEL'S CEMETERY, CHARLESTON

One may depend on these **old cemeteries**
To say the one **charmed** thing there is **to say—**
So here the **silvery seaward outlook** carries
Hints of some other world beyond the bay.

The **sun-warmed tombs, the flowers**. Each faraway
Game-haunted inlet and reed-smothered isle
Speaks of lost **Venices**; and **the South** meanwhile
Has only **to be tragic to beguile**.

Justice inhabits the novelist here by borrowing phrases (in bold) from James's mild contents and deeper discontents:

> In the **old Cemetery** by the lagoon, . . . this influence distils an irresistible poetry—as one has courage **to say** even in remembering how . . . almost anywhere on the American scene, the general place of interment is apt to be invited to testify for the presence of **charm**. The golden afternoon, the low, **silvery, seaward** horizon, as of wide, sleepy, **game-haunted inlets and reed-smothered** banks, possible site of some **Venice** that had never mustered. . . . To what height did he rise . . . at no great distance from this point, and where the **silvery seaward outlook** still prevails. . . . [**T**]**he South** is in the predicament of **having to be tragic** . . . in order **to beguile**. . . . [I]n the sweet old church-yard ancient authority seemed . . . to sit, among the **sun-warmed tombs** and the inter-related slabs and **the** extravagant **flowers**.

By sly adjustments and distortions the poet has taken the novelist in a different direction. The old cemeteries in the poem have something to say, like the aged warriors along the wall of Troy—but the "old Cemetery" remains silent in *The American Scene*, though "apt to be invited to testify." "To say" therefore rests on a hinge of ambivalence, not just a borrowing, but a conversion and creative mutation.

That other world beyond the bay (Justice's notion, not James's) suggests both what the South once was and what it had never been. We're not told what that charmed thing is that the cemeteries, with their burden of lost hopes, will say (they sound very much like antediluvian Southern belles); but Justice's inlet and isle "speak of lost Venices"—that is, a glamour that once gone can never be revived and that in ruin draws a traveler with the Romantic disposition for lost things, like Byron roaming the weedy ground of the Forum. That other world, that sleepy Paradise, is now unreachable. Perhaps it lies across a Southern Lethe in the dominion of death.

James does not go so far. For him that Venice of the South never existed, was never mustered or muttered into existence; but for a Southerner there's an inescapable feeling of something lost and little gained in its stead. ("Game-haunted . . . and reed-smothered" sounds the postbellum dream of the antebellum.) For James, the South is forced to be tragic to beguile; for Justice, like Bernhardt in *Camille*, the South chooses to be. That's the mythic world of the Agrarians, on whom Justice did his master's thesis. He sees what the South never was, what some refused to believe it was not. James's words have quietly been maneuvered, or outmaneuvered, to different purpose.

Justice has concealed nothing—an afternote says "after Henry James"—but he has not only used James's worn clothing but tried on the novelist's impressions over his own, finding through them access to his own ambivalence toward the South. (One of the epigraphs to "My South" is the doomed Quentin Compson's "I dont! I dont hate it! I dont hate it!" from *Absalom, Absalom!*) The penetration into the heart of Justice lies through the mind of James, and just that feeling acquired secondhand secures for the poet the necessary distance from his own mixed feelings.

(3) That poems drenched in the very inadequacies of their art often seem, by analogy, poems about the intermissions and intrusions of the poet's life. Justice never wrote in that mode we call confessional. As a poet, his most naked emotions were masked or concealed in the character of his art. His most affecting (indeed, until he was old his only) love poem was "Ode to a Dressmaker's Dummy."

To take a small example, the incidents in "On the Porch" might have come the summer Justice turned ten, when he was diagnosed with osteomyelitis, a bone infection often fatal before the widespread availability of antibiotics, still a decade in the future. It's not a necessary reading, because the poem reveals nothing about the year, though it probably lies in the thirties. The theme of the poem, the shadow on the shadow of life, would fit a boy already ill with a disease perhaps shortly to be diagnosed—yet the poem exists free of the fact, if fact it is. Curiously, in matters of taste and judgment, Justice was rarely ambivalent. He had strong preferences and delighted in making them known.

(4) That the poems most revealingly and nakedly emotional often be based on translations, as if only in words that begin in the words of others can the concealment of emotion be abandoned. That consolation begins in disguise, that to be unmasked you must have masks to begin with. (The most personal and mortal of Justice's poems is "Variations on a Text

by Vallejo.") If this tension is lodged within Eliot's notion of impersonality, the result haunts the poems, as it does *The Waste Land*, by seeming everywhere permeated by personality, with hardly a shred of the life in sight. You can read a lot of Justice without learning a thing about the consequences or conditions of his life and end by knowing that such facts would have taken you not deeper but further away.

(5) That many of Justice's later poems fix fondly on memories of childhood, but a childhood that seems to deny nostalgia its sentimental character, reminding us that "nostalgia" was first used of Swiss mercenaries who had fallen ill with the sometimes fatal condition known as homesickness. Justice's nearly stoic use of nostalgia finds no consolation, not because it is beyond consolation but because it takes consolation in the mere partiality of the past. It is typical of his ambivalence, of his character of seeing as well as saying, that Justice could say, at a reading in his hometown of Miami, "I miss Miami when I'm away," and then, after a pause, "and I miss Miami when I'm here."

(6) That the poetry remain divided in its loyalties to free verse and form, as if within that division a higher loyalty was implied, a loyalty to what suited the subject, the tone, the instance of conception (because the reader should never discount whim)—loyal to form, then, but with the possibility of accepting, even worshiping, chance and contingency. Such a poet could not have undertaken a sequence of a hundred and fifty sonnets or an epic poem, because his fundamental relation to his art was not obsessive. He knew when to let go. (The reader must be aware, to adapt a remark by Jarrell, that a poet who doesn't go too far may not go far enough.)

These loyalties divided even further, so that despite Justice's belief that one of the pleasures of form lay in obeying the rules, he did not hesitate to disrupt form when it suited him, or when what suited him suited the poem even better. The collusive refrains in his villanelles perhaps answer a need deep in this artistic psyche—yet what poet has written a villanelle truncated like "Women in Love" or jury-rigged and artfully demolished like "Variations for Two Pianos"? Justice loved the form well enough to spoil it when necessary—or for pure delight, or when he thought he could get away with it. Think of the, to my ear, metrically corrupt third line in "On the Porch."

One of the nuances of an artist is his devilishness. Consider "Mrs. Snow":

> Busts of the great composers glimmered in niches,
> Pale stars. Poor Mrs. Snow, who could forget her,
> Calling the time out in that hushed falsetto?
> (How early we begin to grasp what kitsch is!)
> But when she loomed above us like an alp,
> We little towns below could feel her shadow.
> Somehow her nods of approval seemed to matter
> More than the stray flakes drifting from her scalp.
> Her etchings of ruins, her mass-production Mings
> Were our first culture: she put us in awe of things.
> And once, with her help, I composed a waltz,
> Too innocent to be completely false,
> Perhaps, but full of marvelous clichés.
> She beamed and softened then.
>   Ah, those were the days.

Note the small craft, or craftiness, in the rare cross-rhymes between the octet's quatrains (*her* / *matter, falsetto* / *shadow*). The sestet is unusually a series of three couplets. That is very untraditional for so traditional a sonnet. The meter always hits the mark, but the rhyme scheme is delightfully awry, as the schemes of the Romantics sometimes were—think of Shelley's "Ozymandias." It might be too much to suggest that the contrivance is not unlike Mrs. Snow's plummy self-satisfaction. How ludicrous she is—and yet the rhyme is not what makes her so. At the least, such deviations and violations (almost brazenly concealed by the slant rhymes) call attention in their cautious bravura to the poet's controlling ambition, to make the form his own even in the sacrifice of form.

There are smaller matters that show the poet's delight in deviance. Justice avoids the self-conscious, rather Hudibrastic or Byronic feminine rhyme, except when there is something unusual to be gained. (In other words, it is not a sin committed merely for the hell of it.) The rhyme *niches* / *kitsch is* remains part of that mild and almost apologetic condescension of which his memory is composed. The poet knows the risk he takes employing feminine rhymes, but that seems just to make him bolder. There are other examples of farce withheld from such rhymes in "American Scenes (1904–1905)": "The wild frankness and sadness of surrender— / As if our cities ever could be tender!" ("Cambridge in Winter") and "Out of this little hell of spurts and hisses, / . . . Of open gates, of all but bland abysses" ("Railway Junction South of Richmond, Past Midnight"). In both cases, the rhymes refuse to take advantage of the dormant comedy of manners, partly by language that refuses the easy smile, partly by a tone so wry yet full of longing it passes for regret.

There's a related device, used by the artist with an instinct for small but telling import, in the second stanza of "Mrs. Snow":

But when she loomed above us like an alp,
We little towns below could feel her shadow.
Somehow her nods of approval seemed to matter
More than the stray flakes drifting from her scalp.

That bathos of the envelope rhyme, the art of sinking from the alp to the dandruff on her scalp (treated like Snow's snow), places Mrs. Snow at the minor end of the scale of things. She can no longer be Stevens's "Alp at the end of the street," the summit of ambition for the little piano students—yet, though displaying the self-knowledge that raised this one student beyond his teacher's limitations, the poem does not lack fondness. Indeed, the care with which the portrait is managed displays his debt. It would go too far to say that the rhyme, for a poet who cannot forgo such minor tours de force, is tainted with private sorrow (the portrait is devastating, though), yet in its rare address it cannot go unnoticed. To ignore it entirely would not go far enough. The lines introduce the nostalgia while undermining it.

(7) Last, to bring this list of ambivalence ambivalently to an end, that a poetry of ambivalence secure its very nature, perhaps even triumph over it, by admitting that every poem might be other, if only it could be written once more. So Justice sometimes wrote a poem once more. A poet of this character is by nature dissatisfied, and by nature a reviser, leaving as evidence the slight, shy reworkings of some poems (at times restored or revised afresh when they next appeared); the sudden and revealing

change of face (like the removal of the *en face* notes in "Childhood"); and, at the extreme of ambivalence, offering in *New and Selected Poems* two versions of "Incident in a Rose Garden," or, in *The Sunset Maker*, two poems about Mrs. Snow, some images and a couple of lines shared between them, with a memoir as well. In such acts of mutilation and regard the resolution is confessed on the page—the resolution that begins in irresolution, as if to admit that the form of a poem is forever contingent, forever vulnerable, that we must take the poem as found, while realizing that it has come to being through processes vague, marbled with contradiction, by nature occluded and occult.

Justice's contribution, to his students as well as to his poetry, was not a style or even a method easily imitated. His influence lay in the very character—the balance and moderation and ambivalence—of his stance. If such tensions operate at all it is not to create an unalterable stasis but to leave language coiled in its potential, fraught with the murderous mildness of its mots justes, a mildness that by hiding nothing seems to hide all. Think of Greek palimpsests, think of Poe's purloined letter. The lesson to other poets lies embedded in the artist's practice—not in his rush to judgment but in the slow crawl of judgment deliberated and even regretted, not through the rules of Solon but in rulings by Solomon, contingent and humane in their cunning. The lesson is, if this be aesthetics, make the most of it.

A Literary Friendship
(Donald Justice and Richard Stern)

L iterary friendship is based on a terrible longing, the longing to be understood. Every close friendship is a love affair—or, between writers, really four love affairs: between the writers themselves, between each writer and the work of the other, and at last between the two bodies of work. Such bonds may be formed through communion of interest, mutual admiration, desire for flattery, hope of reward, or the need for an acute critical eye—just the odd combination of vices and virtues any friendship requires for what psychologists call "fit." Devotion may also prove a powerful goad to ambition, if the writer doesn't feel worthy of the friendship. Such a desire was perhaps in part responsible for the depth and reach of *Moby-Dick*, which Melville dedicated to Hawthorne.

If writers want an audience in general, they want a reader in specific; and for most writers a single sympathetic and passionate one will do—if he's a fellow writer. Such closeness of spirit gives the writer someone to write to, as well as for. It might be argued that writers write for themselves, but those who have enjoyed intense friendship know that to have a perfect audience of one—the one who does not live in the mirror—is very different. There ought also to be some *mésalliance* between friends, some telling disparity in age or social class, wealth or reputation, some longing on both sides toward an opposite. George Sand and Gustave Flaubert found in their incompatible politics and the gap in their ages precisely what became the strength of friendship. (I'm aware of only three sets of identical twins with literary careers—it would be instructive to know if they possess the bond described. I would hazard that they do not, and perhaps cannot.)

Coleridge and Wordsworth, Byron and Shelley, Emerson and Thoreau, Twain and Howells, Wharton and James, Eliot and Pound, Sartre and Camus, Bishop and Lowell, Larkin and Amis—literature is littered with literary friendships, often more interesting for their asymmetries and disproportions. Emily Dickinson pined for a fellow spirit and came closest to finding one in the somewhat unsuitable Thomas Higginson. Lewis Carroll discovered such a spirit, for a time, in Alice. Perhaps this friendship is one of the strangest—it does not belong simply to that category of worship and bullying that forms the relation between artist and muse. (A muse must be aloof and unreachable—and she is not obliged to give anything back.) Before the breach between Carroll and her family, which prefigured what would have been almost inevitable once she was grown, Alice was more than a muse to him. It was the intensity and intelligence of her pleasure that drove the young deacon to his peculiar fraught ingenuity. None of the other little girls who became his friends had that effect—and afterward there were no books as brilliant as the two written for Alice.

Like love affairs, such *liaisons dangereuses* are quickly contracted and all too easily broken. Literary friendship is rarer than romantic love and comes with its own peculiar liabilities. (It hardly need be said that romance and literary friendship almost never coexist.) Such friendships rarely occur more than once in a life, and when there has been a fatal rupture the loss is often felt permanently. Friendships founder on rivalry, jealousy, mutual incomprehension, petty slights, trivial misunderstandings—such bonds are even more fragile than love's. Fitzgerald was devastated when Hemingway betrayed him—he needed the younger man's approval, the one thing Hemingway could never give. The young and overbearing Melville never understood how he had scared off the shy, prissy Hawthorne. Scholars who want to eroticize literary friendship apparently have no friends—or have been reading too much Freud.

Donald Justice and Richard Stern were unusually fortunate in enjoying a lifelong friendship ending only with Justice's death in 2004. They met in 1944 in the library of the University of North Carolina (now the University of North Carolina at Chapel Hill), where Justice came upon a young man reading an anthology of modern poetry. "Good stuff,"

Justice remarked. There the acquaintance began, though Stern, then only sixteen, admits that he had only recently acquired a taste for poetry. Such chance encounters give friendship the sense of inevitability usually reserved for romance. (Byron wrote that "Friendship is Love without his wings," which says something about Byron but much more about friendship.)

This edition of the Justice and Stern letters reminds us how fluid a young writer's art may be. The art that exists before craft may be plastic, unformed in substance even when driven by the deepest ambition. Though Justice was already leaning toward poetry and Stern toward prose, a range of possibilities seemed latent in the imaginative act. Justice tried stories (eventually writing some prize-winning ones) and fruitlessly attacked a novel, while Stern struggled to compose poems; but their imaginative command, and later achievement, lay close to their early inclinations. Perhaps the division secured their friendship. This record of the first fifteen years of their friendship shows the unsteady progress of their art—the false starts, the good ideas gone bad, and occasionally the bad idea forced to be good. The letters take us from raw apprenticeship to the publication of their first books, Justice's *The Summer Anniversaries* and Stern's *Golk*.

It is rare for a literary friendship to leave such a full account—during the friendship's formative stages, writers usually live within hailing distance. Except for a brief period in the fifties when Justice and Stern were both graduate students in Iowa City, their letters had to supply what they lost to geography. (The letters are one reason to be grateful for the high long-distance phone rates of the day.) Their friendship is uncommon for having begun so early, before either had much hope of success. It is also unusual for having weathered the upheavals of maturity, since the argument with style can become a quarrel with friends, and success can be just as debilitating to *amitié* as failure. Perhaps distance worked to their advantage—the sole occasion they tried to collaborate, while staying two weeks together one summer in Connecticut, was a disaster. The house had a porch, and the porch a single comfy chair. The pair agreed to take turns in the chair while they drafted a play. One morning they argued over who last occupied the chair, and the partnership was over.

If at times the great works of an author can seem an elegy for lost friendship, a wish to prove that the bond should never have been broken, it is perhaps more common for a writer's work never again to reach the heights achieved during such alliance of spirit. To find one person with an intuitive and complete understanding of your work makes a writer feel that the game is not so hopeless after all.

Randall Jarrell at the Y

Had I lived in New York early in 1963 or given a damn about poetry, I might have heard Randall Jarrell read. I was twelve. A year or so later, I happened to stay a few blocks north of the Y with my newly married uncle, but I was too late. All I saw was the World's Fair.

It's spooky listening to a dead man read—far stranger, in its way, than hearing recordings of Hendrix or Joplin or Jim Morrison, all of whom I saw on stage. Writers die with their deaths, while musicians live on after theirs; and all the recordings in the world won't save the writer from his immediate pastness once he's in the grave—indeed, some writers are consigned there long before they die. There is a difference between an artist who lives in the page and one who lives in air. Perhaps that's only a psychological deceit, because we shouldn't be able to hear anyone after he dies—sound is a living thing. The page is twice dead.

On Sunday, April 28, 1963, the *New York Times* reported that Khrushchev would not promise help in Laos, Castro had arrived in Moscow, and the railroad unions were deadlocked in a labor dispute. That's the distance from Jarrell to us. A four-track stereo tape-recorder could be purchased for $359.95, the equivalent of almost $3,000 now. The night before, clocks had moved forward to Daylight Savings Time.

Jarrell was introduced at the Y that evening by Eric Bentley, who began by admitting that he didn't much like the modernists and didn't much care for the Beats, either. He grumbled about Pound and Eliot in a voice that sounded like a mosquito with a liver complaint: "There was something rather awful about that older generation, the whole Harvard–St. Louis–upperclass-and-then-transferred-to-Oxford business of Eliot, and the pseudo-Europeanism of Pound. Although great work was written, it was written through hideous personalities." Bentley preferred his own generation—Jarrell's generation—not poetry of the "pseudo-aristocratic" or the "pseudo-gutter." As introductions go, this could scarcely have been worse.

Jarrell, who had invited Bentley, brushed off the remarks with an offhand amiability, but not without a barb or two:

> I enjoyed very much what Mr. Bentley said, and it even made me think about it. . . . I hope as an audience that you're full of minds too fine to be violated by any ideas, because of course, thinking about the generations, and so on, would be awfully bothersome for the poems. It's kind of enchanting to belong to a good generation between two bad ones. I guess it's the exact opposite of what Arnold said about himself, "Wandering between two worlds, one dead, / The other powerless to be born."

He agreed about Wyndham Lewis, singled out by Bentley for particular abuse, then continued, "On the other hand, I'm crazy about Eliot, his poetry and his criticism both. I think Eliot began, you know, as a bad man, and just neurotic no end, and few people have ever been more superior; but I think, by his poetry and plays, he cured himself; and he became such a good man, in the end he couldn't write any more poetry and plays."

I could listen to that Jarrell all day. One of the virtues of old recordings is that they restore the presence, the hesitations and slight missteps that do more to revive the absent voice than any page of prose. Jarrell was even wittier than I expected—and I recognized in the audience, or thought I did, the same little gasps of pleasure I sometimes hear in my students when I've said something that shocks them to their shoes.

Jarrell explained that he was going to read only new poems, the work of recent months.

> If you don't write poetry, I guess your big fear is that you'll stop breathing, or that people will stop loving you, or something like that. If you write poems, too, the regular thing that scares you so is that

you'll stop writing poems, because a lot of the time you can't write any poems—or, anyway, I can't. Many times, for a year or so, I can't write any at all. . . . At the moment, I feel like a hen with fifteen or sixteen great big eggs! I'm going to read you only nine or ten of them.

It's an unalterable law that, if the poet threatens to read poems before the ink is dry, you must run for the door. The poems Jarrell brought to the podium that evening were among the last he wrote, though he didn't die until two years later. They formed most of the first half of his final book, *The Lost World* (1965), published early the year of his probable suicide.

I love Jarrell's war poems, especially those in the voices of airmen and dead children. He had a sentimental streak as long as an airstrip, but then he'd missed out on the war. Having washed out of flight school, he was consigned stateside to menial camp-jobs—sorting mail, typing, or running a massive dishwasher. (By VE Day he was at least teaching celestial navigation.) Jarrell imagined the war through the voices of those pilots, borrowing the stories from returning flyers. The war drew out something magnificent in him. I can forgive a certain amount of sentiment in the poems spoken by the dead—but however far I'm willing to let him go, Jarrell goes much farther.

The later poems were lesser things. *The Lost World* has its fans, but the poems are precious when not prosaic. As a challenge to *Life Studies* (1959), it failed starkly. Jarrell's late manner is Lowell and barley water, memories that sound like an insurance adjuster's report. If we trust the poems, Jarrell's sickly boyhood must have been not just lonely but, though fondly remembered, insulated as a refrigerator and overseen for a time by grandparents more like—at least as he portrayed them—Ma and Pa Kettle than flesh and blood. His boyhood involved a lot of mooning.

Jarrell, like Browning before him and few poets since, loved personae; but his long poems in the voices of women aren't just unconvincing—they're preposterous. He read "Next Day," the opening poem in *The Lost World*:

Moving from Cheer to Joy, from Joy to All,
I take a box

And add it to my wild rice, my Cornish game hens.
The slacked or shorted, basketed, identical
Food-gathering flocks
Are selves I overlook. Wisdom, said William James,

Is learning what to overlook. And I am wise
If that is wisdom.

I suspect no one in a grocery aisle has ever thought that way, not even
Mrs. William James. Jarrell's portraits of women lost in their lives are
inadvertently condescending (like the joke about brands of detergent),
projections of the poet's psyche not onto the world but onto a movie
screen. Jarrell once groused, in a review of *The Mills of the Kavanaughs*,
that Lowell's characters acted like Lowell, not like real people—and so
Jarrell's women talk like Jarrell, not real people. Had he been a novelist a
second time, he might have written *Mrs. Bridge*—and his reputation
would have been the better for it.

Late Jarrell is the work of a poet who has lost one way and not yet
found another. Worse, his reading voice was corny and affected. He had
a pleasant tenor with deeper notes, not quite the high-pitched voice Lowell and Stanley Kunitz have described—but when he read he sounded
overwrought, piping the lines as if he wanted to dance a jig on them, his
pronunciation as prissily precise as Mr. Gradgrind's. No doubt this
was a period style. I've heard worse, readers of the forties and even the
sixties who couldn't deliver a line without auditioning for Hamlet.
Though it's hard to believe, there are poets who read poems, even their
own poems, more badly than actors—actors have been trained to imitate
a lot of things, but when reading poetry they cannot imitate being natural. Some poets now sound so natural, alas, you think they've just swallowed a handful of Xanax.

We often assume that a reading allows us to overhear the poet's inner
voice, not his outer one—that can't be true, but it's a fond delusion. The
poet's timbre, intonation, and pacing may make the man of paper more
human; but the audience must never suppose the imagination is speaking. It's only the poor lumpish man who happens to be the poet. I enjoy
far more, because off the cuff, the patter between poems, the minor

anecdotes, otherwise lost, in which the poet tries to soften the brute presence of poetry—and, by explaining it to others, explain it to himself.

There's an offness about late Jarrell (and, I fear, much early and even middle Jarrell). The poems have had the life squeezed out, the lines hurtling toward artifice, the sentences poised like marble statues in the gardens of Versailles. Such work gave confessional poetry a bad name. All Jarrell's intelligence could not make his childhood interesting, though it had to happen somewhere, and some of it happened to happen in Hollywood. The poems have the architecture of poems, but the windows have been nailed shut and painted black.

Jarrell wrote in the voices of women and children because he felt at ease with them, or at least easier than he felt around men. He and Robert Lowell once went to Princeton to visit John Berryman. Soon Jarrell was moaning about his hangover, having, he claimed, devoured a poisoned canapé the day before. According to Berryman, he was "walking up and down in my living room, miserable and witty. And very malicious . . . making up a brand-new Lowell poem full of characteristic Lowell properties, Lowell's grandfather and Charon, and the man who did not find this funny at all was Lowell." It's no surprise that at parties Jarrell shunned other guests to talk to the children, if any could be found. Presumably he loved cats because they didn't demand conversation. And they didn't talk back.

Jarrell never found a voice entirely his. (Some of his early verse seems a ventriloquist act by Auden.) Lowell and Bishop were poets immediately themselves. Jarrell sounded like a man trying hard to be a poet—the poetry is fiercely professional, but it is artful without art. The plain clumsy dullness of it was made duller that night by his halting and ponderous reading:

Sometimes as I drive by the factory
That manufactures, after so long, Vicks
VapoRub Ointment, there rises over me
A eucalyptus tree. I feel its stair-sticks
Impressed on my palms, my insteps, as I climb
To my tree house. The gray leaves make me mix
My coughing chest, anointed at bedtime,

With the smell of the sap trickling from the tan
Trunk, where the nails go in.

Imagine that read in winsome monotone, very slowly, and you'll have it. Jarrell's brief introductions, on the other hand, were sometimes hilarious. "Don't you feel as if science fiction had been going on forever—you know, that the little Jesus read science fiction?. . . I can remember the first purely science-fiction magazine. It was named *Amazing Stories*, and I believe it started in the spring of '26. And how I used to read it!" He could be charming even when he had to break the rhythm of reading: "I always hate it when the person reading takes a drink of water. It seems to me to indicate an overweening self-possession on his part. . . . If you won't mind, I'll take a drink of water in midflight, like the bat."

In his remarks about "In Montecito," Jarrell explained that the last name of the character Greenie Taliaferro was pronounced "Toliver." Such vagrant information is just what readings are good at preserving—otherwise the footnote is lost forever. The poem, however, borrows heavily from Elizabeth Bishop's story "In the Village," which Lowell had already pilfered in *Life Studies* for his poem "The Scream"—yet neither Bishop nor Lowell wrote lines as ham-fisted as "there visited me one night at midnight / A scream with breasts."

Jarrell's reputation has fallen a long way, like that of Delmore Schwartz and Theodore Roethke (fairly) and John Berryman (not so fairly). In the work of Lowell and Bishop, you can point and point and point; but for Jarrell, Schwartz, and Roethke, the handful of memorable poems is outweighed by the masses that make no impression, having been written in a period manner (though with better mannerisms than many). The best Berryman is all mannerism, but the mannerism is his own.

If Jarrell's poems figure-skated along the ice, his prose was raised from the dark water below. *Pictures from an Institution* remains one of the great comic novels of the last century. He was a decent translator, a marvel as an anthologist, a standard-bearer for writers out of fashion like Kipling and Graves, and a critic without peer. If you read his essays on Frost or Moore, Whitman or Lowell, you'll hear an original view you'll be tempted to make your own. Some of the things Jarrell said, sixty-odd years ago, we're saying still, as if we'd just thought of them.

The reading at the Y was long, by our standards. We're used now to Freud's fifty-minute hour, though I've heard readers who packed it in after twenty. Their brevity, their short shrift, left me wondering why they'd bothered to appear at all. Late in the evening, Jarrell suffered an odd slip, forgetting a quote by Hofmanstall. He made a joke about forgetting ("It's Freudian, forgetting"), stumbled to recover, then completely lost his train of thought. At last he said in despair, "I shouldn't have got into all this. I beg your pardon." He read the last sections of "The Lost World," and the reading was over. Was that lapse an early sign of the gathering mania and depression that soon overwhelmed him?

His quarrelsome introducer, Eric Bentley, who did important work in the theater, is still alive at ninety-eight. That makes me wish Jarrell were, too.

Flowers of Evil (David Lehman)

Anthologies—aren't they Baudelaire's *Les fleurs du mal*? More than a quarter-century ago, in the wilderness between Ludlowville and Ithaca, David Lehman had a vision. He would go forth and assemble an annual anthology of the best American poetry. Lehman is an enthusiast, the hail-sonnet-well-met type that poetry cannot do without. He soon had a working formula for what has become an institution. A different poet is chosen as editor each year, tasked with choosing some seventy-five poems from all those published. On New Year's Day, the pair sets about reading the year's magazine verse as it appears. They trade favorites back and forth, the final decision always lying with the editor of the moment, and somehow by New Year's Eve the next December the volume is complete.

This is much harder than it sounds. The *New Yorker* publishes a hundred or so poems a year, *Poetry* three times as many; but add dozens of quarterlies, scores of fly-by-night little magazines, then perhaps a hundred websites (for the internet, too, was soon considered), and many editors must have felt they'd made a bargain with the devil—and the devil was David Lehman. Only a masochist would read thirty or forty thousand poems in a year—a few of them wonderful, perhaps, but vast legions published though unpublishable and read though unreadable. It's a tribute to the American character that no editor has thrown up his hands come mid-July and walked away from the whole mess.

The State of the Art is a collection of Lehman's annual forewords, which unfortunately soon succumbed to their own formula: a potted summary of current events; a proud declaration of the range of magazines represented; a list of the poems' odder forms and even odder subjects; praise for the guest editor (the word "distinguished" was used all too frequently); and, as the years went on, an increasingly desperate attempt to find signs that poetry was still part of American culture:

> Dona Nieto, a California performance artist who calls herself La Tigresa, bared her breasts and declaimed "goddess-based, nude Buddhist poetry" at timber sites north of San Francisco to protest the logging of ancient redwoods. Anonymous cyber-scribes adapted familiar lines by Longfellow, Poe, Whitman, Ogden Nash, Joyce Kilmer, Alfred Noyes, and Clement Moore to satirize the post-election stalemate in Florida. Salman Rushdie in the *Guardian* versified the electoral results in the manner of Dr. Seuss.

And so on, in the case of 2001, through traces of poetry during a quiz show, two television dramas, and a movie, followed by news clippings about an investment banker, Shaquille O'Neal, and the financial advisor to Leonardo DiCaprio (whose name is misspelled). These nonevent events, which make poetry sound more marginal than ever, were dull enough to read about at the time—now they're just tedium fossilized. A few years later the editor was compelled to report that Jennifer Lopez had written a poem and that he'd been asked to analyze it for a gossip magazine. This is news that doesn't stay news.

It's an awful thing to say, since the volumes themselves are so inoffensive, full of poems that even when they bore reading don't bear re-reading, that the worst thing about *The Best American Poetry* is the forewords. Lehman's taste for public-relations prose makes the poor reader lightheaded:

> We may take solace in the way the art has been flourishing, against the odds, and in defiance of the gloom-sayers. We may rejoice in the abundance of our common poetic heritage and try to add our own indelible contributions. [1994]

> Modern American poetry is a cultural glory on the level of jazz and abstract expressionism. It is constantly renewing and refreshing itself,

and so the spirit of discovery will always play as great a part in the making of this anthology as the pleasures of abundance. [1995]

I had the vision of an annual anthology that would chronicle the taste of our leading poets and would reflect the vigor and variety of an art that refuses to go quietly into that good night to which one or another commentator is forever consigning it. [1998]

It is tempting to conclude that poetry remains the touchstone art, a supreme signifier, emblematic of soulful artistry, the adventurous imagination, and the creative spirit. [2002]

If you're going to steal from Dylan Thomas for your 1998 come-hither lines, at least have the courtesy not to mangle him. Lehman's endless puffery is exhausting—he might be auditioning for a job as a presidential speechwriter, or just CEO of Blurbwriter Academy: "poetry of high quality is appearing in a dizzying range of publications," "in recent movies poetry is associated with liberation, truth-telling, and self-actualization," "many of us turn instinctively to poetry not only for inspiration and consolation but also as a form of action and for a sense of community."

The Best American Poetry is harmless American hoopla in a country given to hoopla (that similar volumes now appear in Canada, Australia, Ireland, and New Zealand says little about the idea and a lot about the influence of American culture). At a time when there are fewer readers of poetry than ever, perhaps poets feel better when Lehman exclaims, in his Panglossian way, that poetry is getting better and better. We have an American poet laureate, a poetry month (April, of course), and poems on placards in subways and buses; yet most volumes of poetry, even those from major presses, sell fewer than five hundred copies.

Though Lehman knows all this, somehow every year his discovery of scraps of poetry in movies or on television (usually by a poet long dead and sculpted in marble) leaves him convinced that soon poetry will be a major art again and that parents won't wring their hands when their cross-eyed child announces that med school and law school are all very well, but it's poetry, poetry, poetry that makes her heart beat faster. Does anyone believe that American poetry is better off now than half a century ago, when Lowell appeared on the cover of *Time*? An idiot journalist in 1999 apparently predicted that poetry would be the "next great nation-sweeping pop-cultural revolution." Good luck, Nostradamus.

It would be crazy to imagine that more than three or four of the two thousand poems published in the series will be found in poetry anthologies fifty years hence and crazier to try to pick which ones. It would be easier to read the entrails of sheep. (In half a century of scanning magazines, I've only twice read a poem that seemed anointed—Bishop's "One Art" and Larkin's "Aubade.") It's fortunate that the Elizabethans and Jacobeans did not latch onto Lehman's idea first (though they had anthologies, like *Tottel's Miscellany*)—otherwise we'd think their taste ran toward time-serving hacks, now unknown noodles and noddies, with a few bright stars who somehow wandered in by mistake. Had such a volume been published in 1609, an editor might with more justice have dedicated the whole of the contents to Shakespeare's sonnets—but he wouldn't have. More likely he'd have missed Shakespeare completely. In any period, there are likely to be three or four poets writing brilliantly, or nearly so; scores of well-meaning second-raters; and thousands who can't write a line without torturing the innocent reader. The *Best American Poetry* volumes drown the extraordinary in a sea of mediocrity. No wonder it sells.

Amid all the Pollyannaish gush about contemporary poetry, Lehman has his bêtes noires, among them critical theorists (the subject of his book *Sign of the Times*), people who hate workshops, and contemporary poetry critics. Oh, those wretched critics! There's a "vacuum of genuine critical response," an "absence of reliable, disinterested, intellectually strenuous criticism." "Much contemporary criticism," Lehman grumbles, "is singularly shrill, sometimes gratuitously belligerent, even spiteful"— indeed, "it is highly possible that the perennial crisis in poetry is really a crisis in the criticism of poetry." That's a very peculiar thing to say, since many readers are under the impression that, compared to movie and theater critics, poetry critics are far too softhearted. The critics of our day, according to this *medicus medicorum*, suffer from the notion that the "job of the critic is to find fault with the poetry." No critic believes bitching and bellyaching are the sole purpose of criticism; but, without criticism, criticism is just a minor subsidiary of corporate relations. (Better the occasional disgruntled critic, however, than Lehman's goofy delight at the "boost" in a poet's "market value" after she read the inaugural ode for Bill Clinton.)

Lehman eventually unearths the Moriarty behind this crisis, a critic named William Logan, and spends three pages totting up his crimes. Much though I'm bewildered by Lehman's judgment elsewhere, by all evidence this William Logan is a thorough ruffian who may single-handedly be responsible for the decline and fall of American poetry. An anathema (and a fatwa, for good measure) should long ago have been pronounced against this "assassin," as Lehman calls him. Stop this villain, and American poetry will be hunky-dory.

Lehman is a cheerleader for American poetry, and I suppose that if American poetry needs a cheerleader he's as good as any. I like the democracy of *The Best American Poetry*, the divergent tastes of the editors—it's like a frozen biopsy of American verse. The poems are often superficial, alas, and there's an unhappy tendency to favor the quirky and contrived; but contemporary taste is always the product of evanescent fashion, the sentimentalities of the day, and wild prejudices only time will temper. The generation of Lowell and Bishop, the strongest generation of American poets that followed the moderns, has now been reduced almost entirely to Lowell and Bishop, so far as major figures go—with stray poems by Berryman, Jarrell, Roethke, and almost no one else. The kindness and geniality of *The Best American Poetry* does nothing to fend off the savage taste of the future.

In his annual foreword, Lehman has a perfect soapbox. It's a pity that he wastes it on trivia and gossip. He's so busy catching up with the year's news feed and totting up the various forms and subjects that forced his poets into poetry, Lehman says almost nothing of interest about American poetry and little beyond platitudes that would embarrass a self-help guru. His insights are almost always of the cocktail-party kind. Still, in the past decade the forewords have gotten better. Lehman is given now to meditations on the decline of reading, on "Dover Beach," on the career of Billy Collins, and even on anthologies themselves. These are more compelling because more personal, entertaining if not deep.

Even when I agree with his sentiments, Lehman's prose is so clunky, thrown together from hackneyed allusions and used car-parts, that I have to take a handful of aspirin after reading that Wallace Stevens "opined" something or other, a new movie is "slated for summer release," a poet "burst onto the scene," and the singer Jewel is a "sultry songstress." (When "opine" and "slated" move in, all hope of sincerity moves out.) Sometimes the writing descends into lunatic absurdity, no sillier than when Lehman compares poetry to a team sport—"you play for a chance at post-season glory (the sportswriters call it 'immortality')"—or thunders that Maya Angelou has become a "symbol of unity in multicultural diversity," whatever that means.

Lehman's clichés are those of hacks everywhere, from the gobbledygook of "it was a truth universally acknowledged that the book trade now functioned within a vast literary-industrial complex whose corporate masters were ruled by an unforgiving bottom line" (poor Jane Austen!) to the silliness of "the nation's hot romance with poetry shows no sign of cooling off." Worse, the occasionally deranged syntax leaves the reader bemused: "poems that take big, important concepts . . . and render them in compelling terms and true," or, hilariously, the "spontaneous answer given by many was: How can there be not?"

Not even a cynic would deny that good poetry is being written in this country; but, when a man tells you against all evidence that "poetry in the United States today does have a vital readership," you wonder what he's been drinking. *The State of the Art* would have been far better had it consisted of the introductions by the various editors, odd though those introductions and editors have sometimes been. With its small-town boosterism, its stultifying repetitions, and its excruciating prose (by *Time* magazine out of *Variety*), this anthology of forewords is the longest short book I've ever read.

Verse Chronicle: The Glory Days

Louise Glück

Louise Glück's compelling and unsettling new book, *Faithful and Virtuous Night*, is stuffed with morbid fantasies, cracked allegories, offbeat fairy tales, and parables with no name. The speaker, who might be called Glück/un-Glück (if the world of these tales is unstable, so is character), reveals everything while revealing nothing—the poems are a raw look at identity constructed on the fly, which is, after all, not very distant from the way ordinary criminals live. If we trust Freud, we're all ordinary criminals.

Glück's poems display, more than any poet since Plath and Lowell, the mental pressure of invention—they're landmines waiting to be stepped on. The breathless concision and pinchpenny vocabulary that mark them as forms—her brand, in contemporary jargon—have at times proven more burden than blessing. The language is still nervous as a razor (I can't think of any poet as good who takes less pleasure in words), but Glück has found a way to remove the trammels of speech. The slightly woozy voice seems impelled to speak, or perhaps not to stop.

> You're stepping on your father, my mother said,
> and indeed I was standing exactly in the center
> of a bed of grass, mown so neatly it could have been
> my father's grave, although there was no stone saying so.
>
> You're stepping on your father, she repeated,
> louder this time, which began to be strange to me,
> since she was dead herself; even the doctor had admitted it.

Freudian allegory? Haunted confession? Glück has rejected the authority most poets now assume as their birthright—that is, to claim the
authentic by mining nothing but their lives. These new poems may still
derive, in distorted fashion, from the almanac of Glück's experience, in
the same sense that Homer may have filched something he heard for the
Iliad; but mostly they're in the voice of an elderly man, a painter from
Cornwall. One or two seem spoken by Glück (including the most moving, about the death of her mother), the rest by not-Glück, excluding
some surreal capriccios plucked from Mark Strand's waistcoat.

Glück has long taken Greek and biblical myths as her private playground; though these have often given her life grotesque and manic
proportion, in her best work the trifling becomes the spooky embodiment of myth. The speaker has an assistant, a Bartleby to open and answer
letters, but he begins to have doubts:

> Master, he said (which was his name for me),
> I have become useless to you; you must turn me out.
> And I saw that he had packed his bags
> and was prepared to go, though it was night
> and the snow was falling. My heart went out to him.
> Well, I said, if you cannot perform these few duties,
> what can you do? And he pointed to his eyes,
> which were full of tears. I can weep, he said.
> Then you must weep for me, I told him,
> as Christ wept for mankind.

There may be a touch of irony at the last, but Glück sometimes miscal-
culates, sometimes crosses the border from melancholy to farce. (She sees
the problem: the "whole exchange seemed both deeply fraudulent / and
profoundly true.") The Parable of the Talents in Matthew shadows the
scene, however, as perhaps does Frost's spiritually depressing poem
"Snow."

In their subjects, the poems embrace the off-kilter tilt of the bizarre:
a fortune teller's reading, a vision of the kingdom of death, a visit from
dead parents, a fable about a wooden ballerina, a Kafkaesque machine

registering the progress toward death. (It's just a heart monitor; but this is Glück, after all.) One piece is called "Parable," another "A Work of Fiction." In the most disturbing poem, a girl and her grandmother ignore a man sleeping on a stairway, apparently dead. The girl returns. The sleeper speaks:

> She knelt below me, chanting a prayer I recognized as the Hebrew prayer for the dead. Sir, she whispered, my grandmother tells me you are not dead, but I thought perhaps this would soothe you in your terrors, and I will not be here to sing it at the right time.
>
> When you hear this again, she said, perhaps the words will be less intimidating, if you remember how you first heard them, in the voice of a little girl.

That prayer, the hymn of praise called the Kaddish, is not in Hebrew but Aramaic, once the lingua franca of the Jews and much of the Middle East.

Glück's career, the long view shows, has been one string of private fictions worked and reworked, invented, killed off. (I'd compare her to Ovid, that pathologist of myth; but she's more one of his doomed characters.) I want to laugh at the hubris, but she's at last found a way to cast off the burdens of confession. Lowell played fast and loose with the facts—he had the Flaubertian itch—but Glück seems happy to remake her life wholesale. The character at the center of these tales, this not-Glück, was raised by an aunt after losing his parents and baby sister in a car wreck. Born a girl, he becomes a boy, then a man—or so he says. None of this falls from Glück's life—yet fiction can be truer than truth, the facts defective but the psychology pure. In the strangest way, these poems seem posthumous.

JOSHUA MEHIGAN

Joshua Mehigan is a throwback to the Eisenhower days of wary pentameter, Quaker morals, and acid wryness that never goes too far. *Accepting the Disaster*, his second book, often treats Spoon River properties with a modern air—factory, town square, cemetery (with any luck the dead would start yakking at each other). There's a dash of Bishop, a heavy specific of Larkin, and great chunks of Auden—so many poems remind you of other poets, there ought to be a law, or an index.

> Nothing has changed. They have a welcome sign,
> a hill with cows and a white house on top,
> a mall and grocery store where people shop,
> a diner where some people go to dine.

The lack of traction in that diner's dining diners is the point—such towns seem immutable, but the poem's final line ("Nothing here ever changes, till it does") can't quite escape the glassy dullness of the details. The lines are meant to be devastating, but they're just pallid criticism of American Panglossiana, whose textbook has always been *Rebecca of Sunnybrook Farm*.

Mehigan's ideas are too often weighed down by the meagerness of the means and the short payoff of the ends.

> The town had a smokestack.
> It had a church spire.
> The church was prettier,
> but the smokestack was higher.
>
> It was a lone ruined column,
> a single snuffed taper,
> a field gun fired at heaven,
> a tube making vapor.

The poem goes on in this vein for sixty lines or more, describing the smokestack and the smoke at various times in various weathers, here and there very wittily ("when it was resurrected, / the sky turned black, and then white, / as if a new pope were elected"); but the social commentary is more politic than political, and the metaphorical frenzy wears out long before the end. The tone seems borrowed, charm included, from Bishop's "The Burglar of Babylon"; yet the whole doesn't come to much, and it's not clear if it was ever meant to.

Mehigan has a quiet command of form and an intelligence never quite tapped by his designs—it's like watching a Chevy V8 dragging a horse cart. Auden's intellect was always knocking at the edges of form, giving no quarter; and decades ago James Fenton found a heady combination in Audenesque stanzas and high-octane invention. Mehigan's influences have done him no favors except to spoil the reader for anything less.

Where Auden's Everyman seemed a knowing and peculiar case, Mehigan loves the Everyman of Everytown. "No one is special. We grow old. We die," one poem begins, in a hum-ho or ho-hum sort of way; and the various wrestlers with mortality who follow—a devotee of plastic surgery, a gorgeous dancer grown old in a sad toupee, a prince who aspired to be a god and was murdered by his guard—are presented in such bland, passive terms (more diorama than drama), it's hard for any feeling to escape, whether despair or schadenfreude.

At worst, the verse is set on automatic, nattering on without much to say and very few ways of saying it. In the title poem, an attack on the complacency of our modern dystopia, or one almost like ours, the donnish tone (among many nods to Auden: "we, ignoring our leaders' slick assurances / and the timid findings of our so-called experts") sinks into smug and fatty rhetoric:

And our small planet braved the ravages
of constant gamma-ray disturbances,
and it turned counterclockwise. Some of us
blamed aliens. And by small slippages
the moon was drifting.
The cosmos scattered. Its far provinces
were laden with prophetic stillnesses.

If Astronomy 101 were any duller, we'd still believe in the heavens of Ptolemy. (I'll forgive the counterclockwise, though that depends on whether you're looking down on the North Pole or up at the South.) The poems are never bad enough to be interestingly bad but never good enough to be good.

Sometimes you can soft-pedal your ironies until they're scarcely ironies any more. The longest poem in the book is in the voice of a man who has gone off his meds. It collapses, at a length not much short of *The Waste Land*, into a goofy madhouse scene, *One Flew Over the Cuck-oo's Nest* done by refugees from *Alice in Wonderland*. ("'Don't take me!' cried the clozapine. / 'Don't take me!' cried the cure.") In the end, too many of Mehigan's poems, however adroit, however well mannered, however responsibly responsible, offer less to the cookie-cutter suburbs and bankrupt cities than a minor fifties poet like Phyllis McGinley, who knew her limitations and gamely settled for them.

MATTHEA HARVEY

In her charming but annoying new book, Matthea Harvey makes her bid to become the Jeff Koons of contemporary poetry. *If the Tabloids Are True What Are You?* has been interleaved with glossy photos of her schlock art—tiny dolls and doll furniture frozen in ice cubes; tea cups overflow-ing with cotton batting; paper-punch chad printed with the word *yes*; sil-houettes of mermaids whose lower bodies are a pair of scissors, or a revolver, or a Swiss Army knife; and embroidery of unlikely machines—say, a stone piano. The art's just goofy camp, like a tractor-trailer of carny prizes struck by a tornado. As for the poems, the reader can expect a sequence on mermaids; an arty performance piece made by whiting out all but a few words from some pages of Ray Bradbury's "R Is for Rocket"; a tale about women imprisoned in a glass factory, who fashion the living glass-girl who frees them; and an overlong sequence on the frustrations of the maverick Italian inventor Antonio Meucci, who built a precursor of the telephone.

This giddy mishmash of science fiction, Hans Christian Andersen, freak-show silhouettes, and pop obsessions (yes, there's an Elvis poem) is hard to categorize and often hard to bear, unless you like your whimsy in lethal doses. The influence of Anne Carson and the second wave of New York School poets (Ron Padgett, Ted Berrigan, Tom Clark, et al.)—call it Dada with a vengeance—makes the book self-satisfied and unpre-dictable, faux naïf but slickly self-conscious. Take "The Straightforward Mermaid," she of the Swiss Army knife tail:

The Straightforward Mermaid starts every sentence with "Look . . ."
This comes from being raised in a sea full of hooks. She wants to get

points 1, 2 and 3 across, doesn't want to disappear like a river into the ocean. When she is feeling despairing, she goes to eddies at the mouth of the river and tries to comb the water apart with her fingers. The Straightforward Mermaid has already said to five sailors, "Look, I don't think this is going to work," before sinking like a sullen stone. She's supposed to teach Rock Impersonation to the younger mermaids, but every beach field trip devolves into them trying to find shells to match their tail scales.

This could go on forever, and almost seems to. The wincing cuteness is one thing, the heavy-handed message quite another. The rambling never quite gets to the point, though the points are everywhere. The Homemade Mermaid, "top half pimply teenager, bottom half tuna," was created by a modern Dr. Frankenstein; the Inside Out Mermaid has a lover but "secretly loves that he can't touch her here or here"; the Objectified Mermaid, between semi-nude photo shoots (seaweed bra, glycerine), works in a bar where she offers customers Tankside Mertinis, letting them feel up her tail. If you don't understand the symbolism—the billboard notices about women, conformity, torture, self-torture, and of course sex—it's because you've been hit on the head too often with a hammer. That Harvey may at times be lampooning modern proprieties doesn't make the poems much better.

Poetry has a fairly short history of comic improv and few gilt-edged examples (Christopher Smart must be the prime early adopter), because the promise of woolgathering lunacy fades too late to avoid brain rot from the endless blabbery. (Still, the Tankside Mertini may be the best drink ever invented by a poet.) Harvey has a sprightly, devious imagination; and her occasional show of wit makes me wish she'd find better grounds for her talent: for a morning pick-me-up, her Tired Mermaid "bites an electric eel, and the chill in her molars isn't much, but it's something"; her Deadbeat Mermaid "floats on her back and watches the giant sky, stuck on the same stupid cloud channel all day long." In such lines I'm seduced by Harvey's oddball temper—you can go a long way in contemporary poetry without finding anything like her. A girl looks at a thermometer: "the sun has inched up / a few degrees and yes, Monday has a fever." Meanwhile, out in the ocean: "Once, a large square mammal with a wide mouth / of black and white teeth floated up out of a shipwreck. / It's true, we swam away. We'd never seen a piano before."

It's too quirky by half, I admit. Much of the new surreal is written for an audience with an endless appetite for kooky observation. (They never applaud. They smirk.) There's hardly a poem here that doesn't outlast its means—the good news is that you never know where Harvey will go, the bad that you don't care. I can imagine future projects: a documentary about death threats made by scissors, a sitcom called *My Favorite Mermaid*, a talk show with a puppet host and antique dolls for guests, and a rock band whose lead singer is a talking Fender amp.

EDWARD HIRSCH

Edward Hirsch's long, heartbroken elegy for his son reveals undercurrents of rage and guilt more painful than anything actually said. A beautiful adopted baby grows into a nightmare child, impulsive, hapless, destructive, subject to furies beyond any cure but exhaustion. Like dutiful members of the upper-middle class, his parents make appointments with doctors, therapists, and educational consultants, receiving, like dutiful members of the upper-middle class, contradictory diagnoses—depending on the expert, the child suffered from Tourette's, pervasive developmental disorder, obsessive-compulsive disorder, oppositional-defiant disorder, ADHD, or half-a-dozen other things. The parents are packed off with an alphabet of prescriptions for the troubled: the lines "Adderall Depakote Ritalin // Strattera Abilify Concerta" do no more than begin the list.

The loss of a child is the worst fate a parent can imagine, and no parent who loses a child is left unscarred—the bond between them is so profound the parent suffers a grief nearly unbearable. Very few young lives, alas, are riveting enough to sustain 2,300 lines of lament—the dramas of children (where they're not the dramas of adults in disguise) are likely to dissolve, like the death of Little Nell, into tears for the crowd. The hurtling unpunctuated lines in *Gabriel* are as ungoverned as the lost boy, rickety with sentiment, racing on until they collapse:

Perfect fingers perfect toes
Shiny skin blue soulful eyes
Deeply set in a perfectly shaped head

He was a trumpet of laughter
And tears who did not sleep
Through the night even once

O little swimmer in the deeps
Raise up your arms
Ring out your lungs

O wailing messenger
O baleful full-bodied crier
Of the abandoned and the chosen

For all the incidental detail thrown into the poem, the story remains unhappily familiar. Hirsch has never possessed the gift for turning the loose particulars to deeper purpose (a talent Lowell had in spades); and too frequently he lingers on anecdotes that, however beguiling, seem like outtakes from some sappy Hollywood biopic:

There were *Welcome Gabriel* signs in the rafters
The classicists drank gallons of red wine
And hoisted him up like a trophy

Gelsa the Italian nanny overdressed him
And took him all over Trastevere he was known
At the butcher shops the dry cleaners the coffee bars

He had become the unofficial mayor
Of the neighborhood waving from his stroller
At shopkeepers who waved and shouted *Ciao Gabriele*

The great elegies for the young in English poetry have been relatively brief: "Lycidas," which heads the list, is less than two hundred lines, while *In Memoriam*, though long, is a set of discrete lyrics. Hirsch invokes the shades of other poets who have written of their dead children—the Pearl Poet, Ben Jonson, Mallarmé—but they offer a severe comparison to the plodding and tedious verse here.

At twenty-two Gabriel Hirsch died of a heart attack after taking the rave-scene drug GHB, his body lying unidentified while his parents desperately searched for him in the aftermath of Hurricane Irene. The raw facts are more dramatic than anything Hirsch can say about this wasted life, wasted not because his parents were ogres, not because he hung out with the wrong crowd, not because of anything but the bad luck of chemistry or wiring that nothing could fix. Whatever intensity the poet might have brought to this lament has been lost in the prosaic dullness of the writing, in tired metaphors, helter-skelter narrative, deadening anaphora, and odd lapses of syntax ("The funeral director opened the coffin / And there he was alone / From the waist up // I peered down into his face"). The curious reserve that now and then rescues Hirsch from outright sentiment only makes the outbursts of breast-beating unconvincing and embarrassing. There can be no absolution after a crime that has only victims.

Gabriel obeys the conventions of grief without following the poet into the darkness of despair and guilt and self-loathing only hinted at. The most striking passages lie unwritten—the poet casually mentions that in time he left the boy's care largely to his wife, who later divorced him, and admits that he often neglected his son to write poetry. The reader suffers mild whiplash when the wife is replaced without warning by a new girlfriend—the collapse of the marriage in argument and recrimination is alluded to only vaguely, but like the poet's shallow recognition of guilt this suggests the devastating testament the elegy might have been. There was no easy way to write this book. *Gabriel*'s failure is as depressing as the life of the lost boy who could not be saved.

PAUL MULDOON

For forty years Paul Muldoon's poems have come not in a trickle but a flood. Inventive, slapdash, wildly and maddeningly conceived, they're politely freakish, yet especially in the past decade amusing rather than shocking, rarely cutthroat in craft, and so overstuffed with extranea, with the garbage and recycled plastic of culture, they resemble Mr. Boffin's mountains of dust.

There's another Muldoon, one increasingly hard to find. (Poets often contain multitudes even when wholly themselves—Whitman was many, but we recollect him as one.) That would be the fresh-eared poet who was a close student of Heaney and as bog-knowledgeable as an army of peat cutters, a poet who could turn a forgotten poem by Southey into a philosophical epic. Like Newton, that Muldoon picked up seashells until he had a passing acquaintance with the universe.

The later Muldoon, the Muldoon of *One Thousand Things Worth Knowing*, is a monstrous industry, his nose everywhere and his eyes nowhere. Given the kinkiest and most promiscuous gallimaufry of facts, he can turn them into, well, into a Paul Muldoon™ poem (there's a lot of chewing involved—factoids go in, poems come out).

> It was in Eglish that my father kept the shop
> jam-packed with Inglis loaves, butter,
> Fray Bentos corned beef, Omo, Daz, Beechams Powders,
> Andrews liver salts, Halls cough drops,
>
> where I wheezed longingly from my goose-downed truckle
> at a Paris bun's sugared top.
> A tiny bell rang sweetly. The word on the tip
> of my tongue was "honeysuckle."

Beyond the nostalgic litany of Irish grocery stock (Eglish is a tiny village in County Tyrone), the truffle-hunting dialect and linguistic arcana (a truckle bed can be rolled under a taller bed when not in use), the ramifying details take in—like the maw of the Calydonian Boar—Ovid on the Black Sea, the Jahangiri Mahal, Herbert Hoover, Robert Frost, Meleager, Fabergé, surgery on wounded hens, and other matters fowl or fair. (Commissioned to write on a painting in the National Gallery of Ireland, Muldoon chose a trivial genre scene of chickens.)

The poem's partly about the Irish childhood that haunts him still; partly about the rhythms of adult life, the relation of father and son; partly about roosters; and partly about whatever stumbled into Muldoon's head along the way—but there are so many digressions and distractions and culs-de-sac, so many Ogden Nash–full rhymes and Tilt-A-Whirl slants, so many lame jokes and deaf puns ("My new razor / had me on edge"), it's hard to separate the message from the static. (I know, I know, the message *is* the static.) When Muldoon says, "The only thought that crossed // my mind . . . ," it's hard to believe him—his mind is like the Indianapolis 500. Here and elsewhere there's a dodgy fact or two. Is the temperature of chickens really "106 centrigade," beyond the boiling point? Are the best baseball bats "turned from hibiscus"? There may be something serious beneath all the madcappery, antic as an explosion of feathers—but you're so busy scrabbling your way out you can't stop to think.

There's rarely any sense of necessity to Muldoon's poems now, any intention buried deep in reason. He can compact five millennia of Irish history into a stanza or two; but at the end you scarcely recall the subject, the poem's so rich in particulars and starved in substance. It's not too much icing and too little cake—there *is* no cake. The showpiece (Muldoon's poems are all showpieces—that's the problem) is a sonnet sequence in which *Ben Hur* is deported to Ireland, the hero reinvented as Ben Hourihane, the English forced to fill in for the Romans, with Bloody Sunday, Billy the Kid, gerrymandering, and the Mescaleros dragged in for good measure.

> The dog is tense. The dog is tense the day Ben Hourihane
> falls fuel of the new Roman turbine,
> Little Miss Sally hisself, tense enough to set off a chain
> of events that will see Ben mine
>
> warehouse after warehouse of schlock
> and link him via a Roman warship
> to a hell-for-leather chariot race at Antioch.
> Sooner or later Messala will need a lot more than a double hip
>
> replacement while Ben will barely chafe
> at the bit. That's right, Messala, an *amputation* saw!
> The doctor is cocking an ear to your chest's tumble-de-drum
>
> like a man trying to open a safe.

Thomas Pynchon would be jealous.

One Thousand Things Worth Knowing is a roller coaster—not a Frank Gehry–like steel whirligig, but one of the old wooden jobs, rickety as Grandmother's rocker, as likely to pitch you into midair as bring you home and dry. There are so many things I like about Muldoon—all that chutzpah, and sprezzatura, and panache (he's a whole lexicon of naturalized nouns)—it's disappointing that after an hour of such devilish abandon, such endless reruns of the Paul Muldoon Show, I never want to read the poems again.

JOHN BERRYMAN

John Berryman would have turned one hundred this year. Had he lived to that great age, he'd probably still be spouting on the great and sundry with the old bravura self-confidence, meanwhile smoking like a 4-4-2 locomotive. He came from a generation not doomed or damned but acting the part—Dylan Thomas dead at thirty-nine (alcohol and pneumonia), Randall Jarrell at fifty-one (suicide or accident), Delmore Schwartz at fifty-two (heart attack),Theodore Roethke at fifty-five (heart attack), Berryman at fifty-seven (suicide), Robert Lowell at sixty (heart attack). Only Elizabeth Bishop lived to a reasonable sixty-eight. The great moderns—Pound, Eliot, Frost, Stevens, Moore, and Williams—all lived past seventy-five, Pound and Frost surviving until near ninety.

It's not clear in what sense *The Heart Is Strange* can be subtitled *New Selected Poems*. Berryman's publishers have marked the centenary by reprinting *Berryman's Sonnets*, the complete *Dream Songs*, and rather redundantly *77 Dream Songs*, which won the Pulitzer Prize in 1965. The *New Selected* is left to choose from what remains—readers new to Berryman will find here none of his most important work. The subtitle is doltish, but you can't blame the editor for not calling the volume *No Dream Songs! The Dregs of John Berryman*.

Berryman began as a high-flying student (Columbia, Cambridge), cocksure of his gifts, writing like a man whose hot-and-heavy affair with the Muse had left him with not a clue how to write a poem.

> Our superstitions barnacle our eyes
> To the tide, the coming good; or has it come?—
> Insufficient upon the beaches of the world
> To drown that complex and that bestial drum.

*   *   *

Glade grove & ghyll of antique childhood glide
Off; from our grown grief, weathers that appal,
The massive sorrow of the mental hospital,
Friends & our good friends hide.

*　　*　　*

Scotch in his oxter, my Retarded One
Blows in before the midnight; freezing slush
Stamps off, off. Worse of years! . . . no matter, begone.

Yeats, Auden, and Hopkins left their thumbprints all over Berryman's apprentice work, which was earnest and dull when not congealed. The poems are full of special effects filched from his betters and the rhetorical sludge of the day. Apart from one good war poem, "The Moon and the Night and the Men," Berryman had little to show for the decades of poetic drudgery before he published *Homage to Mistress Bradstreet* in 1953.

Anne Bradstreet's bland, doughy verse proved to seventeenth-century England that something resembling poetry could be written in the New World. Berryman revived her in an arch idiom of his own invention, full of crotchets and fidgets and preposterous inversions, yet ragged with the inner life of an educated woman stuck in the wilderness of Massachusetts:

—it is Spring's New England. Pussy willows wedge
up in the wet. Milky crestings, fringed
yellow, in heaven, eyed
by the melting hand-in-hand or mere
desirers single, heavy-footed, rapt,
make surge poor human hearts. Venus is trapt—
the hefty pike shifts, sheer—
in Orion blazing.

The poem was a tour de force of mannerism, rising above the dismal work of the period. What Berryman learned, and forgot, and had to learn again was that his poems in propria persona were so busy proving he was the smartest guy in the room, they were insufferable.

Berryman was an obsessive. Once he settled into the Dream Songs, using a stanza adapted from *Bradstreet*, he found it difficult to quit (Lowell suffered a similar addiction to his unrhymed sonnets). The Songs are terribly uneven, flashes of brilliance interrupting long stretches of crabbed and sometimes impenetrable maundering. Berryman had more to confess than most confessional poets, but it was still garden-variety sinning—mania here, furtive affairs there, drunken bouts abounding. They would have made a decent comic novel.

The Dream Songs, however, found in the character of Henry the way to distance Berryman's know-it-all, peacockish tone—his doppelgänger gave him the right of detachment. All the surface contrivance—maddening inversions, whippy rhymes, smart-alec remarks and minstrelsy and baby talk—became the manifest sign of psychological torment and wrestled intelligence below. The self-indulgence and bitter self-loathing benefited from this bifurcated vision—it was easier to forgive Berryman when, as they say, he wasn't himself.

None of that can be found in this selection. What is offered piecemeal, after the greenhorn work and *Bradstreet*, are the weak later books: *Love & Fame* (1970), *Delusions, Etc.* (1972), and the posthumous *Henry's Fate & Other Poems* (1977). There are long autobiographical poems that couldn't be duller—they read like sub-*Life Studies* sketches (or, given Berryman's major mode, skits). In the better of the dreary sequences in praise of the Lord, the poet quarrels with God while protesting his obsequious submissiveness. The editor, Daniel Swift, picks and chooses among this late work, not always well—having omitted the embarrassing political poems, he includes a silly children's rhyme and a flatfooted elegy for John F. Kennedy while ignoring the witty, scathing "Washington in Love" and "Beethoven Triumphant." The posthumous hooverings include few of the almost fifty post-*Dream Songs* dream songs that gave Henry new life:

Many bore uncomplaining their lives pained
so long and in such weather. Henry complained.
All a Venetian June
the sun raged down on stone & water. Gondoliers slept

    thro' midday on to four. Man was inept
    against the sun, and soon

    humid Henry took boat up the Grand Canal
    where the breeze & the palaces refreshed him, pal,
    palaces bold & demure.

This has all the terrible humor, aggression, and acceleration of Berryman's best work, where he was a sheep in wolf's clothing.

    In his long, cautious introduction, the editor sidles past Berryman's chronic brutishness and spasmodic genius with some public-relations spin. "Taught briefly at the Iowa Writers' Workshop" is code for "fired after being arrested and fined for public intoxication and disorderly conduct" (he took a shit on his landlord's porch). Berryman is ripe for a full volume in the Library of America, containing all the poems—bad, brilliant, and indifferent—as well as the shrewd and knowing criticism (Jarrell the only rival among his peers), not neglecting the idiosyncratic book on Stephen Crane. If space remains, perhaps the flaccid slog of his only novel or the almost forgotten short stories; but even more welcome would be a great gout of the unpublished letters.

Verse Chronicle: Doing as the Romans Do

ROWAN RICARDO PHILLIPS

Rowan Ricardo Phillips's slightly off-kilter poems promise more than they deliver, but they have crotchets and quavers (and notes too flat or sharp) that suggest a poetic imagination still under construction. *Heaven*, his second book, is full of heavens large and small—so many it seems he's been taking backhanders from the heaven lobby for product placement. The poems have an ambitious range, moving trippingly through the minefield of pop culture, with titles that mark off large territory and over-the-shoulder glances at the *Paradiso* and *Hamlet*.

Phillips has a range of styles, though his voice is usually James Earl Jones–ish, as serious as Echo testing echoes.

Perpetual peace. Perpetual light.
From a distance it all seems graffiti.
Gold on gold. Iridescent, torqued phosphors.
But still graffiti. Someone's smear on space.
A name. A neighborhood. X. X was Here.
X in the House. A two-handed engine
Of aerosols hissing Thou Shalt Not Pass
On fiery ground.

I admire a poet who can move so sparely, so choppily, from the sidelong reference to "Kilroy was here" to Milton's "two-handed engine," from the biblical "Thou Shalt Not Pass" to, later, "text me." Phillips is comfortably uncomfortable between worlds, past and present, low and high, hell and heaven—like Mohammed's coffin.

His translation of the meeting between Odysseus and the shade of Ajax has at fifty lines too much filigree and added fat; but he takes on Homer with attitude, giving Odysseus the arrogance not always evident in the original. Where the blind Greek has "the rest of the souls of the perished dead stood near me / grieving, and each one spoke to me and told of his sorrows" (Lattimore translation), Phillips goes on to say, "I must / Admit, they bored me to tears." The classics can use a little havoc, though it's hard to see the Greek Underworld, that dark realm of blood-hungry ghosts, as the modern poet's "High Heaven," which for no good reason has at its center a rowan tree. Have we been hurled out of Hades and into Norse mythology, or is that just a dumb pun on his name?

The poet inflicts upon the poor reader an alarmingly tedious reminiscence of his boyhood, and another about watching *Measure for Measure*:

> All of Shakespeare feels like lead on my chest,
> Not for death, let's face it, death awaits us,
> Usually with less prescient language,
> But death measures us with a noun's contempt
> For our imagination, being death
> But not dying, making do, like when I
> Turn from the Bard, look outside and behold . . .

Like when I? The poem straggles on for another ten lines about a herd of elk, which might as well have been labeled Big Fat Symbol. Weaknesses abound, to be sure: there's a fair amount of takeout politics and Martin Buber–style metaphysics for the middle class (where Phillips seems a more sophisticated version of Mary Oliver), as well as an Elizabethan pastiche of *Hamlet* that stumbles embarrassingly through what the poet seems to think is blank verse.

These poems have a suppleness, a pushy cleverness that in a split-second flees for the worst sort of Romantic pastoral or metaphysical guff. There are everywhere little spasms of overwriting ("Alpenglow ripening the mountain peaks / Into rose-pink pyramids steeped in clouds"), lines that sound like refugees from a travel brochure or a Michelin-star Manhattan menu. Then there are words that long for a Michelin star themselves

("Their world othered by these austere windows") and a passage or two
that tries to out-Stein Stein's patented gibberish ("A poem is a view of
the Pacific / And the Pacific, and the Pacific / Taking in its view of the
Pacific, / And the Pacific as the Pacific . . . / Ends"). The poems about
poetry ("How long ago was it I jotted down / 'Another Nice Poem Written by Rowan' / Before I decided to toss it out?") just make you sorry for
poetry.

A poet who has discovered his powers often resorts to a little grand-
standing ("We are the lost note in the chord of la / Musique éternelle plus
grande that was us," "Nacre-gnarled écorchés of ought / And nought
air"). The book's youthful exuberance, fatuous in its way—like his taste
for sentimental uplift as the poems end—offers a fistful of promissory
notes and scribbled IOUs. If too many poems don't come to much, there
are delicious hints of mastery scattered throughout:

> He sits in a Hawaiian shirt over a bulletproof vest,
> Slumped in a beach chair, its back to the ocean.
> Even his red wine spritzer tastes like Skittles now.

I like the bulletproof vest and Skittle-flavored spritzer, which sound like
Frederick Seidel showing off; but what I love is that beach chair turned
to face the land.

I can give you a dozen reasons why you shouldn't read this book and
only one why you should—the poetic intelligence, though drowned in
run-on sentences and showy detail, suggests that in the next book, or
the next, Phillips will stop trying to make an impression and just write.
That will be something to see.

DOROTHEA LASKY

The poems in *Rome* keep up such an unstoppably hip natter, they might
as well be wearing snap-brim fedoras and hanging out on street corners.
Dorothea Lasky has a plain, off-the-cuff manner, as if she'd written up
whatever she was thinking and dumbed it down a little:

> I walk alone is what came into my head when I was sleeping
> So I wrote you to get the water from which I was so thirsty

Poems are a puzzle
But animals are a beast is
So life is
Quiet life

The lines are trying to do so much at once, it's hard to keep up. O'Hara
might have written the first while missing lunch, but the second gets
snarled in a maze of syntax that must have a Minotaur at the center. It
sounds like a riddle whose answer will open a magic gate or a magic
coffer—"What is that water from which you are so thirsty?" (Um, salt?)
The poem is titled "Horace, to the Romans," but it's hard to see how poor
Horace gets a look in.

Lasky has a grab bag of tricks. There's X-rated sexting:

I want you to eat my menstrual blood
And soft juices
I want to eat your shit until I dream
I want you to come shit all over me.

And dorky science fiction: "I know there is another world / And the
people with their round heads / I know there is a sunset made of sand /
I know they count in fours just to listen to me." There's even a dash
of absurdism à la Ashbery: "I will quench the thirst of my stomach /
And eat the bitter doughnuts / Under the blank sky / Which we have
paid for."

Lasky does more quick changes than a catwalk model; but the poems
all end in the same place, lines overflowing with dread and phony bravado, mingled with deadpan loneliness—with the odd cornball title or
some baby talk thrown in. ("No I don't belong to anyone / Because I
don't and I never did and that's the truth"—that ends with the tag line
of Edith Ann, Lily Tomlin's character, but she would have added a rasp-
berry.) The poems dabble here, sample there, but the more you read the
less there seems to be.

Am I going to die and all I will have are these fucking poems
It doesn't get more real than this

Said the poet
Oh but you hate poems about poetry
And that's fine
Cause I am never going to send you my condolences when I kill it

Such poems ramble along, unpunctuated as a summer dawn, begging for membership in the New Vacuousness. Whatever their miseries, they don't seem to have a care in the world, or anywhere much to get to; and when Lasky can't think of some little twist in rhetoric—you can see the anaphora coming—she just stops dead. One of her articles of faith is that lines should lie on the page like an unraveled ball of yarn. At worst, the poems sound like William Carlos Williams on the day the plums ran out: "Something that I have / Thought of recently / Was my Diet Mountain Dew / Bottle in the kitchen refrigerator."

It's hard to be the latest bad-girl poet when you haven't got acid in your veins. Lasky knows she's not hardcore ("I would have been ok being Plath / But instead I'm Sexton")—she's too garrulous, too needy, to make an impression beyond need, beyond the chatty chatter. Rome has long been a trope for the American empire and its failings. The ancients seem dragged in only to give historical distance to the poet's tears and to pad out the trivia and decocted anxiety with au courant notions of empire and lust, using these antique surrogates as ruthlessly as her lovers apparently use her. The title of the book is merely a come-on—the occasional light wash of classical culture does nothing to give these poems the weight of the past. Much of what she knows about Rome could have been picked up from *Spartacus*.

Reviewers and blurb writers have been more than usually kind to Lasky: "You'll wish your journals sounded this profound," "No one else is writing poetry as boldly colored, unabashed, and wildly human." It's embarrassing when such highly touted poems sound more like cheesy pop songs, Taylor Swift out of Hank Williams Jr.: "It meant nothing / It means nothing / There is nothing / But this / But this," "I always loved you / And I didn't love him / And I used you." Deprived of soulful twang, they're just as banal as lyrics often are—long on longing, short on depth. Indeed, the whole book might have been better had it been sung in four-part harmony.

JOHN ASHBERY

John Ashbery turns eighty-eight this summer and shows no sign of slowing down. The poems continue to pour out—not like the tsunami of his sixties, but still a freshet at an age when most poets have dried up completely. The rumors that an Ashbery app will go on writing his poems long into the next century are as scurrilous as the accusation that the app is writing his poems now.

> Will research tell us tomorrow
> of normal morals? Take a Brooklyn family
> in fracture mode, vivid,
> energizing, throbs to the earlobes. Thanks
> to a snakeskin toupee, my grayish push boots
> exhale new patina/prestige. Exeunt the Kardashians.

Breezeway is the latest example of Ashbery's late-age manner, stuffed with knockabout comedy and droll observations on contemporary mores, with an up-to-date sense of fashion and pop culture. The poems stutter along, always charming, often empty-headed, elusive as the ivory-billed woodpecker—they seem to mean more than they say, while the cynic suspects they say far more than they mean. No matter—Ashbery changes the subject so often you feel you've been mugged. Houdini could not have imagined a better poet, because every poem requires handcuffs, chains, and a key hidden somewhere unmentionable.

Book by book, however, Ashbery has hardened into a crude imitation of himself. Does each generation get the Ashbery it deserves? We expect of him what we expect from any poet—to break new ground. Hardy was boringly and bracingly himself decade after decade—and when he wasn't he produced the disaster that is *The Dynasts*. Yet in the past quarter-century, while scarcely moving a muscle, Ashbery has scribbled some fifteen hundred pages with hardly a memorable poem in them.

He can still write lines so hilariously offbeat you want to quote them until you keel over: "OK, I said it. Sarabande. A dance no one dances anymore. Except maybe in heaven, where they don't have better things to do" or "We walked all the way here in the eighteenth century. / Century of closures! I'm not sure of that though." Or "Those who help me understood / henbane is box office poison. Same for midlength weepies" or "We had a few people over to / celebrate the monotony of the new place" or "Bilingual bullying was on the next floor."

Then there are lines that are mere gibberish: "minute entries blown together / weed house sleep with men / comes after not too bad" or "Last winning people told me to sit on the toilet" or "You wood have too oracle snow." Has the app gone rogue? Pop quiz. Which is Ashbery?

(1)

How to be in the city my loved one.
Men in underwear . . . A biography field
like where we live in the mountains,
a falling. Yes, I know you have.
Troves of merchandise, you know, "boomer buzz."
Hillbilly sculptures of the outside.
(They won't see anybody.)

(2)

Why I never . . . That came from a tree.
For whatever reason,
the salt has lost its savior.
J'accuse. The open system showing its age,
they said. I can't tell the doctor about it.
Is that such a big deal, Danny boy?

Trick question. Both are! The second example consists of the last sentences of the opening poems in the book. That it's impossible to tell the difference tells us a lot about Ashbery, and a little about ourselves.

Ashbery's aleatoric rants have been a delight for sixty years or more. Our poetry would have been poorer without this dash of Dada, though like all sugary things you can overdose on it. He took a small part of O'Hara's manner and blew it up into five-alarm farce. Ashbery's impeccable sense of pastiche, of snappy repartee that bursts like a bubble and is immediately forgotten, has expanded the notion of what poetry can be—yet it's hard to say that American poetry would be much the worse had he never written a word—or, rather, had he written nothing except "Self-Portrait in a Convex Mirror," which remains the stunning party piece it always was.

Ashbery has kept our poetry in touch with slang, his ear having caught on the fly "sockdolager" and "so's your old man," "neat-o" and "bummer," "pod cast" and "morphs" and "OMG." He's an archive of sound bites from the days of Hoover to those of Obama. When I feel the world too much with me and need a pick-me-up, I go to Ashbery, just as I go to Carroll or Swift. If I think the old master has lost his touch, that he's entirely forgotten how to bang out a poem, he wakes me from my torpor. The best poem in *Breezeway* is a dialogue in a commuter bar car:

> Pardon my sarong. I'll have a Shirley Temple.
> Certainly, sir. Do you want a cherry with that?
> I guess so. It's part of it, isn't it?
> Strictly speaking, yes. Some of them likes it,
> others not so much. Well, I'll have a cherry.
> I can be forgiven for not knowing it's de rigueur.
> In my commuter mug, please. Certainly.

It sounds like slow-burning Beckett, but it ends, "Do I wake or sleep?" For a poet whose lines often seem to forget the lines just slapped down, Lethe always awaits. How nice to close with Keats.

EAVAN BOLAND

Dragged from Dublin to London to New York before she was a teenager, Eavan Boland has spent her adult life between countries. The daughter of a respected painter of still lifes and a former Irish ambassador to the United Nations, she wars against the legacy of Ireland almost as much as she embraces it. A book titled *A Woman Without a Country* has certain obvious themes available, and Boland doesn't hesitate to pick them up and throttle them as often as possible.

Boland is a fluent, serious poet with peat under her nails. She sculpts her lines with a mattock. When she's patient, open to the crabbed beauties of experience rather than some PowerPoint version of them, the poems bear the minor grandeurs of the world without disregarding the scars:

> I have a word for it—
> the way the surface waited all day
> to be a silvery pause between sky and city—
> which is *elver*.
>
> And another one for how
> the bay shelved cirrus clouds
> piled up at the edge of the Irish Sea,
> which is *elver*, too.

The observation lives within silence, the pauses between one vision and another. The lines wait for such moments of detachment, visual predation, even neglect.

Too many poems, however, have been issued a road map in advance. Boland knows where they're going and all too soon the reader does, too. She imagines watching the terrible Victorian poet Speranza at work: "She is / busy with / the transformation. / She is writing to Ireland. / Ireland. She is." In her memoir, *A Journey with Two Maps* (2011), Boland wrote far more compellingly and critically of this minor poet, Oscar Wilde's mother—but in poems Boland can't help climbing on a soapbox: "You will not like it, Clio, this menial task / I have in mind for you: speak for me, / say *history* say *famine* / say *fever* say *Trevelyan*." That would be Charles Trevelyan, the despised English administrator of Irish famine relief.

Such arguments with history seem prejudged, with little left to learn the second or third time around. (Boland dealt with Trevelyan forty years ago in "The Famine Road.") After lines here and there like "He has no language for the Empire that owns him," or "she lived in a dying Empire," or "1890. Empire, attitude," the reader may look at his watch while the ax is being ground, even if he likes axes. In such a hymnal, no questions of faith are permitted. One of the many virtues of Auden's and Heaney's political poems is that they are comfortable with ambiguity.

The low point in the book is a sequence for the poet's grandmother, divided by six didactic prose "lessons" that batter the poems to death: "The issue between an artist and a nation is not a faith, but a self. The issue between the artist and a truth is not a self, but an image." Such terms could be juggled for a year without becoming a whit less opaque.

The themes of history, empire, and oppression keep surfacing without quite being gripped. Boland knows the burden of the past, yet the past rarely seems more than set decoration. For all her invocations of the famine, the Irish War of Independence, the Troubles, for all the sorrows in the extended portrait of her grandmother, the poems often lie lifeless on the page. The glints and hints of ambition are overwhelmed by the finger-shaking. Boland's a vivid and emotional poet who too often dresses in sackcloth.

When she's not hectoring the reader or succumbing to sentiment (she's got a romantic streak as broad as the Irish Sea), Boland can let in the extranea of the world:

Yellow vestments took in light
A chalice hid underneath its veil.

Her hands were full of calla and cold weather lilies.
The mail packet dropped anchor.
A black-headed gull swerved across the harbor.

Without knowing more, the reader will understand that something has come to an end. It was not the poet but her grandmother, after living in Ireland all her life, who had no country.

The question that haunts poets as they age is whether they've become some dull ghost of the younger poet who breathed fire. There's a radical difference between the dissipation of elderly Pound and the sharp renewals of Yeats, the shallow sludge of ancient Frost and the religious depths of wartime Eliot. The promising manner in this book can be found not in poems already predicted by the oddsmakers in Las Vegas but in quieter, unexpected things—sly moments of fancy, the shame of having an ancestor who was master of a workhouse, the delirious image of Eurydice "walking beside ditches brimming with dactyls."

ROWAN WILLIAMS

Rowan Williams served a long decade as Archbishop of Canterbury, so it's fortunate the post is not a requirement for budding poets. (Besides, too many believe themselves archbishops already.) Williams has a reputation for formidable intelligence and undogmatic religiosity. The poetry in *The Other Mountain* possesses both, despite being mannered, clotted, and weighed down by the chainmail of rhetoric—it's the poetry academics write on holiday.

> Sliced clean as marble; a glassy mourner
> bending to read the blunt letters, the routines
> of leavetaking. But glass will splinter: ragged bites
> stand open and the port-red ooze, crusted
> like scale in kettles, wanders, slow as a winter fly,
> across the arctic slope. Gashed bodies
> push out their sickness through the skin:
> the marble mourner has leached up the fevers
> from the rubbed lives piled round its roots.

The subject is a bleeding yew in the graveyard of the Norman church of St. Brynach at Nevern in Wales. Had Williams not mentioned that in the title, the poor reader could not have discovered it in a month of Sundays. The opening jumble of phrases with little syntactic relation—the "glassy mourner" is the tree—would baffle even a CIA codebreaker until that late reference to roots. The glass will splinter because it's wood, "ooze" is not verb but noun, and the rubbed lives are presumably the dead whose gravestones have been eroded by time, with perhaps a glance at the pastime of grave rubbing. (Marble isn't sliced clean—it's laboriously sawn and then polished smooth.) That mourner bends to read the letters left on the stones. Are the gashed bodies soldiers dead in ancient battle, or is that another reference to the antique tree, which has lost a few of its limbs? Is "sickness" blood or some sap-ridden arboreal infection?

None of this is particularly obscure, but there seems small advantage in language that strains so to deliver itself of meaning. A poet who contemplates the world in such terms must be a master of depths, like Geoffrey Hill—otherwise the poems will choke on the musty atmosphere of long-shut libraries. It's sometimes claimed that the yews needed for longbows were grown in fenced-off churchyards because the tree was poisonous to cattle. The tale is no doubt apocryphal—church yews probably survived because no one was allowed to fell them. The tree, now often identified with Yggdrasil, may have benefited from pagan respect for its long life. Some are perhaps two thousand years old.

It's almost the job description of archbishops to hunt for symbols and cobble up allegories. (Sermons are too often a degraded form of poetic craft.) Williams has a taste for overripe phrases and Byzantine syntax, without being able to use all that rhetorical force to produce anything but overdecorated Morris wallpaper. There are faint notes of Hughes and Heaney throughout, without the muscular bustle of thought beneath; and too often the poems fall into sentimental charities that would exasperate even Hopkins: "night // Where the stars' little wounds drop streams / of slender clarity, no less than days of mist / and the mumbled theatre of waking dreams." *The mumbled theatre of waking dreams*! That will show Hart Crane a thing or two.

Williams has the seriousness of his original calling, but seriousness is not always a good thing for a poet—a little humor might substitute for humility. Instead, the former archbishop hoards metaphors like a miser, eggs the emotion into overrich pudding, and, whenever he nears the inhumanity of man, can't help himself:

When, in the starburst's centre,
the little black mouth opens, then clenches,
and the flaying wind smoothes down the grass,
and prints its news black on bright blinding
walls, when it sucks back the milk
and breath and skin, and all the world's vowels
drown in flayed throats, the hard things,
bone and tooth, fuse into consonants of stone.

The world's vowels drown in flayed throats! Consonants of stone! The scene is Nagasaki, where the shadows of the dead were burnt into walls, where the milk in the breasts of dead mothers was vaporized. All the pity in the world, all our sorrow for the dead, can't justify writing so self-conscious and suffocating. *Feel! Feel!* the poems plead. The word "heavy-handed" was invented for such occasions.

A striking fable or two and the poet's love for the thinginess of things are not enough. Williams is not the shallow, frivolous noodle that celebrity poets usually are, all cassock and no crosier. Randall Jarrell once wrote, scanning the books of bad verse before him, "How cruel that a cardinal—for one of these books is a cardinal's—should write verses worse than his youngest choir-boy's!" *Plus ça change.* Yet the wet-eared choir-boy could no longer write better than Williams, not on a bet.

HENRI COLE

Henri Cole's *Nothing to Declare* starts by beating a dead horse:

> sucked out to sea and washed up again—
> with uprooted trees, crumpled cars, and collapsed houses—
> facedown in dirt, and tied to a telephone pole,
> as if trying to raise herself still, though one leg is broken,
> to look around at the grotesque unbelievable landscape.

Something has happened, but Cole refuses the reader the solace of history. The moment, presented as if snipped out of air, ends with the mystery of a boy, probably the beast's owner, "stroking the majestic rowing legs, / stiff now, that could not outrun / the heavy, black, frothing water." When you realize a tsunami has passed, that provides no solace, either.

After more than a decade writing quasi-sonnets, Cole has cast most of his new poems in clipped five-line stanzas. Anxieties still surround him like a miasma—the broken family (hard-faced father, wounded mother); the ridiculously louche lovers; and a strange cast of animals, half-Grimm, half-Disney. The new poems have a lightness of touch but the same bleak affect that haunts his later books. Their power derives from the reader's recognition of their pained privacy, even though they've been left in the open, like a scandalous letter dropped casually on a table.

Cole loves to shock, and it doesn't take much to bring out his inner Grand Guignol:

> Eating a sugar sandwich, I sit at the kitchen table
> admiring the geraniums outside the window,
> their big heads as American as Martha Washington.
> I grew them from seeds, and now the leaves are frilly like genitalia.

The cheerful luridness promises a series of aftershocks, though that "sugar sandwich" (a Depression staple) does not sweeten the self-admiration. Cole must know that a popular geranium (perhaps the very one he planted) is called the Martha Washington—though it looks not a thing like her. He's probably the first poet to put the first First Lady anywhere near frilly genitalia. The poem eventually gets round to the poet's clamor of identity, but that's a sideshow after the bizarre, flamboyant geraniums.

The morose poet of desk and kitchen, who admits, "I like invisible-ness," and calls himself a "piece of meat with eyes," is Jekyll. Hyde demands subjects startling as the front page of the *New York Post*—a girl who speaks after being murdered by a serial killer, a bizarre dream in which his mother's hands have been amputated, the autopsy of Lincoln, and a birth partly magnificent and partly freak show:

> Her teats were fat as ticks and her udder was heavy.
> A little pink poked out from her vulva,
> and she grunted softly while making small defecations
> all around the stall. Pacing, pawing, standing up, and lying down,
> she was waiting for the cover of darkness,
> but when she started to sweat, the baby—perfectly well-made—
> came quickly, groggy and gleaming from her insides.

The mother might be cow or horse; but the newborn, "calling to mind remnants of defeated armies, / fleeing slaves, and refugees herded across / all the borders of the earth," makes us think again. The udder isn't human; yet after the poet christens the calf or foal a baby, trots out those slaves and refugees, and titles the poem "Mother and Child" it's hard not to think this also the Virgin Mary, given back some of the animal nature religion has removed. Cole would have had Freud scrabbling for his notebook.

The poet has long turned to the animal kingdom for his alter egos— it's as if all the beasts of forest and field have gathered around him like the bluebirds in Disney's *Snow White*. This engagement with the animal (unlike Marianne Moore's, but not that unlike) always keeps the self at center. Cole can sometimes talk about himself only through proxy sufferers: the buffalo who resists when all his fellows go charging over a cliff, the dying bee outside the window, the sardines gutted for dinner and providing life lessons along the way. Then there's the gelding, seen in an advertisement, named Henri. There are dangers in using animals to say what cannot be said—in the weakest of his recent books, *Blackbird and Wolf*, the brutes practically took over.

Cole has a shapeshifting ability to discard adulthood and see the world afresh, before succumbing again to gloom. (The poems sometimes start as Bishop and end as Glück.) I can't help but fall in love with a poet who declares, offhandedly, "Sometimes, / during breakfast, // I speak French with / a taxidermied wren," or listens "to the mantel clock's / kind, minimalist / *Don't be afraid*." There are missteps. Cole turns the rutting of stags into a symbol of romance only at the cost of baroque grandiosity— the beasts bear too much psychological burden. There are stray moments of teary sentiment and now and again a medicinal dose of self-pity.

It has been apparent for some time that Cole is the most important American poet under sixty. His late work has made the bland, generic poems of so many in his generation an embarrassment. His unsparing portraits are as scarifying as any poems we have. (I'm surprised there's no poem about St. Sebastian—ah, but he wrote that two or three books ago.) These poems record moments of cruelty, murder, even birth—but beneath lies the terrifying will to survive. To survive, and suffer.

Meeting Mr. Hill

I arrived in England shortly after the Brixton riots and in the midst of the Ashes, won largely through the heroics of Ian Botham. He was a legend then—a decade later, when he could neither bowl like a demon nor hit for six with the old careless, magisterial command, a columnist said that the legend had become a myth. Over the streets, nailed to hoardings, were large signs that advised TAKE COURAGE. Courage was a brand of ale. It was high summer, 1981.

We rented a modest terrace-house in Cambridge on a back street near the river, an apple tree in the garden and a chiropractor next door. Up and down the Cam trailed the stately swans, dying of lead poisoning. Because we knew no one, I dropped notes to local poets and critics—I suppose that's what Eliot did when he arrived in London almost seventy years before. The only poet in Cambridge, so far as I was concerned, was Geoffrey Hill. A note was returned, asking me to come on a certain afternoon to his rooms in Emmanuel College.

Hill was not quite fifty, slightly barrel-chested, with a dark scurf of beard. He lodged in a small set of rooms up one of the staircases in a modern wing of the college—the rooms were neither austere nor overdressed. Hill was courtly in his coolness, but he took boyish pleasure in showing off the knickknacks and arcana displayed on a coffee table. He was proudest of the small pistol his father had carried as a police constable in Bromsgrove. I mentioned that I had been reading a lot of Larkin. "Larkin!" he exclaimed from the little kitchen, where he had gone to fix us tea. "That yobbo!"

For the two years Debora Greger and I lived in Cambridge, we met Geoffrey for lunch every month or so, or invited him to dinner on Pretoria Road. He dressed in black, like some English Johnny Cash, except for a pair of lurid socks—fuchsia and acid yellow were favorite colors, the rakish touch in that monkish wardrobe. Each time it was as if we were meeting as strangers. He would be stiff, heavy with a formality that lasted a quarter-hour or so; then at last, by infinitesimal degrees, he would warm to the company (or just give in to the burden of friendliness). Once he did a wicked imitation of a hedgehog.

Hill was breathtakingly shy, nearly as shy as a hedgehog—formality and bluster were his protections against the world. We attended three or four of his lectures, which were grave, learned, delivered as if composed of death notices—they were also ponderously slow. (By the end of a series of lectures, only a few true believers were left in the hall.) His method, which did not endear him to students, revealed the pressure of learning within, while tending to hide the grace. Indeed, that seemed part of the poet's character—he was not an example of grace under pressure but of pressure under grace.

There were also, I now recall, one or two Dinky toys on that table, additional relics of his childhood. (These perhaps make more important the references in poems to his toys.) "I am certain," he once admitted, "that on a back street, in a cathedral town, there stands a shop, its windows coated in dust. Inside there are still shelves of old Dinky toys, pristine in their original boxes, and bearing their original prices."

Toward the end of 1982, Hill loaned us the typescript of *The Mystery of the Charity of Charles Péguy*. He mentioned that, where he had changed his mind, he had tried to find a word with the same number of letters, so the compositor wouldn't be put to trouble. When I innocently pointed out that different letters took up different amounts of space, he looked crestfallen, as if some terrible secret had been revealed.

Faced with the petty annoyances of life, Hill often adopted a rueful tone. Once, in the upper stacks of the university library, he came round a corner, having loudly pronounced his frustration at not being able to find some book crucial to a footnote. Seeing me with my head buried in a book, he stopped short. "You are always there," he said, "to observe my inadequacies and misdemeanors." I no longer recall what prior accident had elevated me to that status—but the hound-dog mournfulness was his way of being funny.

We both had a taste for rare books acquired on the cheap. One day something went wrong with his car, and I offered to look at it. My competence as a mechanic was open to question, but there was some complication in the fuses I was able to figure out—and soon the thing was running again. In celebration, he decided to drive us into the fens to a bookshop in the horse-racing village of Newmarket, a shop long heard of but never visited. Geoffrey's fantasy was that we would discover there a pristine copy of *Land of Unlikeness*, probably for tuppence—and that we would each race to grab it.

This was perhaps not as impossible as might appear. On the 50p table at a local bookseller's, I had found the original edition of *Typee*, and on the shelves of another shop a signed copy of Bret Harte stories for £6. Indeed, there was a tale circulating in Cambridge of a man who, visiting a dusty bookshop in Prague or Budapest, no doubt on a back street, had spirited away a copy of the Second Folio for a couple hundred pounds. Our appetites had been whetted. We arrived at the shop. The door was locked. A hand-lettered sign on the glass read "Closed Due to Death of the Owner." As we turned away, Geoffrey muttered, "The man knew we were coming." Then he smiled.

We left England late in the summer of 1983. As a farewell, Geoffrey invited us to lunch at Emmanuel, a departure from custom, as he preferred to meet in pubs. Having greeted us in his rooms, he led us down to the dining hall. Before we entered, he turned and said, with courtly gravity, "If I do not introduce you, it is only because I . . . have forgotten . . . your names."

Those were about the last words spoken between us for a quarter-century. In time, somehow or other, I ended up with two copies of *Land of Unlikeness*.

The Death of Geoffrey Hill

G eoffrey Hill was the major English poet of the last half of the twentieth century. Hill's intransigence, his clotted difficulty, his passion
for the redolent fineries of English landscape—he eyed the woods and
fields like a plant hunter—have stood in magnificent solitude. Among the
poets long set for A-level examinations in Britain, Thom Gunn and Ted
Hughes, good poets in their way, had neither the depth nor the irritating
brilliance of Hill—both Gunn and Hughes seem poets of their day, with
the manners of that day. That's the fate of most poets—for many, their
highest aim. Hill was never on the syllabus.

That Hill from the start was trying to escape his time—perhaps to
wrestle his way out—was apparent in the coiled syntax and lush imagery
of his first books, *For the Unfallen* (1959) and *King Log* (1968):

> The Word has been abroad, is back, with a tanned look
> From its subsistence in the stiffening-mire.
> Cleansing has become killing, the reward
> Touchable, overt, clean to the touch.
> Now at a distance from the steam of beasts,
> The loathly neckings and fat shook spawn
> (Each specimen-jar fed with delicate spawn)
> The searchers with the curers sit at meat
> And are satisfied.
>
> ("Annunciations, I")

These were the poems of a young man at odds with the Movement, but
the influence of the Metaphysicals (and of poets as rarely embraced, at

least on such terms, as Southwell and Blake) showed that Hill had set himself tasks that made most of his contemporaries look like the pale imitations they were.

The death of a great poet leaves a gap, even an abyss. (It's remarkable how many poets once considered great end with a period, not an ellipsis. What afterlife has de la Mare enjoyed, or John Masefield, or Stephen Vincent Benét?) In "Tradition and the Individual Talent," Eliot famously remarked,

> the existing monuments [of art] form an ideal order among themselves, which is modified by the introduction of the new (the really new) work of art among them. The existing order is complete before the new work arrives; for order to persist after the supervention of novelty, the *whole* existing order must be, if ever so slightly, altered.

So of poets. After a death, those remaining form a new order, their relation to one another forever changed. Indeed, it is by sensing that alteration that we realize greatness has passed—like the perturbations in the orbit of Uranus that marked the presence of an unknown planet.

Which deaths over the past century have had such affect? The modernists, of course, though their careers ended long before they died—before obituaries were written for Eliot, Pound, Moore, Frost, and Williams, their absence had been calculated and digested. (Stevens died closer to some of his major work, but perhaps after a certain age a poet writes posthumously.) Who else, then? Yeats. Auden. Lowell and Bishop, certainly. Heaney, of a generation younger. Now Hill. (In a more minor register, Larkin. Plath, after the publication of *Ariel*. Berryman, perhaps, though his influence was fatal to poets who tried to form a School of John.)

Hill's father was a police constable in a Worcestershire market village. The poet came, certainly in the private myth of his making, from the old stock of nailmakers. Similar stock once provided the bowmen at Agincourt, their skills passed through families, with nothing ahead but a twisted spine, muddy death, some gristly pride. Hill's hardbitten splendor was a wound in the blood, in other words.

Autumn resumes the land, ruffles the woods
with smoky wings, entangles them. Trees shine
out from their leaves, rocks mildew to moss-green;
the avenues are spread with brittle floods.

Platonic England, house of solitudes,
rests in its laurels and its injured stone.

("An Apology for the Revival of Christian
Architecture in England," 9)

His poetry was recognized even at Oxford, where he took a first in English, as exacting and formidable—forged not in new language but in an older language still glorious, but indrawn, out of key with his time (in Pound's phrase) and in key with times long past, as if Donne or Vaughan had been drummed out of the seventeenth century and into the twentieth. Indeed, in *Mercian Hymns* (1971) Hill hauled the ashes of King Offa from the Dark Age of the Midlands to dump them in the Dark Age of modern England. The poetry of stony certitudes, glistening with primal ardor, fertile but intellective, yet often dry (though not so dry as late Eliot), had only a small clutch of readers from the start.

Hill wrote "memorable speech," Auden's definition of poetry, which like all such definitions casts a net too broad. (Pilfering the phrase from Arthur Quiller-Couch, Auden left out "set down in metre with strict rhythms.") Hill created his own world—or the rhetoric and style that required a world. If you wished to enter, you had to accept its terms—the contract demanded a measure of punishment. It was hard for him to imagine a poetry that did not tax the reader's intelligence. He armored the poems against loss of attention and therefore made them hard to attend to. For poetry that often left a touch of religion at the edges—Christianity variously rejected, scolded, hedged—some sacrifice was necessary. His second wife, an Anglican rector, said that her husband knelt at the altar, "communicant but resentful."

The wise men, vulnerable in ageing plaster,
are borne as gifts

to be set down among the other treasures
in their familial strangeness, mystery's toys.

("Epiphany at Saint Mary and All Saints")

After the age of sixty, we all live in penalty time—but his gift allowed
Hill to remake himself at the outset of great age. When the clockworks
of most poets are winding down, Prozac proved a specific against throt-
tling depression, releasing him from the trammels. He became what earlier he might have sneered at—industrious. We are rightly suspicious of
poets who pour ink onto the page, yet the fluency of Byron is very different from the fluency of Southey. Wordsworth had workaday grace
when young but only facile and disastrous ease in old age. Shakespeare—
well, Shakespeare. Yet with Hill, even when he wrote rapidly, the
poems seem dragged from the depths. (Recall that line from bad police-
procedurals, "Order the men to drag the harbor.") I imagine that he
reacted to the onset of the late work with some elation and some alarm—
he was the sort to feel that every silver cloud had a lead lining.

Above Dunkirk, the sheared anvil-
head of the oil-smoke column, the wind
beginning to turn, turning on itself, spiralling,
shaped on its potter's wheel. But no fire-storm:
such phenomena were as yet unvisited
upon Judeo-Christian-Senecan Europe.

("The Triumph of Love," XI)

Looking over the wreckage of the later books, especially *The Daybooks*, composed over the last decade of his life, it's hard to imagine a
race of readers that could find much beyond the browbeating and cater-
wauling. Hill became a voice crying in the wilderness, like an Old
Testament grandee—prophet, I mean. Short passages rise beyond the
sensibility of the vexed, hermetic mind that composed them—as if the
sharpened pales Hill erected against the common reader, the reader he
so often held in contempt (let's face it, the common reader is a poor
judge of what will last), had become a stronghold the poems could
rarely escape.

This might equally be a description of the ravaged landscape of Pound's *Cantos*—local beauties abound, but apart from the early cantos, and others in a limited way, the willful obscurity and vast stretches of sludge have not grown more attractive since his death, however thoroughly the poems have been excavated. The work for Hill went far enough until it went too far. You can fail to seduce a reader by despising him, but you should not despise him for wanting to be seduced. And yet. And yet.

After the torrent of the last poems, book after unlikely book wallowing forth—growly, leg-pulling, sometimes tortured into rhyme, obscure as Linear A (or were the poems closer to the Kensington stela or the Spirit Pond runestones?)—suddenly the millwheel stopped and the millrace was closed. Perhaps someone, somewhere, is preparing a *Key to All Mythologies* to explain poems almost immune to the reader's eye (as Hill, if we believe him, seems to have wished, though beneath every resistant child lurks a desire for love). What they offer is so partial, so demanding, at best they might come to have the reputation of *Finnegans Wake*—preposterous, brilliant, but who but an Aquinas can find the time? The grim pride did Hill no favors.

The great work, the work likely to last because it can be read with stony-eyed (but not stony-hearted) pleasure, will be the best of the early poems, the shocking swerve of *Mercian Hymns*, the magnificent long poem *The Mystery of the Charity of Charles Péguy*, and, among the books of the Flood, *Canaan*, *The Triumph of Love*, *The Orchards of Syon*, *Without Title*, and *A Treatise of Civil Power*, books more focused if not easy to compass. After publication of his collected poems five years ago, Hill lapsed into the quietude—perhaps, in his case, a fraught quietude—that often befalls poets in their eighties. He became Grand Old Mannish in his last years, with his Brillo of white beard and a straw hat only slightly larger than a hubcap. Then there was a quiet click as he slipped out the door.

Two Strangers (Marie Ponsot and Ishion Hutchinson)

MARIE PONSOT

Most of Marie Ponsot's career has been belated. Her first book was published in the City Lights Pocket Poets series in 1956, when she was already thirty-five—late, but not as late as Frost or Stevens. Her next, not until she was sixty. Now ninety-five, she has continued to publish a book every decade or so, as if she had all the time in the world. *Complete Poems* is the model for every poet who worships procrastination.

Being a minor Beat might have been more than enough reason to fall silent. Her early poems were overstuffed with preening twists of rhetoric: "Let no word with its thinking threat / Thrust betwixt our kissing touch," "It is not ring-magic nor the faithing leap of sex," "Coming out of ether I might cry on reed and rood of sacredness." These sound like passages dropped from *The Lord of the Rings*. Secondhand Tolkien is one thing—bad Allen Ginsberg quite another:

> Bring me that truth love-ridden whose black blaze makes
> A comfort in the ice-bitten ghettos of cities, that wise
> Love whose intemperate told truth thrusts into the aching
> Arms of old men old women's lonely bodies with a cry.

Nevertheless, the first poems have hints of modernism (in the French titles, among other places) and faint whispers of Marianne Moore—though perhaps Moore seen through a spyglass. Only a quarter-century later in that second book, *Admit Impediment* (1981), did the rabid hectoring, schoolmarmish decorum, and jumbled syntax (sometimes Ponsot seemed to be rewiring Donne) start to fade away.

Ponsot found her vein of expression by attending to the small. The poems were still overbearing, but more modest now. Though she continued to turn the emoting up to eleven at times, gradually she accepted the poetic virtues of a workaday life. That wasn't settling for restraint (though the private details were dull enough) so much as allowing restriction to free her from ambitions unsuited to her talent. She was always aware that freedom for men meant constraint for women—it's not surprising that sometimes this boiled up as rage.

Ponsot was an observer like Moore, a noticer of things unnoticed—or unheard. Few poets would have bothered to eavesdrop on a senior citizen gabbling on about her husband: "'He was just like my father, he / didn't know I was alive. / With him it wasn't business it was socialism.'" There's a whole novel by Zola or Dickens there.

Poets usually begin by writing loads of rubbish, and few ever write anything else. Ponsot long struggled toward a style that would yield to the particulars of imagination. Her mature poems show the restlessness of a poet who kept writing but simply chose not to publish. In those long decades there was a certain rustiness, as if the talent were partly out of use, with here and there a line of almost shocking clarity. It did not take much to stir up again whatever had been buried back in the fifties. *The Green Dark* (1988), published at an age when most poets would have been cashing Social Security checks, revealed a late-blooming richness comparable to Amy Clampitt's.

Ponsot discovered poems not just in psychological mini-portraits of friends but in life lived through nature. Gradually she abandoned the hollow immensities ("Yet it is the personal / that links us body to body / in the gigantic intercourse, fugal / among the spheres"), applying a metaphysics of observation to aesthetics of feeling: "Sudden awe sudden dread: the visible / fontanelle just under the scalp / of the delicate new-born head." She became at times imposingly charming:

I explain ontology, mathematics, theophily,
Symbolic & Aristotelean logic, says the tree.

I demonstrate perspective's & proportion's ways.
I elucidate even greyness by my greys & greys & greys.

The history of landscape painting lies deep in that outburst. A cynical humor also kept breaking in: "'I'm moving from Grief Street. / Taxes are high here / though the mortgage's cheap.'"

If she rarely achieved the difficult balance between wearying naiveté and knowing longwindedness (Elizabeth Bishop is the rare poet who could make faux naiveté sound like wise innocence), Ponsot was always a poet inconsistent in her triumphs, often succeeding and failing in the same poem. The risks she took produced depths otherwise impossible. Her poems early and late are slightly ungainly, impossible constructions (like a Louis XVI settee made from an Erector Set), but her oddities turned more lovable as she aged.

What begins as craft for a poet sooner or later has to become second nature—and in the poems of age Ponsot found that the offhand remark, the small scene deftly rendered, could suggest more than suggestion can. (Emily Dickinson said, "Tell all the truth but tell it slant," and Ponsot took the advice with a protractor.) Her casual manner was terrifying because seemingly never calculated. A poet who can write, of a flicker, "It chisels toward the fault"; or of a lover, "We make love and other excuses"; or of Pascal's brilliant sister, "In her convent Jacqueline kept the rules. / On or under every desert there are pools," can write, at off-angles, on subjects difficult if not impossible:

> Suicide, in a village of forty heads,
> is loud language—mythic but personal.
> This year's been hard. A father hanged himself
> in time for New Year's. Now at noon on May Day
> the son's found drowned, sand in his redblond hair
> facedown in the shallows of a river
> a fox can walk across, head above water—
> a week before the hay comes in. Despair's
> not a word they use.

Willing to see what is hard to watch, Ponsot was never afraid of cunning. She's a fox, not a hedgehog.

Not all her poems come to much. Many come to nothing at all—but then for most poets poetry is not hit or miss but miss and miss and miss.

A good poem is as rare as an old canary in a coal mine. Ponsot has a weakness for poetic forms like the sestina, though her sestinas are recommended only for insomniacs. She's best not in the crown of sonnets or the occasional villanelle but in poems where she lets her will-o'-the-wisp imagination find its own course. The titles and subjects of her most recent book, *Easy* (2009), are fearless, which cannot be said of many poets in their late eighties—"Peter Rabbit's Middle Sister," "Drive Like a Lady Blues," and, for subjects, a Mesopotamian lute four thousand years old, Mozart and his starling, a soliloquy by a turkey, a desert gas station.

You could overrate Ponsot, but she's much more interesting when underrated. You happen on a line like an albino rhinoceros and immediately want to possess it. She reminds me of another undervalued poet of her generation, Eleanor Ross Taylor. We read such poets because we want to know how a poetic intelligence inhabits the world—or invents it. Ponsot found her way through nature (she might have been happiest as a Metaphysical garden poet), but she promises nothing like consolation. Readers after solace or revelation will find bad poets enough to supply them. Ponsot works where being is not contempt.

ISHION HUTCHINSON

Ishion Hutchinson's darkly tinged yet exuberant new poems are the strongest to come out of the Caribbean in a generation. Haunted by his country's fractured past, by memories of an upbringing starved of books, he escaped from history through literature. If his heart still lies in Jamaica, writers have given him a landscape beyond memory. His touchstone is the magnificent passage in Xenophon where the Greek mercenaries, having fought their way across the Persian Empire, come to the Black Sea, shouting "Thalatta! Thalatta!" ("The sea! The sea!"). The moment would brand any poet trying to find his way home.

If this resembles Derek Walcott's poetry, the heavy influence is lightly worn. The saturated descriptions of island flora, the pen portraits (as they once were called) of local characters, the stranger-in-a-strange-land displacement, the visceral love of Europe and the classics—all these make *House of Lords and Commons* indebted to the poet who for half a century has cast a long shadow over Caribbean literature. Hutchinson's elegant, rough-edged poems have wrestled with influence without being overwhelmed.

> The streetlights shed pearls that night,
> stray dogs ran but did not bark at the strange
> shadows; the Minister of All could not sleep,
> mosquitoes swarmed around his net,
> his portrait and his picture and drinking glass;
> the flags stiffened on the embassy building but
> did not fall when the machine guns
> flared.

Soaked in the intelligence of cities and towns where nature seems the dominating grace, these poems try to negotiate a treaty between Jamaica and the foreign world for which the poet abandoned it. In memories of the near riot of cane cutters stiffed by their bosses or the mysterious classroom hierarchies of primary school in St. Thomas Parish, the country Hutchinson left behind has rarely been so vividly rendered.

After college in Jamaica, the poet flew to America. He now teaches at Cornell. His descriptions find their urgency in his unsettled place between two worlds. (Poetry, for the exile, may be a surrogate home.) The fraught self-examination of these poems defines their achievement. Where Walcott's point of view was established in his thirties and rarely wavered, Hutchinson seems still in the midst of inventing himself. His rooted suspicion of academic views of Empire is no more savagely expressed than during a lecture by a "tweeded rodent scholar":

> a bore
> was harping in dead metaphor
> the horror of colonial heritage.
> I sank in the dark, hemorrhaged.
> There I remembered the peninsula
> of my sea, the breeze opening the water
> to no book but dusk; no electricity,
> just stars pulsing over shanties.

The poet may perhaps be forgiven the touch of sentiment at the end. (Night sky makes him mawkish.) The whole of *House of Lords and Commons*, the title an ancient term for the houses of Parliament, is a rejection of the unctuous jargon of academia, its gaseous clichés about the post-colonial Other and the anthropological gaze. Hutchinson writes poetry with an estrangement that doesn't need the justifications of theory or its distaste for drenched metaphors that escape the political realm.

The books that infuse these poems look back to the generation of poets post-Eliot, a generation that found inspiration in literature as much as life—that considered literature, indeed, a higher form of life. A casual allusion to Sir Thomas Browne and sidelong references to Heidegger and Lévi-Strauss set the tone; but Hutchinson can leap in a stanza from Chaucer to Frederick Douglass or, with music in mind, title a poem "Sibelius and Marley." The shotgun wedding of the latter takes not the sublime to the ridiculous but one sublime to another—alas, the poet's just as cack-handed as most poets who try to turn music into poetry. When Marley "wails and a comet impales the sky," the reader can't help but cringe.

Hutchinson's affectionate portraits of local characters have the finesse and generosity of Chaucer (rather than the cartoonish burlesque of Browning), and the poems in persona create their voices with an easy command that always eluded Walcott, whose attempts at island patois sound forced. Hutchinson marks the rhythms of local speech without trying to mimic the voice, say, of the record producer Lee "Scratch" Perry:

> consider
> the nest of wasps in the heart of the Bush Doctor,
> consider the nest of locusts in the gut of the Black Heart Man,
> I put them there, and the others that vibrate at the feast of the
> Passover when the collie weed
> is passed over the roast fish and cornbread. I Upsetter, I Django
> on the black wax.

This may be a bit arch, but the spirited aggression is preferable to the studious self-regard of third-generation confessional poetry.

Back home, Hutchinson becomes a Baudelairean flâneur, a tourist in a land more vivid for no longer being his own:

Let the cerement of light, the silent snow
covering the bells frozen in the towers, speak

a country of tired bays, where rain hesitates
to break the seamless yellow of toil; let this

coffin-shaped light balance on the negative
compass, the shock and stun, the heart's

sudden brace for a jealous thunder.

The metaphors are elsewhere laid on with a trowel, and too many poems descend into lists that run out of steam long before they're finished. Hutchinson arrives in Venice like a yokel with a passport: "I hop off the vaporetto mooring in / the after-storm harbour, puff-chested, shouting: / 'Keep up your bright swords, for the dew will rust them.'" OK, *Othello*— but the trace of self-mockery in "puff-chested" isn't enough. Call it the preening of a gifted young artist.

This is a young man's book, with the expected flaws of excess and overreaching—before a poet can break the wild horses of invention, he has to capture them. Hutchinson's poems are prosy, often not quite wholes, just fragments of sensibility. Perhaps the occasional straining for intensity ("I circled half-mad a dead azalea scent that framed / my room; I licked anointed oil off a sardine tin") will relax into the giddy accuracy of the best lines here: "the white detonating curtain, the sea, our sea," "a rusty mule, / statue-frozen in the punishable heat," "God grumbles in his mirrored palace."

If the voice is sometimes monotonous, the rhetoric often inflated ("they steam chromatic, these Elijahs / in their cloud wheels, fatherless and man-killing"—the "cloud wheels" are just automobiles), Hutchinson has a mature sense of tone and a wary detachment that gives the ordinary the glossy depths of a Vermeer. In a landscape of younger American poets increasingly shy of language rich with responsibility, increasingly suspicious of literature, Hutchinson is like fresh air. *House of Lords and Commons* is his American debut (an earlier book was published in England). Sometimes it takes an outsider to shake things up.

The Jill Bialosky Case

J ill Bialosky's *Poetry Will Save Your Life* is a memoir concealed within
an anthology of poems. The world is crowded with memoirs, which
universities sometimes insist on calling "life-writing," a term so unlovely
that writers have stabbed themselves with a pen rather than use it. The
idea of using poetry in service of autobiography is an old one. Dante's
La Vita Nuova is the best known of medieval prosimetrum works; but in
the wake of Rousseau the Romantics had a taste for leaving behind—
in prose, poetry, or both—a private record of poetic life. Coleridge's *Bio-
graphia Literaria* and Wordsworth's *The Prelude* are not the only access
to those complicated men, but their force and intuition make them indis-
pensable to each poet's version of poetic evolution.

Poets are formed by poems, just as Lego sculptures are formed of, well,
Lego. You get some insight into Shakespeare's mind from Shakespeare's
borrowings, but it would be far better to have a manuscript in which he
remarked on the poems he blamed for his growth and development.
Occasionally a poet will refer in an interview to one poem or another
crucial to his nascent imagination, but we have few documents that do
so in depth. Some revelations might be slightly embarrassing, because
not all sources are worthy of their heirs—Dickinson, for example, loved
more than her share of trashy poems. We would be richer had Eliot, or
Lowell, or Bishop compiled such an anthology, leaving a portrait of the
"growth of a poet's mind," as Pound did in *ABC of Reading*.

Bialosky tells how her life has been touched by various poems, arrang-
ing incidents more or less chronologically, more or less by theme (Danger, Shame, Sexuality, Friendship). The themes have been bolted on,

more marketing than memoir; but the real problem is that this book intended for adults has been written in a style that would embarrass a child of twelve. The editor of W. W. Norton's distinguished poetry list writes as clumsily as a newborn calf.

> One day, a new girl moves into the house behind mine. I'll call her Marie. She has blond hair and dark-brown, sensitive eyes. . . . In the winter we huddle in her bedroom or mine and play with our Barbie dolls, imitating the seductive world of adults. Sometimes we go into the clubhouse behind her house and show each other our flat chests[,] wondering when we'll get bumps.

Her punctuation is often a little wayward, but that naive tone has rarely been heard in such gosh-gee-willikers purity since Shirley Temple hung up her taps. It's bad enough when applied to childhood; but after the poet grows up she describes herself, having arrived in New York, as a "girl from Cleveland, struggling to find my way in America's largest metropolis[,] filled with inhabitants from around the globe here for the very reasons I am—to push their limits and reinvent themselves from the obscurity from which they came." Later comes 9/11:

> All of us who were in New York City will remember the glaringly perfect blue skies of that day, so incongruous with the terrorists' act, and the overall atmosphere of disbelief as the vibrant city mourned the thousands of loved ones lost, and Americans stood frozen in front of their television sets trying to comprehend the improbable act of destruction while somewhere the executioners sang.

The tone-deafness of her prose is almost as wearying as the gush of clichés.

Bialosky has chosen some fifty poems, most by Americans, most from the twentieth century. A lot of the usual suspects are here, but it would be odd if a lot were not. Her choices are sometimes peculiar, as should be true of any good anthology: Keats and Wordsworth, not Coleridge; Dickinson, not Whitman; Frost and Stevens, not Eliot, Pound, Moore, or Williams. Instead, there are Robert Louis Stevenson, Louise Bogan,

Gerald Stern, and Li-Young Lee. There's no living poet younger than sixty; but this is, after all, a private anthology—poets can scarcely help which poems invented them.

Bialosky unhappily shows little talent for interpreting these poems or explaining why they mean so much to her. Though the ways the interpretations go wrong are small, they suggest that she has never thought deeply about the poems she loves. In "The Road Not Taken," "two roads diverged," so it is much more likely that Frost meant not a "crossroad" but a fork. (At a crossroads, there would be three choices, not two.) When Robert Hayden's working-class father gets up, circa 1920, to make the "banked fires blaze," that would be in a coal or wood stove, not "roaring in the fireplace."

Further, Plath's poppies ("Poppies in October") were probably not found "in the stalls at the greengrocer"—the poem is set months after field poppies in England have blown. They're probably the red paper poppies, called remembrance poppies, sold late in October and worn until Remembrance Day, November 11. Though in warm years poppies may bloom again in fall, Plath's last line mentions cornflowers, which bloom in May—the "dawn of cornflowers" may be a cornflower-blue sky. The paper poppies would be another reminder that nature is out of joint, that she's not in the country but in a city where there's a "forest of frost." (Real poppies would have withered in the frost.) The title bears a cutting irony. Like a high-school freshman, Bialosky explains Wordsworth's "I wandered lonely as a cloud" simply by rearranging his words. She interprets "In pensive mood, / They flash upon that inward eye / Which is the bliss of solitude; / And then my heart with pleasure fills" by explaining, "When the poet is pensive and his 'inward eye' recalls the daffodils, the memory fills his solitude with pleasure."

The deeper problem is that Bialosky is uncomfortable with what poems are, if they are anything but simpleminded—she wants poems to console the reader or offer rude guidelines for living. (That's the point of her title.) Can she really believe that most problems with the young could be solved if "We Real Cool," a "cautionary tale," were "taped on the refrigerator of every house with a teenager"? "Poems," she declares, on her way to a panacea, "are a form of mythmaking, as they seek to create a unified vision of cosmic, social, and primal life order." *Primal life order*? I'm not sure what the heck that is, but I very much hope that isn't the point of poetry.

Perhaps a reader must accept a certain amount of blather when a poet talks about poetry (though you won't find it in Coleridge, or Wordsworth, or Eliot), but Bialosky gabbles on about the "mystery and wonder of a poem":

> I allow its seductive voice to take me to the enchantments of the unknown world where father, legacy, and prayer are all intertwined. Surely this is one of the reasons poetry enriches us. A poem links us to a universe at once intimate and communal.

Reading this, I felt I'd been imprisoned in a poetry theme-park.

Most of the memoir is a bland coming-of-age tale, no different from a hundred others except that it's duller than most, no different except that it has been written excruciatingly in the present tense. Still, some of the incidents reveal a subtlety of feeling the prose refuses to explore: the lost dog never found, the expensive sweater Bialosky can't bring herself to wear, the college that goes bankrupt after her freshman year, and the inconsolable loss of two babies. Unfortunately, prose is an unforgiving master—it can reveal depths unseen and shallows better concealed.

Instead of an intimate sense of the little that poems can do at the worst of times, chapter after chapter offers a sales pitch. Bialosky jabbers on about (re: Stevens's "The Snow Man") the "iconic association of building a snowman as a child," informing us (ditto) that the "poem unites us. We are all essentially alone, and yet also part of a larger humanity," confiding (re: Robert Frost) that "I am privy to the tough pulse of another being's consciousness" or (re: Emily Dickinson) "I let the dark undercurrent of loss pulsate in my own life and unleash a well of sorrow." *Unleash a well?* The innocent reader might be forgiven for never picking up a poem again. When she says, of Sylvia Plath and Ted Hughes, that "they birthed two children and numerous collections of poems," I almost choked to death with laughter.

Bialosky is on no more certain ground with poetics, declaring that a "sonnet is a fourteen-line poem that rhymes in a particular pattern." Quite a few different patterns are common in sonnets, but to leave out iambic pentameter is to leave out much that makes a sonnet a sonnet. A villanelle, to her, is a "verse poem with a particular rhyme scheme that repeats certain end words, assigning it complex musicality. Its power is restraint. The rhyme sequence allows for its song-like quality and its surface fun." *Assigning it*? *Surface fun*? Her definition is so vague and silly a reader couldn't recognize a villanelle in broad daylight.

Memoirs no more require a raison d'etre than the writer's desire, or neediness. Still, it's hard to imagine Bialosky's intended audience. Her past offers little beyond the experience of Everyman, and many of the poems will already be familiar to anyone who suffered through high-school English. Most poets will know half-a-dozen or a dozen by heart: "Bright Star! would I were steadfast as thou art," "After great pain, a formal feeling comes," "The Road Not Taken," "Stopping by Woods on a Snowy Evening," "Musée des Beaux Arts," "My Papa's Waltz." The publisher apparently couldn't afford a copy editor, so niggling errors have wriggled in—the scene setting for Gwendolyn Brooks's "We Real Cool" ("The Pool Players. / Seven at the Golden Shovel") is printed as if it were the first stanza; a character given a pseudonym is now Mary, now Marie; Rilke was born in 1875, not 1874, and Adrienne Rich in 1929, not 1950; Paul Laurence Dunbar's middle name is spelled "Lawrence" in a chapter heading; "Richard Cory" was written in 1897, not during the Great Depression; and Bialosky says that Plath's "Nick and the Candlestick" ends, "The pain / You wake to is not yours." Her statement lies just beneath the four stanzas that follow that line.

Bialosky's naive, dispiriting book shows throughout that, despite her love of poetry, one of the most important editors of contemporary verse has a narrow comprehension of her art, not just in her love of the rankly sentimental, but in her failure to include many poems the least challenging. Worse, she has plagiarized numerous passages from Wikipedia and the websites of the Academy of American Poets and the Poetry Foundation. I have underlined her borrowings below.

The Academy on Robert Louis Stevenson:

Born on November 13, 1850, in Edinburgh, Scotland, Robert Louis Balfour Stevenson came from a long line of prominent lighthouse engineers. During his boyhood, he spent holidays with his maternal grandfather. . . . Prone to illness, Stevenson spent many of his early winters in bed, entertained only by . . . love of reading, especially William Shakespeare . . . and *The Arabian Nights*.

Bialosky on Stevenson:

> **Robert Louis Stevenson** was **born in Edinburgh, Scotland, on November 13, 1850. He came from** a family **of lighthouse engineers. During his boyhood he** was **prone to illness** and **spent many of his** childhood **winters in bed, entertained by reading Shakespeare and** *The Arabian Nights*.

The Academy on Emily Dickinson:

> She attended Mount Holyoke Female Seminary . . . , but only for one year. Throughout her life, she seldom left her home and visitors were few. The people with whom she did come in contact, however, had an enormous impact on her poetry. She was particularly stirred by the Reverend Charles Wadsworth, whom she first met on a trip to Philadelphia. He left for the West Coast shortly after a visit to her home in 1860, and some critics believe his departure gave rise to the heartsick flow of verse from Dickinson in the years that followed. . . . By the 1860s, Dickinson lived in almost complete isolation from the outside world.

Bialosky on Dickinson:

> After **attending Mount Holyoke** College **for a year, she** barely **left her home and had few** acquaintances. . . . Those she held close **had an enormous impact on her** verse. One such figure was **Reverend Charles Wadsworth, whom she met on a trip to Philadelphia. He left for the West Coast shortly after a visit to her home in 1860, and some critics believe his departure** unleashed **the** wistful, at times **heartsick**, always profound **flow of verse in the years that** followed. From that time, **Dickinson lived in almost total isolation from the outside world.**

She repeats the Academy's error of "shortly after"—Wadsworth left for San Francisco more than two years after the visit. Many of Bialosky's changes here and elsewhere—"barely" for "seldom," "verse" for "poetry," "unleashed" for "gave rise to," "total" for "complete"—are the slight, guilty revisions of the serial plagiarist. "Mount Holyoke College" is simply a mistake. The school, as the Academy site correctly says, was then called Mount Holyoke Female Seminary.

The Academy on Paul Laurence Dunbar:

> Paul Laurence Dunbar was one of the first African American poets to gain national recognition. His parents . . . were freed slaves from Kentucky. . . . Dunbar had poems published in the *Dayton Herald*. While in high school he edited the *Dayton Tattler*. . . . Dunbar was financially unable to attend college and took a job as an elevator operator. . . . Dunbar moved to Chicago, hoping to find work at the first World's Fair. He befriended Frederick Douglass, who found him a job as a clerk, and also arranged for him to read a selection of his poems.

Bialosky on Dunbar:

> **Paul Dunbar was one of the first African American poets to gain** wide **recognition. His parents were freed slaves from Kentucky.** . . . **In high school, he** published his **poems in the *Dayton Herald*** but he did not have money **to attend college and took a job as an elevator operator.** He eventually **moved to Chicago** in hopes of getting a job **at the World's Fair,** and there **he befriended Frederick Douglass, who found him a job as a clerk and arranged for him to read** from **his** poetry.

The Poetry Foundation on Louise Glück:

> Her poetry is noted for its technical precision . . . and insight into . . . family relationships.

Bialosky on Glück:

> Glück . . . is known **for her technical precision and** sharp **insights into family relationships.**

The Poetry Foundation on Elizabeth Bishop:

> Her father died before she was a year old. Her mother suffered through serious bouts of mental instability and was permanently committed to an institution when Elizabeth was only five years old.

Bialosky on Bishop:

> **Her father died before she was a year old.** After **suffering** from **mental instability, her mother was committed to an institution. Elizabeth** Bishop **was five.**

Wikipedia on Robert Lowell:

> Although Lowell's manic depression was often a great burden (for himself and his family), the subject of that mental illness led to some of his most important poetry, particularly as it manifested itself in his book *Life Studies*. When he was fifty, Lowell began taking lithium to treat his mental illness.

Bialosky on Lowell:

> **Although Lowell's manic depression was a great burden for** him **and his family, the** exploration **of mental illness** in his verse **led to some of his most important poetry, particularly as it manifested** itself in *Life Studies*. **When he was fifty, Lowell began taking lithium to treat his mental illness.**

A quotation by the editor of Lowell's *Letters* that follows in Wikipedia also follows in Bialosky. Her pilfering is not limited to the pocket biographies of her poets. She lifts lines on poetic history and technique as well:

Wikipedia on a line from Wordsworth:

"Child is father of the man" is an idiom originating from the poem "My Heart Leaps Up" by William Wordsworth.

Bialosky on the line from Wordsworth:

"The **child is father of the man" is an idiom originating from the poem "My Heart Leaps Up" by William Wordsworth.**

The Poetry Foundation on Deep Image poetry:

A term originally coined by poets Jerome Rothenberg and Robert Kelly. . . . The idea was later redeveloped by the poet Robert Bly, and deep image became associated with a group of midcentury American poets including . . . James Wright. . . . , focusing on allowing concrete images and experiences to generate poetic meaning.

Bialosky on Deep Image poetry:

A literary **term originally coined by poets Robert Kelly and Jerome Rothenberg** and **redeveloped** . . . **by Robert Bly, James Wright,** and other **midcentury American poets.** It is a poetic technique that **allows concrete** elements **and experiences** . . . **to generate poetic meaning.**

Helen Vendler in *Last Looks, Last Books* on Plath's "Poppies in October":

Plath, under a wintry dawn sky . . . , finds herself on a street where poppies are for sale and where businessmen wearing bowler hats are walking by while an ambulance hurtles past, carrying a hemorrhaging woman.

Bialosky on "Poppies in October":

> **Under a wintery** [*sic*] **sky,** she **finds herself on a street where pop-**
> **pies are for sale and businessmen wearing bowler hats** and **an**
> **ambulance carrying** a bleeding **woman** pass **by.**

This last malfeasance is made worse because Bialosky quotes from
Vendler's book just before stealing her prose. There are other passages
almost as damning, but these are damning enough.

Jill Bialosky, New Revelations

The psychology of plagiarism is more twisted than the house of the Minotaur. Plagiarists rarely confess their sin, the worst a writer can commit. Almost all, when caught, make excuses. The most common are: (1) Everyone does it; (2) It's not really plagiarism; (3) Any similarities are slight or irrelevant; (4) I forgot to cite the sources; (5) Quotation marks and citations were accidentally removed; (6) The passages are only a small part of the book; (7) I unconsciously memorized the original; (8) My researcher is to blame; (9) Drinking, drugs, or mental illness is to blame; and (10) The critic who caught me is to blame.

In my October 2017 review of Jill Bialosky's memoir *Poetry Will Save Your Life* for the magazine *Tourniquet Review*, I accused her of having plagiarized numerous passages from Wikipedia, the websites of the Poetry Foundation and the Academy of American Poets, and a book by the critic Helen Vendler. I printed eight extracts in which Bialosky routinely copied phrase and sentence. (Five other significant passages were not included.) Bialosky is an executive editor and vice president at W. W. Norton, one of the champagne firms of New York publishing, where she has for many years been in charge of one of the most important poetry lists in the country. Having published four books of poems and a previous memoir, she is no novice writer.

Responding to an article about the accusation in the *New York Times* on October 8, Bialosky insisted that the plagiarism amounted to a "few ancillary and limited phrases from my 222-page memoir that inadvertently include fragments of prior common biographical sources and tropes after a multiyear writing process." (Excuses 3 and 6, with 4 perhaps implied.) By a "few . . . phrases" she apparently meant the fifty or sixty phrases duplicated in the damning excerpts. Whole sentences showed minor variations, or none at all. It's not clear what she meant by "prior," except that the prose she copied preceded her own. "Ancillary," "limited," "fragments," and "common" attempt to minimize the plagiarism by suggesting that the things she borrowed were plain facts, piecemeal and isolated; but any examination of the parallel passages will reveal how often she shamelessly appropriated the work of other writers.

A student who copies web sources for a term paper is usually failed outright. In Bialosky's case, seventy-two writers calling themselves "friends of literature" signed a letter to the *Times*, protesting the publication of a story that, they claimed, "tainted the reputation of this accomplished editor, poet and memoirist." Bialosky's borrowings are not, as the Friends of Literature declared, a "handful of commonly known biographical facts gleaned from outside sources." Terming the plagiarism a "mishandling," the Friends further asserted that this was merely a "small offense" and that the "inadvertent repetition of biographical boilerplate was not an egregious theft intentionally performed." This soft-pedaled the persistent feature of her memoir, the uncontrollable kleptomania practiced on other writers not just for the brief biographies of poets but for her interpretation of poems and her notes on poetic technique. The Friends referred to her response as a "statement of apology," though there was not a hint of apology to it. That is not the worst of it.

Five years ago, Bialosky published a best-selling memoir, *History of a Suicide: My Sister's Unfinished Life*. The book suffers from sloppy citation (referring to editions that do not exist) and numerous errors: the title of *The Waste Land* is misspelled throughout (and Eliot never wrote a poem titled "East Cocker"), Donne's *Biathanatos* is not a "religious defense of poetry," and the adjuration in Leviticus 18:21 against sacrificing children to strange gods is not the 613th commandment of the Hebrew Bible. In addition, she plagiarized numerous passages, just as she did later in *Poetry Will Save Your Life*.

Plagiarism is rarely the simple cutting and pasting of another author's work. Most often the later author tries to conceal the source with trivial changes, cloaking the identity of the original with a synonym or two, collapsing phrases from long paragraphs into a new whole. The language and structure of the original can be very difficult, however, to keep secret. In the parallel passages that follow, the wholesale copying of previous sources is so plain they must be characterized as outright theft. Mere shifts in tense or number have been marked as verbatim.

Wikipedia on Charon (Wikipedia version of March 24, 2011):

> In Greek mythology, Charon . . . is the ferryman of Hades who carries souls of the newly deceased across the rivers Styx and Acheron that divided the world of the living from the world of the dead. A coin to pay Charon for passage . . . was sometimes placed in or on the mouth of a dead person. . . . [T]hose who could not pay the fee, or those whose bodies were left unburied, had to wander the shores for one hundred years.

Bialosky on Charon:

> **In Greek mythology Charon is the ferryman who carries the souls of** the dead **across the River Styx, which divides the world of the living from** that **of the dead.** As fee **for passage,** the survivors must **place a coin in or on the mouth of** the **dead person. Those who cannot pay the fee, or those whose bodies are left unburied, have to wander the shores for one hundred years.**

Alfred Bates, ed., *The Drama: Its History, Literature, and Influence on Civilization* (London, 1903), 1:192–94, on *Medea*:

> The *Medea* tells the story of the jealousy and revenge of a woman betrayed by her husband. She has left home and father for Jason's sake, and he, after she has borne him children, forsakes her, and betroths himself to Glauce, the daughter of Creon, ruler of Corinth. . . . Jason arrives and reproaches Medea with having provoked her sentence by her own violent temper. . . . In reply she reminds her husband of what she had once done for him; how for him she had betrayed her father and her people. . . ."I have brought you from a barbarous land to Greece [says Jason], and in Greece you are esteemed for your wisdom. . . . [I]t is not for love that I have promised to marry the

princess, but to win wealth and power for myself and my sons." . . .
She leads her two children to the house, and that no other may slay
them in revenge, murders them herself.

Bialosky on *Medea*:

> *Medea* **tells the story of the jealousy and revenge of** Medea after
> she is **betrayed by her husband,** Jason. . . . Medea **leaves** her **home
> and** her **father for Jason. After she has borne him children,** Jason
> betrays **her and betroths himself to Glauce, the daughter of
> Creon, ruler of Corinth. . . . Jason arrives and** blames **Medea for
> having provoked her** exile through **her own** rage. **In reply she
> reminds** Jason **of what she has done for him: how she betrayed
> her father and her people for him.** . . . Jason replies that it is he who
> saved her, **having brought her to Greece** where **she is esteemed for
> her wisdom.** He tells her **it was not for love that he promised to
> marry the princess, but to win wealth and power for himself and
> their sons.** . . . Medea fears retaliation on her sons **and,** so **that no
> others may slay them,** she **murders them herself.**

Several websites on Zeus (these repeat the same information almost
word for word, sometimes with the same typos—and all may derive from
some unknown print source):

> Zeus was the sixth child born to Cronus and Rhea. . . . But, unlike
> many gods in other religions he was neither omnipotent nor omni-
> scient. He could be, and in fact was, opposed, deceived and tricked
> by gods and men alike. His power, although great, was not bound-
> less[.] Zeus had no control over The Fates and Destiny. Like all Greek
> divinities, Zeus was subject to pleasure, pain, grief, and anger, but he
> was most susceptible to the power of Eros—love, which often got the
> objects of his desire in a lot of trouble with his wife, Hera.

Bialosky on Zeus:

> **Zeus was the sixth child born to Cronus and Rhea. But, unlike
> many gods in other religions,** Zeus **was neither omnipotent nor**

omniscient. He was often **tricked, deceived, and** threatened **by gods and men alike.** . . . **His power, although great, was not** unlimited. **Zeus had no control over the Fates** or **Destiny. Like all Greek divinities, Zeus was** not inured **to pleasure, pain, grief, and anger, but he was most** vulnerable **to the power of Eros, love, which often got** his lovers into terrible entanglements **with his wife, Hera.**

The citation she gives for the passages on *Medea* and Zeus, Edith Hamilton's old warhorse, *Mythology* (1942), is either a wholesale error or knowing misdirection. Bialosky cannot herself be the source of the websites on Zeus, because they go on at greater length in the same style.

Wikipedia on *Mrs. Dalloway* (Wikipedia version of January 6, 2011):

Septimus Warren Smith, a veteran of World War I suffering from deferred traumatic stress. . . . is visited by frequent . . . hallucinations. . . . Later . . . he commits suicide by jumping out of a window.

Bialosky on *Mrs. Dalloway*:

Septimus Smith, a veteran of World War I, suffers from recurring **hallucinations** and eventually **commits suicide by jumping out of a window.**

Even where she cites a source, in at least one instance Bialosky borrows liberally without putting her thefts in quotation marks.

Stanton Peele on Romeo ("Romeo and Juliet's Death Trip: Addictive Love and Teen Suicide," *Psychology Today* website, posted online November 1, 2008):

[T]wo unformed-maladjusted youths meet at vulnerable points in their lives. . . . [D]isconsolate over his lost paramour, Rosaline. . . . Romeo . . . expects to "expire the term of a despised life." . . . Juliet is a 13-year-old virgin . . . who has just been told that she is to marry an older man she is to meet . . . at the party. Instead, she and Romeo . . . kiss passionately. Juliet doesn't yet know if Romeo is married, and if he is, "My grave is like to be my wedding bed."

Jill Bialosky on *Romeo and Juliet*:

> **Two** young people **meet** when they are both in **maladjusted** and
> **vulnerable** states. . . . [M]ourning the loss of his previous lover,
> **Rosaline**. . . . [Romeo] hopes **to "expire the term of a despised**
> **life."** . . . [T]hirteen-year-old Juliet has been told that she is to
> **marry an older man she** will **meet at the party.** . . . [S]he meets
> **Romeo** and they **kiss passionately.** Not **knowing if Romeo is**
> **married,** she says **if he is, "my grave is like to be my wedding**
> **bed."**

Though Bialosky credits Peele in her notes, she uses his prose willy-nilly,
just touching it up here and there. The reader has no idea what's Peele
and what's Bialosky. The passages that follow were found by the poet Ira
Lightman, whose discoveries provoked my further investigation.

David Lester, "Understanding Suicide Through Studies of Diaries:
The Case of Cesare Pavese," *Archives of Suicide Research* 10:3 (2006)
(abstract):

> The diary left by Cesare Pavese covering the 15 years prior to his sui-
> cide is examined. . . . [M]ention of failure with women was immedi-
> ately followed in his diary by denigration of his literary work. Other
> features of his life, such as the loss of his father when he was six, are
> also discussed.

Bialosky on the diaries:

> Pavese's **diaries examine fifteen years** of the Italian poet's life **prior to**
> **his suicide** and document his **failure with women,** the **denigration**
> **of his literary works,** and **the loss of his father when he was six.**

New Columbia Encyclopedia (Columbia University Press, 1975) on
tragedy:

> Tragedy, form of drama . . . in which a person of superior intelli-
> gence and character . . . is overcome by the very obstacles he is

struggling to remove. . . . Aristotle points out its ritual function: The spectators . . . are purged of their own emotions of pity and fear through their vicarious participation in the drama.

Bialosky on tragedy:

[T]ragedy is defined as a **form of drama in which a person of superior intelligence . . . and character is overcome by the very** struggles he is trying **to remove. . . . Aristotle pointed out** tragedy's **ritual function: the spectators are purged of their own emotions of pity and fear through their vicarious participation in the drama.**

The plagiarism is not limited to Bialosky's memoirs. Lightman discovered a further theft in her essay "The Unreasoning Mask: The Shared Interior Architecture of Poetry and Memoir."

Richard Gilbert, review of Sven Birkerts, *The Art of Time in Memoir* (posted online July 26, 2010):

[A] memoir is of course made of memory shaped and dramatized. . . . *The Art of Time in Memoir* by Sven Birkerts posits that memoir is defined and distinguished by its dual perspective: the writer *now* looking back, trying to understand a past version of herself or himself. The glory of the genre, Birkerts says, is in the writer's search for patterns and connections; in using the "vantage point of the present to gain access to what might be called the hidden narrative of the past."

Bialosky on Birkerts ("The Unreasoning Mask: The Shared Interior Architecture of Poetry and Memoir," *KROnline*, Spring 2013):

Sven Birkerts in his book *The Art of Time in Memoir* writes, "**memoir is of course made of memory shaped and dramatized.**" He **posits that memoir is defined and distinguished by its dual perspective: the writer *now* looking back, trying to understand a past version of herself or himself. The glory of the genre, Birkerts says, is in the writer's search for patterns and connections;**

in using the "vantage point of the present to gain access to what might be called the hidden narrative of the past."

Bialosky has muddled Birkerts's ideas with those of the critic from whom she stole: Gilbert, not Birkerts, wrote that "memoir is of course made of memory shaped and dramatized." She has copied even Gilbert's italicized "now" and his erroneous semicolon. Rather than laboring to put research into her own words or to cite her sources honestly, Bialosky has habitually drawn nearly verbatim from the very places students are warned against: websites, encyclopedias, and even the work of writers not anonymous. It will be difficult for anyone to pretend that her trivial and occasionally clumsy rewriting is inadvertent duplication, rather than conscious theft.

Cases of plagiarism do not depend on an author copying everything in sight. The disturbing thing about Bialosky's memoirs, largely composed of personal anecdotes, is how often she plagiarizes the little that is not. Though in rare cases critics are obliged to write about this sad and sorry business, no one can do so without feeling tainted or without sympathy for a writer who has violated the cardinal rule of the trade. As an editor for a major New York publisher, Bialosky knows how serious this transgression is. *History of a Suicide* formed the template for the literary piracy in her later essay and memoir. Her defense of the wholesale copying in *Poetry Will Save Your Life* as "inadvertent" can no longer be sustained.

Verse Chronicle: Under the Skin

LAVINIA GREENLAW

The romance of *Troilus and Criseyde* was a fairly recent invention when Chaucer borrowed the tale. Troilus had a bit part as a corpse in the *Iliad* but was otherwise a tabula rasa. It took medieval poets, chiefly Boccaccio, to make the back story a love story. *Troilus* was an attempt to apply medieval romance to characters more than two millennia old, cast in an epic about a war half a millennium older, if it occurred at all. For all the praise scholars have lavished on Chaucer's nearly endless tapestry in rime royal, more than half as long as the *Iliad*, the poem in its staginess is like an early talkie. You have to go to the *Canterbury Tales* for a medieval world out of Breughel.

Chaucer's Middle English catches the language in the frenzy of transition from its guttural Germanic roots to the flexible gallimaufry known as modern English. Synonym heavy, shaved of most case endings, old conjugations dumbed down, the language grew as empires do, gorging on pan-European migrants, mainly French and Latin, and not a few additions from the later reaches of dominion. Rime royal is a punishing form, its *ababbcc* quickly exhausting the obvious rhymes and forcing the poor poet either to repeat himself or—as Byron did in *Don Juan*'s ottava rima—invent rhymes so preposterous they're worth the price of admission.

In *A Double Sorrow*, Lavinia Greenlaw has taken gobbets from the original, sometimes reinforced by a line or two from Boccaccio, and boiled them down to a stanza apiece. These snapshots reduce Chaucer's eight thousand lines by more than eighty percent—*Troilus* has been put on a killer diet. Her "corrupt version" of rime royal, as she calls it, retains

only the bad memory of rhyme—appearing, disappearing, clanking like a
rusty chain:

> So composed
> Her every gesture confirms her grace.
> Of such noblesse
> A perfect woman, perfectly made.
> (He only glimpsed her face.)
> The prince must hide this joy, this fright.
> He's never felt so full, so light.

Prince Troilus sounds as if he'd just finished a bag of Cheetos. This epi-
sodic vision is a flicker book hard to follow unless you have the Chaucer
in hand. When you're forced to look back at the original, however, you
repeatedly find that little or nothing has made its way into translation.

The tale has been pilfered so often, it's hardly a felony to revive *Troilus
and Criseyde* for a modern audience; but any new version lies upon the
palimpsest of older ones (Chaucer filched about a third of his lines from
Boccaccio's hip pocket). Sometimes in this hall of echoes the poor reader
is deafened by lines done far more clumsily than those of Boccaccio,
Chaucer, and Shakespeare. You wonder if the world is ready for a *Chaucer for Dummies*.

Greenlaw's "extrapolation" has been made no better by her addiction
to clichés: after "each is on the edge of her seat," "I must play my cards
well," "this is love not war," and dozens of others, it's not clear if she even
hears them. Worse, there are passages so embarrassing they would have
been red-penciled from a Harlequin novel ("his attention folds like a
dying star / As he takes her—black and white—to his core") or drop-
kicked out of a Spike Milligan sketch ("He holds a broken thing / And
after a while arranges her / As if a mortician in search of the person").
The first thing a translator requires is an ear, and if he doesn't have one
for the guest language he ought to have one for the host.

Moments layered with subtle intention have been turned into soap-
opera dialogue:

> If I have any fear
> It is that I may be the cause

Of damage to her.
I will only go so far as is proper.
I put myself in your hands.
Commend me to she who me commands
But do not use force.

Commend me to she who me commands! You'd need a crowbar to straighten
that out. (It doesn't go down quite that way in *Troilus*—but why update
Chaucer only to mire him in Middle English syntax?) Greenlaw's Troilus might as well be some idiot surgeon from *General Hospital*. If you long
for soapy emotion, there's soapy emotion on steroids. Criseyde speaks:

How could any one person contain
Such agony?
So much torment there can be none left
Beyond this body.
All the world's woe, complaint, distress
Anguish, rage, dread and bitterness . . .
I have been made to take it all in.

Match that, Ophelia. *Troilus and Criseyde* bears as much relation to such
scraps as *Hamlet* to badly written instructions for assembling a bicycle.
    Many radical translations from the classics have a hole in the center.
Poems like Alice Oswald's *Memorial*, which consists of obits from the
Iliad, are interesting because provocative—they let us look at the original from a different angle. Chaucer's homiletics about the price of vanity
would be unlikely to win a modern hearing, even if to later readers Middle English weren't mostly gibberish.
    Troilus is fussy, longwinded, stiff-necked, and for long stretches with-
out humor; but whenever Greenlaw draws directly from Chaucer her version gets a little better. This confetti translation does not suffer the
longueurs of the original, but to drag the poem into this century would
require the quartz clarity of Pound's Chinese translations or a yahoo version like Logue's *Iliad*. I can imagine a modernist vision that focused
only on Troilus's horse, the ruby-heart brooch given to Criseyde, her
widow's weeds of brown silk, and the cloak of Diomedes—the tale might
be inferred entirely from material objects.

Greenlaw's love story leaves no one unstained—her Troilus is an adolescent horndog, Criseyde a witless pawn, and Diomedes a snake-eyed
stinker—but this undernourished footnote to a masterpiece is an opportunity missed. (Had Greenlaw let the Wife of Bath spin the tale, it would
have been racier and far funnier.) Translating our greatest medieval poet
into lackluster English, with clichés and a shotgun scattering of relics, is
not nearly enough.

YUSEF KOMUNYAKAA

Yusef Komunyakaa's new book is a mad dash through cultures classical
and modern, an *If It's Tuesday This Must Be Belgium* tour with H. G. Wells
at the controls. Beneath the lush adjectives and lavish detail (often exer-
cises in sublime excess) lies the estrangement of a poet for whom being
in the world is not being of it. Who would have thought Komunyakaa a
secret pre-Raphaelite? The poems in *The Emperor of Water Clocks*, even
more than those in his last book, are haunted by Derek Walcott, who
managed to compound a sense of historical presence with a painterly
encaustic that buried any scene in its own description.

There's a new authority to Komunyakaa's work, a command that rarely
dissolves into comfort:

> The middle ground
> is a flotilla of stars, a peacock carousel
> & Ferris wheel spinning in the water
> as vines unstitch the leach-work of salt,
> thick mud sewn up like bodies fallen
> into a ditch, blooming, about to erupt.
> Water lily & spider fern.

Walcott's major flaw is that beneath the detail he has little to say—and,
when he does say something, it tends to be about empire, or St. Lucia,
or women, women, women. Having tapped the resources of influence,
Komunyakaa often seems unsure what to do with them. The poems are
at times drowned in the classical world; and a few take place in some
unnamed empire inhabited by an emperor, a fool, a raven master, and

others, though their characters are blandly anonymous. This is the fan-boy approach to *Game of Thrones*.

Most of the historical detail redeems not a minute of history. (One can perhaps forgive the poet for thinking that *Beowulf* was written in dactyls, but he should know better.) The poems lie lost in some vast Borgesian library, bereft of complexity, of raw causes for these cooked-up effects. There seems no reason that, dislocated in time, Komunyakaa floats from Isadora Duncan, Rimbaud, and Second Empire décor in one poem to another where a woman's "T-shirt says THESE GUNS ARE LOADED"—he seems equally moved, or unmoved, by each subject in turn. Without more connection than poetic sensibility, the poems, however beautiful, veer toward narcissism—or the infinite choices in some cafeteria of history.

The poet has his romantic side, and his romantic side a romantic side. The reader may be mesmerized by breathtaking stretches of landscape, details out of Constable or Gainsborough; but then Komunyakaa throws in some mystical or metaphysical love potion, as if he can't help himself. When he writes of a "secret icon / filled with belief, / bloody philosophy, / & a drop of stardust," or says, "Please / look into my eyes & tap a finger / against my heart to undo / every wrong I've ever done," he's grabbing your lapels and waiting for tears to gush:

> I see the tip
> of a purple mountain, but sweetheart,
> if it weren't for your late April kisses
> I would have turned around days ago.

The reader might turn around long before that. It's unclear just how much back-patting has gone into his chummy dual elegy for Derek Walcott and Joseph Brodsky, but my guess is a good deal:

> They are one small republic of ideas,
> three good friends, & almost one mind
> when they lift their eyes to greet
> a woman walking in from the day's
> blinding array of disorder & chance.

Given Walcott's and Brodsky's reputations as *roués extraordinaires*, one feels sorry for that woman. The infections of sentiment mar even the elegy for Galway Kinnell, which ends, "Galway, / thanks for going down into our fierce hush / at the crossroads to look fear in the eye."

The poet's historical eye finds purpose only in the rare flight from shopworn romanticism. He looks back at J. M. W. Turner:

> one day while walking in windy rain
> on the Thames he felt he was descending
> a hemp ladder into the galley of a ship,
> down in the swollen belly of the beast
> with a curse, hook, & a bailing bucket,
> into whimper & howl, into piss & shit.

Despite the whiff here of a self-indulgent ars poetica, Komunyakaa finds more in such visions than in the endless piling up of detail that makes the poems a flea market from Hell. (Perhaps more poets, however, should adopt Lightnin' Hopkins and Chuck Berry as their tutelary gods.) He has become a broader and more redolent poet in this new work, but too often beneath the surface lies nothing but surface.

John Crowe Ransom

John Crowe Ransom has always been a minority taste—even when he was alive the reviewers, some of them former students, made excuses. This *Collected Poems*, long needed if not long awaited, suffers from high-minded guff, slightly cracked fantasies, and barrels of magnolia-scented language from antebellum storehouses (sometimes Poe seems to be look-ing over the poet's shoulder in a rictus of grinning). In the handful of Ransom's best poems, however—the work of a very narrow period in his thirties—the pressure of the Southern past and the peculiarities of his own psychology produced, as they did in Faulkner, a mannerism responsive to the darkest currents of character—ingrown secrets, like a rare species of pike, breasting still waters, then vanishing again.

Ransom was a more buttoned-up character than Faulkner—in most photographs, he's dwarfed by a heavy wool suit that would strangle a sheep. The poet was one of the first teachers of "creative writing": his students at Vanderbilt and Kenyon included Allen Tate, Peter Taylor, Randall Jarrell, and Robert Lowell. Robert Penn Warren and Cleanth Brooks, the editors of *Understanding Poetry*, which introduced half a century of English majors to close reading, were also Ransom students. He's the key figure behind the manners of attention used in writing workshops almost a century later.

Ransom was a member of the Fugitives and later stood at the center of the Agrarians, the Southern writers responsible for *I'll Take My Stand*, a manifesto proposing that the South remain a traditional agrarian society, "reconstructed but unregenerate." Though he broke with the group, his poems rarely acknowledged the modern world. He thought the moderns major poets, most of them; but his work was profoundly backward looking—Ransom ignored the harrowing of convention that made Pound, Eliot, Moore, Stevens, Frost, and Williams the most influential generation in American poetry, ignored them as if their poems suffered a case of bad manners. A few of Ransom's early poems, even so, read like outtakes from *North of Boston*, written by a Frost who had stumbled over the Mason-Dixon and kept going:

A hundred times I've taken the mules
And started early through the lane,
And come to the broken gate and looked,
And there my partner was again,
Sitting on top of a sorrel horse
And picking the burrs from its matted mane.

Ransom's memorable poems are off-center, strange in their strangeness. He had an eccentric ear, and a clumsiness of expression reminiscent of Hardy's, but without Hardy's bleak comprehension of human frailty. You have to put up with a lot of lines knocked together with a sledgehammer, lines it's hard to imagine anyone reading without choking to death from laughter: "Yet of evasions even she made a snare. / The heart was bold that clanged within her bosom"; "Abbott said several dooms with firm intone"; "And beautiful else had been their bosoms poutering by! / 'But ye are a cloud,' I said." When you add the bale or two of archaisms ("previsal I made," "so vengeant for his vine," "a depth of woody grot," "up clomb the enemy," "toughly I hope ye may thole," "his gloomy halidom," "his egregious beauty richly dight," "duly appeared I at the very clock-throb appointed," "the diuturnity was still"), it's as if Ransom were trying to recreate cockentrice or snake soup, with nettle pudding and live-frog pie for dessert. As a stylistic choice, it's a disaster.

Ransom seems never to have gotten over his years as a Rhodes scholar, when Oxford dons apparently still spoke Middle English. (Jarrell thought the ill-fitting language derived from biblical pedantry or Southern preach-ifying, among other things; but Ransom likely dreamed it up on his own.) He wasn't a high-flying student, though his degree was the "best of the Seconds." When you read the Georgian poets of the day, his style makes better sense—but it's a sense that makes sense only if you wanted your poems to sound like little chats with Milton.

However old-fashioned the eye, Ransom's subjects, if not his style, were at times more up to date than those of Frost, who wrote pastoral with the old New England farms already in sharp decline. Can you imag-ine Frost writing a verse narrative that required a good deal of vomit-ing? Or poems about prostitutes, or dumbbells, or drinking as a man's path to God? Ransom's most desolate subject was marriage, that long war between two countries now allies, now enemies—there you see the filial connection to Frost and Hardy at their most crippling. If Ransom wrote slightly disturbing poems about young girls, he also took an interest in the superannuated. If he wrote too many about trivialities like a children's argument or the death of a chicken named Chucky, and too many lines like bad Stevens, who also had problems with the antique (Ransom: "my scholars, the young simple snails, / Treading their tumuli to holy grails"), for all his maudlin gestures the Southerner could write matter-of-factly about brutality.

Ransom's most devastating poems were often character studies. Had he been more morbid, he might have produced a Southern *Spoon River Anthology*, or rather something that outmastered that talking graveyard with vignettes closer to Chaucer's miniatures of his pilgrims. Ransom's portraits of Miriam Tazewell, Miss Euphemia, Emily Hardcastle, Con-rad, Minnie, and others unnamed have their heavy-handed ironies, and even their cruelties; but they come from looking hard at other people and refusing to look away.

When that intensity moved a step or two into absurdity, Ransom produced one of his few extraordinary poems, "Captain Carpenter," about a latter-day man-at-arms who tussle by tussle loses nose, arms, ears, eyes, and more. The black humor lies halfway between *Der Besuch der Alten Dame* and *Monty Python*'s Black Knight:

> But God's deep curses follow after those
> That shore him of his goodly nose and ears
> His legs and strong arms at the two elbows
> And eyes that had not watered seventy years.
>
> The curse of hell upon the sleek upstart
> That got the Captain finally on his back
> And took the red red vitals of his heart
> And made the kites to whet their beaks clack clack.

It's hard not to see, in this adventurer who keeps looking for a fight until he has no more anatomy to trade, something of Ransom himself, a perversity in no small way heroic. As poet and critic, he was a gentleman amateur of the best sort.

Ransom published only three collections, all during his thirties, and in the near half-century that remained added just half-a-dozen new poems, while occasionally issuing a volume of selected work. Like Rimbaud, he walked away from poetry, though he'd crack the workshop door once in a while to tinker with his old verse, sometimes ruinously. His revisions proved a torment to critics, who in the midst of praising a selection might send readers back to versions in earlier books. The continual changes, sometimes niggling, sometimes whole hog, must have made editing the *Collected Poems* a nightmare. No reader will sit still for four or five versions of the same poem, and a variorum is of practical use only to scholars.

Ben Mazer deserves praise for taking on a task much harder than it seems, though this handsome book has a shape too bulky to be read comfortably. (I have a volume of *The Works of Geoffrey Chaucer* smaller in every dimension.) Mazer has reprinted the poems of Ransom's three volumes in their original order, substituting versions from his 1945 *Selected*, the edition most admired by critics. The notes, which limit themselves to standard scholarly information and a collation of texts, might have been more helpful had they explained some of Ransom's references. The editor has attempted to bridge the chasm between main text and variorum apparatus by providing a section of "distinct versions"—it's a half-measure, but a welcome one. The wilderness of notes, alas, is a map that needs a map—page headings like "Notes for Pages 127–207" (repeated for a dozen pages) are worse than useless. As Ransom's poems are unlikely to be edited again, it's a pity that this book, beautifully printed and bound, will in small ways prove so frustrating.

You ignore the manner of Ransom at your peril, the way you ignore the manner of Poe, because what you lose by scraping it off you don't regain from what little lies beneath. The manner *is* the poems. Ransom's outdated rhetoric ignored the corruptions of style modern poetry invented, ignored them to protect fading dioramas in the back quarters of a natural history museum. You know Ransom's poems better when you remember what Pound and Eliot and Moore were doing at that hour, but when you think about those poets it's hard to remember Ransom at all. I feel about him the way Churchill felt about Stafford Cripps: "He has all the virtues I dislike and none of the vices I admire."

The afterlife of such a real but slightly freakish talent is always tentative. The small group of poems worth revisiting includes "Captain Carpenter," "Here Lies a Lady," "Bells for John Whiteside's Daughter," "The Equilibrists," and some lesser pieces like "Miriam Tazewell," "Conrad in Twilight," "Blackberry Winter," "Piazza Piece," and "Puncture." Know those, and you may want to know more; but there are few more worth knowing so well.

JUAN FELIPE HERRERA

Juan Felipe Herrera's wildly uneven post-Beat Beat poems are a throwback to a time when hip poetry seemed revolutionary. What you find, paging through this dispiriting book, is Ginsberg without animation, Ferlinghetti without the giddy innocence, Corso without the—well, whatever it was that made people read Corso. The new poet laureate takes the worst qualities of these poets and makes a hash of them. He's still living for the days of coffee houses and bongos.

The devil-may-care insouciance of *Notes on the Assemblage*, slapdash lines thrown on the page with the swaggering aggression of Jackson Pollock, sentences sprinting along until they collapse from exhaustion, comes at a price:

> we were protesting for funds that is all we were
> surrounded by police and their cronies they fired their guns they
> burned us they dismembered us in trash bags they threw us into the
> river yet we continue yet we march from here from the bowels of
> Mexico

Herrera harkens back to street-corner preachers, Hyde Park Corner debaters, and the occasional lunatic ranter. The free association spills out like a torrent from a ruptured dam, often liberated from the bounds of punctuation. (Is punctuation necessary? W. S. Merwin has been punctuation free for half a century, with no ill effects except incurable dullness.) When the message is so urgent the poet can't stop for a stop or two, you worry about his blood pressure.

Herrera grabs his headlines off the front page—they're a news recap of depressing tragedies from the past year or two: the forty-three murdered Mexican students, the Japanese journalist beheaded in Syria, the young black men killed by police. One poem is dedicated to the nine black pastors and parishioners murdered in a church shooting in Charleston, South Carolina, just weeks before the book was published. About the only poem to reach further than the day before yesterday is an elegy for a black farmhand lynched in Texas in 1916.

The dominant note is outrage, but rage takes poetry only so far. The usual problem of political poetry is that, if the politics are your politics, the message is superfluous; if they aren't, the message is bullying. The masters of political poetry over the last century—Yeats, Auden, Lowell, Hill, Heaney—never let the message destroy the fidelities or ambivalence of language. If that seems no great difficulty, find a single decent poem written against the war in Vietnam, or Iraq, or Afghanistan. For all Herrera's honorable attempts to speak for migrant laborers, undocumented immigrants, and the poor, there's scarcely a line worth re-reading. It's the old argument out of Jonson, Poems of an Age vs. Those for All Time.

Political poems are only part of the book. Paging through Herrera's dreary renderings of daily events, you realize that he has assembled a mini-anthology of poets whose heyday was the sixties: Beats, mountaintop eco-warriors, and half the New York School. Here's Frank O'Hara ("In Soho, NYC—at Dunkin' Donuts of all places, a year ago—hanging out with Gerald Stern"), there's Gary Snyder ("I sit and meditate—my dog licks her paws / on the red-brown sofa"), and over there, why, it must be Bukowski:

> you should have seen the Pig Act
> the pig   a real pig with a wig in flames
> in pinkish pajamas & a cigar doing a Fatty Arbuckle shtick
> he even ordered 18 eggs over easy with 18 sides of sourdough

Herrera reads at a poetry festival. Herrera writes elegies for Jose Montoya, Philip Levine, Jack Gilbert, and Wanda Coleman. Herrera rescues a white dove. This isn't life transformed by confession, it's the diary jottings of a poet doing the poet thing—that sickly sweet perfume is the smell of rotting orchids.

Herrera is so eager to please, so insistent on having his populist heart in the right populist place, it's hard to dislike him. A number of poems are produced *en face* in Spanish, a nod to the poet's heritage (he's the son of migrant farm-workers), though the translations had to be provided by one of his friends. Despite all the worthy messages, too many of these poems stagger into sentimental gush ("and the moon the wild sickle swan and / i ascended / through the fire"), uplifting drivel ("Wanda Coleman word-caster of live / coals of love // in gratitude / we stand & rise"), images that would embarrass even Ashbery ("the dog violins that sniff-sniff you"), or just plain silliness ("your voice dooby-dooby-doo-wop / paint me the flying coat color of flame & tutti-frutti"). Then there are passages that would confound Augustine or Champollion:

> O, what to do, chile peppers, Mrs. Oops
> Dr. What, Mr. Space Station unscrewed

The *Redbook of Ants* says you better run
No sirree, LOL, blowin' my bubble gum sun

The publicity flacks have done the poet laureate no favors by proclaiming that "at the heart of his work is the poet as technician of multiple registers, advocate of multicultural voices and . . . devotee of interbeing, that is, tearing down the walls that separate us personally, culturally and globally." *Interbeing*! The disdain of its enemies won't drag poetry down, only the insidious pitchman's language of its friends.

CLAUDIA EMERSON

Claudia Emerson died last December at fifty-seven, in her last months writing feverishly, fiendishly, with the clock always at her shoulder. *Impossible Bottle* is a book surrounded by death, finished under a pressure that did not often allow the leisures of recollection—the immediacies are quickening and painful. The staccato phrases of a sequence of chemo diaries have trouble taking in what amounts to a death sentence (Emerson would have heard the ironies in the phrase). The moment most fraught comes when her doctor, knowing that things are beyond hope, refuses to face her and "speaks to his screen / instead."

Knowledge of the darkening present infuses old memories of accident, mishap, and death: a neighborhood where a family was slaughtered, a man skinning a bird in a museum, a wedding party now half gone to the grave, a hurricane rising. The reader can't shut out the death to come, which makes these poems unbearable even when they can be borne.

Emerson knew how to structure a poem to reveal its secrets by the way:

Fog that morning all of them waded.
They were used to her

voice, her hand on their spines, their flanks, her fingers
in their manes, their tails,

the pressure she brought to bear on the bits they let her
slip into their mouths.

The pastoral seems innocuous, lovely, but it's all canny preparation; then something happens, and a life is ruined. These poems of death postponed but not denied are heartless, Gothic, and without consolation. She sketches a portrait of marriage:

> Her daughters were born fast, three in a row,
> the older two the ordinary
>
> disappointment most girls are to their fathers,
> the third one *God's child*,
>
> she said, declaring it so; *bird-stupid*, he called it,
> *slow as a log chain*
>
> *through mud.*

The Southern inflections have a cruelty they come by honestly. In another poem, a fellow patient must go back to work because a new guy is "some brand new kind of stupid."

In the aftermath of a poet's death, images become metaphors; metaphors, symbols; and symbols turn into neon signs. Gestures otherwise innocent come to mean more than they should. The reader has to take scenes plain to prevent the language from escaping into elegy or eulogy. In the hospital, Emerson meets an old woman who does not speak:

> Her eyes occluded,
> clouded over, the older woman appears
>
> to look me in the eye, though, to hold me in
> an iron-steady gaze, the cataracts
>
> small blinds she has early drawn down,
> defiant, and she stands behind having done it.

I can recall few books of such presence carrying such a burden of absence. Emerson never tried to overwhelm the reader with a lot of curtain chewing and scene stealing. She was a solitary, an off-in-the-corner type, a classic observer—as observant as a sniper. Poems are often the sum of a poet's nature—only the rare poet like Frost, who kept the ill-natured parts of his personality under wraps, can fake it.

Long illness tends to infuse the world of the ill—the dying turn to their dying because that is what they know. The poems Emerson wrote about her treatment, her hospital stays, are familiar from all the cancer narratives that have gone before, though hers have a poet's eye (an MRI technician is "talking / with someone in the glassed // control booth about Dixie Donuts") and an irony that never succumbs to *ressentiment*. The tensions of these poems plead for a resolution they cannot provide—they leap from metaphor to metaphor like a moth battering inside a light fixture. These remnants are constant reminders of a life cut short.

I knew Emerson in passing and reviewed her, and then I knew her better and could review her no longer. She was a poet who demanded the reader's patience not just to acknowledge her effects but to absorb them. The best poems here escape the trappings of illness, turning almost in desperation to the natural world that was her natural home. "Well," "*Chain Chain Chain*," "Pasture Accident," "Last the Night," "The Scar," and in a lesser way "Ecology" and "Fast" are poems darkly moving, unsentimental, drenched in regret, loss, and what Emerson calls the "familiar art of sorrow." They embody the vigilance on which illness insisted. These little narratives might have been afterthoughts; but they became a necessary reckoning with the past, a final act of salvage. In her last months, Emerson added much to an art that was delicate but indomitable. There is another book to come.

Verse Chronicle: Foreign Affairs

FREDERICK SEIDEL

Frederick Seidel's long devotion to Savile Row suits, Cleverley shoes, Ducati motorcycles, and Patek Philippe watches—accoutrements of the one percent, or at worst the two percent—has made him seem, though he grew up among bobby soxers, a Beau Brummell past his sell-by date. If at eighty he's finally aged into himself, he's a man no less at odds with the world. Seidel lives in a bespoke suit of amused rage and disappointment.

The poems in *Widening Income Inequality*, a phrase much in the news (and a splendid name for a grunge band), display Seidel's poems at their most fetid and triumphant, their subjects often nipped from the headlines, phrases strewn like salt on an open wound, with a strong dose of political incorrectness added.

> I'm Mussolini,
> And the woman spread out on my enormous *Duce* desk looks teeny.
> The desk becomes an altar, sacred.
> The woman's naked.
>
> I call the woman teeny only because I need the rhyme.
> The shock of naked looks huge on top of a desktop and the slime.
> *Duce! Duce! Duce!* is what girls get wet with.
> This one's perhaps the wettest one's ever met with.

It's hard to shock readers these days. Though Seidel's late poems court a blend of crassness and bad taste, wearing a boater and toting a bouquet, he's still the little boy—a naughty little boy of eighty—who's learned a few bad words and wants to try them out. Short lines are followed by lines longer than the Lackawanna, syntax is pretzeled into shape; then there's the embarrassing but delicious admission that "teeny" isn't the right word at all—it's there just to catch the rhyme.

Seidel decided in midcareer to channel Ogden Nash. (That might have bewildered Nash more than anyone.) Nash's light verse, mostly forgotten now, often made the reader wait for a rhyme devised by some contortionist—sublime only because it was ridiculous. His "In the Vanities / No one wears panities" compares favorably with Seidel's "In my astronomy, I lick her cunt / Until the nations say they can't make war no more. / Her orgasm is violunt. / I get the maid to mop the floor." Once or twice in this collection, Seidel becomes a latter-day Byron (who, after all, rhymed "intellectual" and "henpecked you all"), but mostly it's Ogden Nash all the way down.

Seidel has invented a world—a world half Fellini, half fantasized by some rancid uncle with a taste for porn, overpriced haberdashery, and dirty jokes. In his lurid snapshots of the rich and shameless, Seidel has become a late-blooming Weegee, ready with his Speed Graphic and a pocketful of flashbulbs. The bon ton of Manhattan and elsewhere hasn't had such an anatomist since Wharton.

Still, many of these poems are no more plotted than a train wreck: "Pussy Days" begins with contact lenses, followed by an odd moment in the Tokyo subway, an incident in Bombay, tropical disease, a beautiful woman named Shireen, the Shah of Iran, the Shah's cancer, a parenthetical remark about the boss of Fiat, back to the Shah, then to the surgeon Michael DeBakey, tropical disease again, Hemingway in Paris, *A Farewell to Arms*, French riot police in 1960, the Algerian War, and at last Newark Airport. Having dipped into the swamps of memory, the poems often dredge up a load of muck.

On occasion this method, if it amounts to method, makes me want to rethink everything I dislike about Seidel. He watches a model train in a Christmas display:

It circles the department store's Christmas tree all day,
Into and out of a tunnel made of papier-mâché.
It's a passenger train, but something queer,
A freight train caboose brings up the rear.

That's not the only thing.

> It's a freight train with a yellow star,
> And has a Michelin yellow-star dining car.
> Sleeper compartments under sweeping-searchlight guard towers.
> Hissing Zyklon B gas showers.

This dream vision, superimposing the Holocaust on children's toys, is as brutal and terrifying as Anthony Hecht's "'More Light! More Light!'" or "The Book of Yolek." It would be, that is, if not for the penultimate stanza, which shows Seidel's compulsion to wreck what he creates:

> In God's department store at Christmastime are many choo-choos.
> Chuff-chuffing to their death are many Jew-Jews.
> And then there are the Hutus,
> And Tutsis vastly murdering them, producing Hutu boo-hoos.

The descent into bathos is rarely so steep.

Seidel began as a follower of Lowell in *Life Studies* mode, an imitator so canny you couldn't always tell them apart. He's become the ultimate Peck's Bad Boy, not by drinking or drugging or whoring too much, but by setting down what others think but wouldn't dare express—or don't think and are sorry someone does. His poems begin like car bombs (the real thing, not the drink), and he has a sense of *discordia concors* that would have shocked poor Sam Johnson. Seidel is perverse, ludicrous, exhibitionistic, goofy, and so delighted by schoolyard vulgarity he has made it an Olympic event. He's a man who thinks it clever to rhyme "stool cards," "prison guards," "stool bards," "drool hards," and "school yards." Byron wept! Yet if you don't read him, for the rude fancy as well as the occasional flights of terror, you'll have missed something crudely eccentric—no, carnivalesque—in contemporary poetry.

MAUREEN N. MCLANE

It's hard to know what Maureen N. McLane's *Mz N: the serial* wants to be, it tries so hard to be something. Next year with any luck we'll have

Mz N: the movie, then *Mz N: the cookbook*, and, if the sequels come hot and fast, eventually *Mz N: for dummies*. This breezy little book lives under the Falstaffian shadow of Berryman's *Dream Songs*, though Mz N is just a scarecrow imitation of Henry. Many poets have tried to counterfeit Berryman's crackpot sequence, three-fifths brilliant and two-fifths mere sludge. The results have shown how difficult it is to imitate the inimitable.

McLane's ragged lines, often bobbed to a word or two, are only occasionally wrapped around a subject; really she's happiest nattering on with no destination in sight. The titles are not much help—"Mz N Trans," "Mz N Meadow," "Mz N Monster," "Mz N Thirteenth Floor," and so through a clatter of identities to places even Rand McNally would have trouble finding. The titles are just hooks on which to hang a jazzy monologue ("Mz N Hermit" opens with a hermit thrush), and often the only grounding lies in literature. The poems are as chock-a-block with allusion as Eliot, but a poet whose lines are rarely more appealing than day-old oatmeal might be cautioned against throwing in, like a handful of raisins, the "Poet's self-centred / seclusion" (Shelley), "look into thy heart" (Sidney, sort of), "why not say what happened?" (Lowell), or "with how sad steps / o moon" (a triple play, Sidney to Wordsworth to Larkin). The echoes offer a devastating criticism of the language in which the poems are cast.

In some ways these rags of poems are strung together, like T-shirts on a clothesline, by Wordsworth's "growth of a poet's mind," as the second title of *The Prelude* had it. The great panjandrum of the Romantic era tried to write in the "real language of men"; and *Mz N* in plucky imitation offers a splash of slang here ("haters," "why don't you / chill out"), comic obscenity there ("a hermit thrush / says fuck all"), with scattered outbreaks of contemporary theory ("a classed grid / a kind of massive erection of the self / amidst the machinery / of institutions").

I have trouble disliking a book that in a few lines goes from "Those that have the power / to hurt and will do none" (Shakespeare, also misquoted) to "death metal." Yet Mz N's preferred mode is angsty free association, if association is ever free. She brings up Mary Shelley:

What should we do
Après le déluge

Victor left Geneva
Alien now alien in his natal home
The Monster would have left
for South America with his mate
but for her murder & his ice rage
Mary and Shelley left
for France with Claire
Then they left for Italy

It's hard to see the point of what seems torn from a page of term-paper notes.

In *Mz N*, a lot of things get said, or "sd": Hume, Arendt, Brecht, Gertrude Stein, even Beyoncé, among others, have things to say. Perhaps Robert Creeley can be blamed for "sd," blamed as well for the frantic short lines, weary concentration on trivia, and prosaic blandness. *Mz N* might be arch satire on the aimlessness of contemporary verse, but that would give it too much credit. The intelligence beneath the lines is never in focus.

When her sister asks her to be a surrogate mother, Mz N's response is curiously affectless:

This was intriguing
this was frightening
as there had been no babies
come thru her
& to have a baby
not her baby
seemed a strong hard thing
to split the body for.

(Then, more pungently, "Shitting / a pumpkin / is what a friend / of Shulamith Firestone / said in the late '60s / it was like.") However much these poems talk about thinking, or think about talking, they're almost immune to the life beneath.

The old resentments and flyweight anguish of these underdeveloped scenes (the subtitle's subtitle is "A Poem-in-Episodes") might have been better diagnosed than embodied. McLane is so quiveringly sensitive to poetry, as her autobiographical criticism in *My Poets* made plain, she might think that dumbing down her work makes it performance art; but *Mz N* lacks the bravado of exposure or bravura language of the *Dream Songs*. McLane is a knowing poetry critic and Romantics scholar with three earlier books of poems not so unprepossessing. Much as I like the frenzied sprezzatura of these poems, the desperation never quite followed up, the rare flashes of description ("maples liquefy / into a queer green flame"), in the end reading them is like being trapped in an elevator with a meth head.

LES MURRAY

Les Murray writes poems galumphing, a bit tone deaf, out at elbows and knees. *Waiting for the Past* sounds like, not verse post-Eliot, post-Lowell, but the lost poems of McGonagall. You can read pages of Murray and wonder if he's a poet at all; then your eye lights on a passage so strange, so breaknecked and roughnecked, you'd mistake a pile of broken glass for uncut diamonds:

> the steel houses it threw
> all over Hindmarsh Island,
>
> the barrages de richesse,
> film culture, horseradish farms,
> steamboats kneading heron-blue
>
> lake, the river full again.
> Upstream, the iron cattle bridges.

There have been very few poets who could turn pastoral description into a Piranesi engraving or think through landscape like Wordsworth— Murray makes Australia seem the next county over from the Lake District. The description is rarely ornament. It would be beneath him not to write with a purpose in mind.

Purpose, of course, is double edged. Murray's books suffer from long stretches of rabid hectoring, poems like scripts from a reality show called

Demagogues Go Wild. He has little time for the Outback bucko going
walkabout with his billycan, while sharing his cocksure traits—a Ned
Kelly rage over obscure grievances, distaste for culture with a capital C,
and of course hatred of nobs and experts of all sorts.

Such rants spiral into the sheer blithering of "Persistence of the
Reformation":

> four hundred years of ship-spread
> jihad at first called
> the Thirty Years War
> buff coats and ships' cannon
> the Christian civil war
> of worldwide estrangement
>
> freemasons, side massacres
> the nun-harem, Old Red Socks
> wives "turning" for husbands
> those forbidden their loves
> bitter chews of an old plug
> from Ireland and Britain.

A lot of history has been put into the op-ed trash compactor here. Old
Red Socks was Ian Paisley's name for the pope, but when a poet's shouting in your ear you don't want him to stop to explain. You just want him
to stop.

There's a kind of Murray garble-speak—sentences malformed, metaphors skew-jawed:

> The oblique rudder lever mis-thumbed
> against its chisel opposite
> crimps awry, gets re-occluded
> biting corners off middle dabs.

Give up? A nail clipper cutting toenails. The title spells it out, but that's
not always the case. Some lines that seem mysterious, however, need only
the twist of a pocket-watch key:

Cervantes. This one-strum pueblo
seen beyond acorn banksia
along a Benedictine surf—
never the Oz end of a cable, though.

How Spanish was the Indian Ocean?

Well, not.

This appears perfectly impenetrable unless you know that Cervantes is a small town north of Perth on the Indian Ocean. A ship named the *Cervantes* had been wrecked close by. Acorn banksia (orange banksia) is a tree, or further north a shrub, with large orange flower spikes. For "one-strum," perhaps read "hick"; for Benedictine, "mostly silent." The cable would presumably be transoceanic.

Murray shows a beautiful recklessness in his subjects. It's not just that *humani nihil a me alienum puto* must be tattooed on his forearm but that he writes about things few poets would bother with: a cargo plane full of horses, English as a second language, the expansion of universities, a Bollywood video in an Indian restaurant, a girl who lets a boy cut off her finger. Consider Murray's titles: "Nuclear Family Bees," "Tap Dogs Music," "The Privacy of Typewriters," "Diabetica," "Big Rabbit at the Verandah," "Eating from the Dictionary"—the capaciousness of his imagination is often a little eaten away by the trivia it prefers.

If Murray is a Demosthenes with pebbles still in his mouth, if the poems are too often factory-floor leavings swept up with a push broom, if he's all too capable of overbearing images (chickens "crying in tin hell-ships / warmed all night by shit-haloed bulbs") or lines that need a CIA codebook ("Balconious kung fu of Shanghai," "all that axed splinter cookery"), that's just Murray being Murray, though I sometimes wish he were Murray less often. He's a nonpareil like Whitman—and about as much of a rough as that autodidact Brooklyn editor. Murray possesses many of the qualities of an extraordinary poet, but the talents are so frequently mismanaged you're surprised he's a poet at all. Nonpareils are like that.

MELISSA GREEN

Melissa Green published a gorgeous, flawed book in 1987, drenched in
intoxicating description that concealed any intimations of damaged personality. Then she vanished. *The Squanicook Eclogues* should have been the
beginning of a stunning career, but Green spent the following year in a
mental ward. Apart from a memoir published in 1994 and a chapbook
issued in a small edition almost a decade ago—I had to bribe a man with
lunch to get a copy—she has lived on the margins of poetry, almost forgotten. When a writer disappears, unless he's J. D. Salinger no one goes
looking.

Magpiety: New and Selected Poems is the wretched refuse of a career cut
short, or cut to pieces. *The Squanicook Eclogues* looks as gorgeous as it did
thirty years ago, poems drifting along in deft alexandrines, surviving on
the ghost of rhyme:

> After a blustery, fretful March, the fields have yawned,
> Tossing off their goosedown coverlets to thaw.
> In airing upstairs farmhouse rooms, the sunlight paints
> A sudden gold leaf on the dresser drawers and wall.
> In his oldest jacket, I wade the oxen road,
> And under my boots, a gingery leaf-fall breeds new growth.

In the midst of this Keatsian drowse, it's easy to overlook the resourceful meter or the rhymes that go beyond even Wilfred Owen, letting a
couple of consonants or a vowel compose the echo. However lovely the
layers of impasto, the sequence is a fever dream that leaves no recollection of what was said. When you return to the poems a second time, a
third, what seemed an argument is just a series of beguiling images, the
traffic of sensibility without sense—or perhaps where sense lies locked
away. What she borrowed from Derek Walcott is clearer now.

The early poems nose along in a mood, offering arpeggios and variations like a young Mozart. Here and there something harsher emerges,
showing how much Green needed a polemical angel like early Lowell,
who planed away at the world, rarely able to resist a savage point for more

than a line or two. She swallowed him, like other influences, without becoming him:

> Does broken Carthage most resemble death,
> or do those workmen on the roof who lift
> a horizontal beam, stripped to the waist,
> still forge the final crosspiece of the West?

That might have been an outtake from *Lord Weary's Castle*, but the cautions of hope suggest how often her poems are a defensive withdrawal from her sources.

Green never lost the desire to write, however much circumstance conspired against her. The fragments of unpublished books collected here—poems mourning Joseph Brodsky or deriving from "Tom O'Bedlam's Song," a sequence about Heloise and Abélard, a clutch of poems she thought would be her last—reveal a mind dark with longing, driving toward extremities of expression, or language. This is Heloise:

> They dolved my mother's cophin when I was five.
> But at Argenteuil, I had a hundred mothers.
> The nuns nantled me with kisses, governed me
> with love, fed me on sculsh and sugared flawns.

For these lines not to be precious is a triumph. She says of the sequence, "I nearly had to invent a language," and at "nearly" the reader's ears should twitch—the words are English, but antique: *dolve*, a variant of "delve" (here, "to put . . . into the ground by digging," *OED*); *cophin*, coffin; *nantle*, to lift up; *sculsh*, rubbish; *flawn*, a custard or cheesecake.

Green often lets ideas run away with her. There's scarcely a sequence here, however truncated, that would not have been better even shorter. These haunting, haunted poems, the lines often airy as feathers, are scarred by psychic damage, by a life not fully lived—the imagination never finds a way fully to integrate itself, and the poems remain postcards from the abyss. In their scattershot focus, their trawlings from manuscripts lying in drawers, they do not avoid the fraught condition of their

writing (she once almost lost a foot to infection), particularly in the valedictory poems:

> The reeds are writing their wills.
> Wind has given up braiding the white wisps of the salt hay's hair.
>
> There's no telling when the weather will turn. There's [*sic*] isn't a
>   place
> in the world where I'm allowed to say—*I'm tired to death of life.*

Magpiety is not a selected poems in the usual sense. Like some whimsy
of Borges, these fractioned books may never be whole. I'd guessed that
"magpiety" was a portmanteau, letting "magpie" draw too near "piety,"
but not that it was first used by Thomas Hood in 1832. That catches her
peculiar blend of chatty seriousness marked by touches of affectation, or
affection. It's almost as if Green had been on a desert island for the past
thirty years, or perhaps two centuries, with palm leaves for paper and
ink made of soot and fish blood. Now she's back.

MARIANNE MOORE

Marianne Moore is the most underrated of the great moderns. Frost,
Pound, Eliot, Stevens, and Williams attracted critics galore, and each
poet proved a major influence on the poetry of the next century. Pound
was a maker of manifestos—but the poetry of the other men became
manifestos of their own. Moore, whose ambitions were more cryptic, was
such an unlikely poet, her subjects so absurd, her poems so off-kilter and
difficult to grasp, she never had nearly such effect. Others attracted disciples by the hundred, Moore only a few—like Elizabeth Bishop—as sin-
gular as herself.

During the years of her greatest popularity, in the 1950s and 60s,
Moore was writing her weakest work, having become a poetry mascot
dragged out whenever the public needed to be reminded how peculiar
poets were. Though she was asked to write liner notes for a spoken-word
album by Cassius Clay and to name Ford Motor Company's latest

showboat (eventually baptized the Edsel, through no fault of hers), such acceptance might as well be called refusal—these honors had nothing to do with her poems. Quirky poets rarely establish schools of poetry, at least not since Byzantium. Feeding her reputation for oddity was a way of denying how radical and original a poet she was.

Moore was thirty-three when friends in England secretly arranged to print her first book, *Poems* (1921). She had not been eager to publish and was appalled when the volume arrived in the mail unannounced. (Many reviews were unkind or uncomprehending.) Three years later, the editors of the *Dial* convinced her to publish a second book, incorporating most of the early poems. Moore's work attracted conspirators—the editors promptly awarded the book, *Observations*, the annual *Dial* prize (given in 1922 to *The Waste Land*). That had been their plan all along. The reissue of the book now is an occasion to mark the work of a woman who, as great poets do, redefined the poetic.

Reading Moore's poetry is like getting slapped in the face with a frozen haddock. Who else would begin a poem about roses,

> You do not seem to realize that beauty is a liability rather than
> an asset—that in view of the fact that spirit creates form we are
> justified in supposing
> that you must have brains,

or one titled (her titles sometimes stood as the first line) "England,"

> with its baby rivers and little towns, each with its abbey or its
> cathedral,
> with voices—one voice perhaps, echoing through the
> transept—the
> criterion of suitability and convenience,

or a poem called "The Labors of Hercules" ("To popularize the mule, its neat exterior / expressing the principle of accommodation reduced to a minimum")? Often you have to read her lines two or three times to take in the subtleties. Her poems are a triumph of empirical passion.

This is the poetry of an actuary from the sub-basement of the Hartford Accident and Indemnity Company or some browbeaten minion crawling from the archives of Faber and Faber, a poet part Harvard professor, part safari guide, part fossil hunter. Poets are their influences; but Moore arrived full blown, possessing, like Whitman, only a scrappy relation to the poetry that came before. When you think of her precursors, you think, Darwin.

Moore never had a lyrical ear—she wrote in a thorny prose broken into the syllabics of intricate stanzas. Her rhymes, at first embarrassingly amateurish, later became far more daring, half-hidden like overgrown wayposts. Though her tightly bound family was fond of joky pet-names (Moore was usually Rat, but also Weaz, Pidge, and Fangs), her poems lacked warmth or sentiment. The modernists were more personal than critics once thought, but their tone (except for Frost and Williams) could be Arctic or bookish. Moore's habit of dropping lines from books or newspaper articles into her poems may seem like Cubist collage; but her thinking was provoked by the stray trash of reading—like Pound, who wrote the Adams Cantos with *The Works of John Adams* propped open on his desk. She was at home among discards. Consider her abecedary of animals—chameleon, dock rat, jerboa, pangolin, paper nautilus, snail, wood weasel. One of her animals was a steam roller.

The animal kingdom offered Moore a realm from which human behavior could be observed without intimacy. A poet who revealed emotion by displacement, she knew herself perfectly well when she wrote, "'The deepest feeling always shows itself in silence; / not in silence, but restraint.'" Almost inevitably, she attributed the lines to someone else. You learn about Moore from the way she observes: the "elephants with their fog-colored skin," the mussel shell "opening and shutting itself like // an / injured fan," or, from what is possibly a self-portrait, "your cheeks, those rosettes / of blood on the stone floors of French châteaux." No one could have invented her; she had to invent herself.

Linda Leavell, who wrote a biography of the poet, has used the text of the second edition of *Observations*. The first had been produced quickly; after it sold out, Moore made one radical revision, one addition, and numerous small cuts and corrections, especially to punctuation. (She was an inveterate reviser whose fiddling bedevils critics even now.) The introduction, unfortunately, tries to drag Moore into the twenty-first century by the scruff of her neck, touting her as a poet who could "look beyond racial and national stereotypes" a "socially engaged poet, whose views about multicultural tolerance, biodiversity, . . . and individual liberty we are only now beginning to appreciate." Really? Moore would have laughed in her face—or scurried away, shaking her head. Had Aristotle somehow been transported to New York in the Coolidge years and happened across *Observations*, he would have said of this poetry always at right angles to itself, "There, there is poetry as I understand it."

CHRISTOPHER LOGUE

Christopher Logue died in 2011, his translation of the *Iliad* unfinished. *War Music* collects the shattered parts of the greatest modern translation of Homer, on which Logue labored in fits and starts for half a century. Though often true to the spirit of the poem, the translation radically revises the details, giving us an *Iliad* more vulgar, more brutish—and breathtakingly up to date. Pope, who reinvented Homer for the Augustans, looks like a piker in comparison.

Logue took a page from Pound, whose *Cathay* and *Homage to Sextus Propertius* gave poets license to alter an original wholesale. As Samuel Johnson remarked, "We must try its effect as an English poem; that is the way to judge of the merit of a translation." Boswell, in the same passage from his life of Johnson, says about Pope's Homer, "The truth is, it is impossible perfectly to translate poetry. In a different language it may be the same tune, but it has not the same tone. Homer plays it on a bassoon; Pope on a flagelet." Logue plays Homer with a bullhorn.

War Music starts like a film treatment:

Picture the east Aegean sea by night,
And on a beach aslant its shimmering
Upwards of 50,000 men
Asleep like spoons beside their lethal Fleet.

Now look along that beach, and see
Between the keels hatching its western dunes

A ten-foot-high reed wall faced with black clay
Split by a double-doored gate;
Then through the gate a naked man
Run with what seems to break the speed of light
Across the dry, then damp, then sand invisible
Beneath inch-high waves that slide
Over each other's luminescent panes;
Then kneel among those panes, burst into tears.

That's Achilles. The characters are everywhere rich with subtle attention. In a later scene, Hera and Athena approach. The gods turn around to see "(Steadying her red-sepal hat with the russet-silk flutes) / Creamy-armed Hera with teenaged Athene / (Holding their scallop-edged parasol high) / As they wobble their way down the dunes, / Shouting."

Donald Carne-Ross, the classicist and BBC producer who goaded Logue into tackling the poem, said in his foreword to Logue's *Patrocleia* (1963) that the poet was "far less 'civilized'" than Homer. Indeed, he's scarcely civil at all—Logue's gods are squabbling and vengeful ninnies; Agamemnon a high-handed tyrant, the Trump of his day; Achilles a petulant man-boy. No one comes off well, and the reader is reminded, despite the modern exaggerations, what a subtle psychologist Homer was.

Logue's *Iliad* is both contracted and accelerated. He's capable of metaphors soaked in finesse and penetration: "when the armies met, they paused, / And then they swayed, and then they moved / Much like a forest making its way through a forest"; Hector's "spear's tip flickers in the smoky light / Like the head of a crested adder over fern." Logue also delighted in grating anachronism. Still, it would be overly prissy to give up Ajax "grim underneath his tan as Rommel after 'Alamein"; Diomedes "brimming with homicidal joy"; or Achilles:

Observe his muscles as they move beneath his skin,
His fine, small-eared, investigative head,
His shoulders' bridge, the deep sweep of his back
Down which (plaited with Irish gold)
His never-cut redcurrant-coloured hair

Hangs in a glossy cable till its tuft
Brushes the combat-belt gripping his rump.

The description, however out of place (Irish gold in ancient Greece?), is brutally effective.

When Logue writes, "It was so quiet in Heaven that you could hear / The north wind pluck a chicken in Australia," the reader might be forgiven for wondering how many chickens lived Down Under three thousand years ago. But who would want to miss seeing a deadly arrow "float on / Over the strip for a beat, a beat; and then / Carry a tunnel the width of a lipstick through Quist's neck"? (Logue frequently had his way with Homeric names—Troy's bit characters seem to have wandered in from the Klingon Empire.) An Uzi here, a fighter plane there, some bread trucks trundling along—all remind us of our distance from Homer, and oddly sometimes our nearness, too. Men still kill each other hand to hand.

Logue knew no Greek, like Pound and Lowell translating piggy-back on the translations of others. That may seem akin to using a glove box to handle radioactive isotopes, but the method offers great freedom in exchange for loss of fidelity. Whoever Homer was, if he was anyone at all, he inherited a poetic form and a hoard of phrases from what may have been half a millennium of bardic singers. The *Iliad* was the work of centuries, with a jumble of arms and armor never seen on a battlefield together. The epic was likely no closer to the original than *Hamlet* had an ancient society of Shakespeare fanatics preserved the play in public recitals, knowing only iambic pentameter, the major incidents, and phrases lodged in memory. Logue has given us piecemeal, from the burnt scrolls of Herculaneum or the rubbish dumps at Oxyrhynchus, an *Iliad* Homer would still have recognized as his own.

Mrs. Custer's Tennyson

Our books read us as we read them; but those—those readers, I mean—who read pen in hand are now nearly extinct. When we write in antiphonal chorus to what we're reading, we engage in that conversation time and distance make impossible. Coleridge, one of the most obsessive of marginal annotators, those graffiti artists of the book, was so addicted to the practice that any book he borrowed became a hostage to fortune. If he ever managed to return it, the margins were often heavily defaced—he crowded his arguments into the side aisles.

Before the middle of the nineteenth century, reading in this wrangling or reciprocal manner required more preparation—your quills, your knife to sharpen those former pinions, and your pot of ink (India) all ready to hand. You needed a flat place to display these furnishings—a nearby table or lapboard. For the traveler, there were inkpots with latched tops, because spilled ink in your trunk would ruin your finery. Though the pencil was far more convenient—even Coleridge used one on occasion—most readers preferred ink.

The main abusers now of the pages of a book are probably college students. Months back, I bought a used copy of a new edition of T. S. Eliot's poems, allegedly unmarred by some scribbler's notes; alas, the major poems had all been rendered unreadable, words circled or underlined or double-underlined, margins stuffed with explanations and, I suspect, the parroted jargon of some professor. Against the line "I sat upon the shore" in *The Waste Land* stood the sad word "liminal"; near the opening of "The Burial of the Dead," "speaker is a flaneur."

This unnamed reader did not know the words *burnished*, *unguent*, *clairvoyante*, *propitious*, or *demotic* (which does not mean, as the professor perhaps thought, "imperfect")—and, more worryingly, not *patronising* or *antique*. Though the reader had never heard of Mylae ("ancient war") or Tiresias ("blind prophet"), he helpfully reminded himself, next to the lines "A crowd flowed over London Bridge, so many, / I had not thought death had undone so many," that the professor had explained, "like zombies." At least I suspect it was the professor, in a fit of idiotic genius, trying to make the text "relevant" at the expense of meaning or sense. Eliot's dead were not zombies. Readers bury their mistakes in the bone-yard of the margins.

Readers also reveal themselves in the passages they mark, reveal themselves in ways they might only to someone deeply loved. A decade ago, I happened to buy Elizabeth Custer's copy of Tennyson's poems, a small duodecimo volume (3 1/2" × 5 1/2") bound in blue buckram, front and rear boards blindstamped, page edges gilt, with gilt decoration to a spine that bore the title *Alfred Tennyson's Poems*. The title page, opposite a portrait of the clean-shaven young author, read *The Poetical Words of Alfred Tennyson, Poet Laureate, Etc.* The book was published in 1859 by Ticknor and Fields, the most famous Boston house of the day, publishers of Dickens, Hawthorne, Emerson, Thoreau, Stowe, Longfellow, and later Twain. On the front flyleaf, in faint pencil, was inscribed "Libbie Bacon / Monroe / Mich / March 1860," when she was seventeen. The earliest marginal note was dated September that year. In the upper corner of the leaf she had written in bold blunt pencil, some years after, "E. B. Custer."

Such a small volume was meant to be carried about, convenient for handbag or reticule or a man's coat pocket. The book shows considerable wear, the edges of the covers having in places rubbed through to the boards, the front hinge separating, many page edges dirtied by a thumb. At some point it suffered mild water damage—Libbie may have taken the book into the field with her husband.

Elizabeth Clift Bacon was born April 8, 1842, in Monroe, Michigan. Two decades before, her father had headed west from upstate New York toward what was then the frontier, intending to make his way by keeping school. Traveling by boat and stage, though later claiming he had walked, the young man arrived in lower Michigan Territory in the fall of 1822. By spring he was teaching in Raisinville, later part of the town of Monroe, which lies on the western shore of Lake Erie. He cleared land for a farm despite recurrent bouts of ague, the major disease endemic to that region, the Mississippi River Valley, the Carolinas, and even the District of Columbia. Also called the shaking ague, we know it as malaria. He wrote his parents, "Doctors here? Aye, and good ones, but they hew you to the verry stump, nor is there quinine enough to go round."

Daniel Bacon did not marry until nearly forty. He raised a family, becoming judge of probate, bank president, and influential man of business. Libbie, his only child to survive into adulthood, was sent as a day student to the Boyd Seminary nearby. After her mother died in 1854, she became a boarder, later returning after three years at a girl's school in upstate New York. She was headstrong, high-spirited, by turns frivolous and serious, a pretty girl used to getting her way.

Libbie met George Armstrong Custer, captain in the Union Army, at a Thanksgiving party at the seminary in 1862. This somewhat feckless young man, who the year before graduated last in his class at West Point, had begun to prove himself in battle. For some years, he had lived in Monroe with his half-sister. Though the houses stood on the same street no very great distance apart, the families did not know each other. Social circles of the day were often circumscribed by churches—hers, Presbyterian; his sister's, Methodist. Custer did not become a professing Christian—that is, did not accept Christ as his Savior—until after his marriage. Libbie was cool to him when introduced, he somewhat shy. Soon he was pressing his suit.

Apart from a few weeks in the east, Custer stayed in Monroe from November until the following April. Their courtship was not *All's Well That Ends Well*, but it possessed the Shakespearean comic impediments. Judge Bacon did not approve of Libbie's suitors in uniform, writing that many were "of the mustached, gilt-striped and Button kind"—implying that Union officers were foppish, insincere. Not long after the party, however, the judge met Custer at Humphrey House, a local hotel that served as a social club, finding him a sensible and direct young man, knowledgeable about the war. Bacon had, however, forbidden Libbie from seeking Custer's company or inviting him into the family home. That did not prevent them from meeting at other parties; once at a supper, when she put her head on his shoulder, he asked to kiss her. She refused. (It was improper for a girl to kiss a beau until he became her fiancé.) On his return to the army that spring, the couple wrote each other surreptitiously, using her best friend as a go-between. Judge Bacon and the young captain meanwhile struck up a warm correspondence.

The long-distance lovers suffered their share of misunderstandings, second guesses, second thoughts. That summer Custer was promoted to brigadier general, at twenty-three the youngest general in the Union Army. It was no surprise that newspapers called him the "boy general of the golden locks." Having suffered a bullet wound to his lower leg at the Battle of Culpeper Court House, that September he returned to Monroe on fifteen days' leave. At a costume ball in his honor the twenty-eighth—she dressed as a gypsy, Custer as Louis XVI—Libbie apparently told the new-minted general she would marry him if he could obtain her father's consent.

A few days later they probably became engaged, at least in their own eyes, though where and when is not clear. In *Cavalier in Buckskin*, the historian Robert Utley says that Libbie's promise on a sofa at the ball was only indirect. Her literary executor and biographer Marguerite Merington claims that the couple "plighted their troth" beneath a tree in the Bacons' garden, at the house he had been banned from visiting. (She may have heard this from Libbie herself.) In her journal of those years, its whereabouts now unknown, Libbie wrote after Custer's departure that she had seen him three times a day in the parlor at Humphrey House, but with "no clandestine meeting." Here the book of Tennyson's poems casts a raking light. Libbie's habit was to mark lines by drawing a vertical pencil stroke in the margin or by enclosing them with square brackets, parentheses, or even hash marks. Of more than a hundred passages she dated only twenty-two, a few of these lacking the year. (All quotations that follow are from her edition.)

Apart from the last stanza of "The Charge of the Light Brigade," dated soon after she acquired the volume, the earliest lines to receive Libbie's pencil are "'Come / With all good things, and war shall be no more'" ("Morte d'Arthur"). In the margin she wrote, "May 8, 1863," a month after Custer had returned east. He had reached the front near the start of the Battle of Chancellorsville, May 1–5, which ended in a Union defeat.

Libbie may have read reports of the battle with some anxiety—and sought the comfort of poetry. She also wrote on a rear blank leaf, dated the same day, "The flowers are the hand writing [*sic*] of God." I have found no source for this.

The most interesting early dates, however, are clustered in September and early October 1863. Four passages have been dated September, at least two before Custer received the wound at Culpeper Court House that brought him leave in Monroe. Though she had been conflicted during their months apart, by fall she was certain she and Custer were meant for each other. (She wrote in her journal, "Try as I did to suppress the 'fancy' for six months it did no good.") This conjecture is supported by two passages in "The Lotos Eaters," dated September 4, 1863 ("To hear each other's whispered speech; / Eating the Lotos, day by day, / To watch the crisping ripples on the beach, / And tender-curving lines of creamy spray"—she may have marked only the last two or three lines), and September 6 ("Only to hear were sweet, stretched out beneath the pine"). Libbie did not have another serious suitor then, so far as is known, though the idea that she was using Tennyson for a bit of double-dealing would otherwise be amusing.

The next group is dated October 3, five days after the ball and two before Custer left Monroe. A stanza from "The Miller's Daughter" hints at the atmosphere of this meeting:

> Look through mine eyes with thine. True wife
> 　　Round my true heart thine arms entwine;
> My other dearer life in life,
> 　　Look through my very soul with thine!
> Untouched with any shade of years,
> 　　May those kind eyes forever dwell!
> They have not shed a many tears,
> 　　Dear eyes, since first I knew them well.

The lines "True wife / Round my true heart thine arms entwine" have been placed in parentheses, the word "wife" underlined. Libbie added "Saturday afternoon," and then "October 3," written around the date "Sept," which has been crossed through. (The original date might have been "Sept" or "Sept 3.") This suggests that the couple plighted their troth on October 3 while reading the laureate together. Whatever she had said at the masquerade a few days before became a formal promise. The extraordinary portrayal of these lines—of that perfect oneness between two lovers, the marital bliss to come—made them the more significant, significant enough to be revisited the following day. Probably on this second reading the whole stanza, dated in each margin "Sund Oct 4th 1863" (in one case "/63"), was set off by a vertical line.

Tennyson was among the authors Libbie loved most at seminary. Made poet laureate in 1850, he was popular on two continents, his many poems on love obviously attractive to the young couple. Mrs. Custer's Tennyson is the private account of a woman of twenty-one finding in lines of poetry the words for her feelings. It may also record—we cannot know the circumstances of what was probably a joint reading—the words that gratified, that answered the emotions of, the twenty-three-year-old one-star general. The following summer, after they were married, Custer purchased a gift for Libbie—Tennyson's new book *Enoch Arden*, just published in America.

Two further passages are dated October 3, a line from "Love and Duty" ("In that last kiss, which never was the last") and a quatrain from *Maud*:

> O that 'twere possible
> After long grief and pain
> To find the arms of my true love
> Round me once again!

(Tennyson's echo of the lyric "Westron winde, when wilt thou blow" has long been noted.) Over the lines lies the date "September" and, below that, "October 3, 63," as well as the initials L A (Libbie and Armstrong—or Autie, Custer's family nickname). In the left-hand margin, the same initials have been intertwined. Though it is difficult to read, on the rear flyleaf she has also written "Sunday afternoon Oct 4 63," followed by those same intertwined initials. Recall the line "Round my true heart thine arms entwine," also read that afternoon—any intertwining had to take place on the page, if the sweethearts were sitting in the Bacon garden, where they might have been observed.

When Custer had returned to Monroe, Libbie and her father were boarding at Humphrey House, having shut up their home while her stepmother was away. Libbie wrote in her journal, the night of Custer's departure, "for two weeks I've been at Nett's"—that is, at the hotel. (Nettie Humphrey, her best friend, lived there with her father, the owner.) The Bacon house was therefore still unoccupied the days just before, and the couple might have stolen into the garden—a good lawyer in romantic law might have argued that Custer had not been barred from the grounds.

The September date on this passage could have been after Custer's arrival the 16th or, like the lines from "The Miller's Daughter," a possible trace of Libbie's growing hopes. It might have been wise to erase the date, had she later started reading the book with Custer—unless she confessed that she had been thinking only of him.

In his biography of Libbie, Lawrence Frost says that early the previous February, at a party where Custer pretended to flirt with her rival, he sat with Libbie in the parlor. She gave him her ring unobserved, a ring engraved with the initials "L A." Frost provides no source—it may be her missing journal—but why her ring possessed those initials is uncertain. They were neither hers nor her late mother's. Perhaps they were the abbreviation of a phrase like "Love Always," though I've found no similar examples from the period. Again giving no source (perhaps the journal once more), Frost later states that Custer had marked a passage in her Tennyson. This same passage about the "arms of my true love." It's certainly possible—the writing looks very much like hers—only an expert could determine. Whoever marked the lines and intertwined their initials, the importance is plain. Though the couple did not have permission to marry, they were already seeking permission in the poetry they read.

Facing the page with the stanza from "The Miller's Daughter," part of another stanza has been noticed, also dated "Sund Oct 4th 1863":

The kiss,
The woven arms, seem but to be

Weak symbols of the settled bliss,
    The comfort, I have found in thee.

Each individual word is underlined. Apart from the single word "wife" on the previous page, only two other lines have been underlined in the scores of passages where Libbie employed her pencil ("sweetly, my heart beat stronger," in *Maud*, and a line from *The Princess*). The intertwined initials and the line in which "thine arms entwine" find further echo here in "woven arms."

On the following page, in the poem "Fatima," one of the lovers bracketed another passage:

My whole soul waiting silently,
All naked in a sultry sky,
Droops blinded with his shining eye:
I *will* possess her [*handwritten above deleted* him] or will die.

Either might have blacked out Tennyson's "him" and inserted "her"— Custer to show his passion, or tenderly mocking hers; Libbie just the opposite. "Possess" from at least the time of *The Spanish Tragedy* was used for sexual possession; if that meaning had occurred to the couple, the nearby presence of "naked" might have secured the thrill. In Thomas Bowdler's *Family Shakespeare* (1818), Rosalind's "Now tell me, how long you would have her, after you have possessed her" was Bowdlerized by substituting "married her" for "possessed."

The lines from "Fatima" are dated that same Sunday, October 4; though above them a stanza is bracketed but undated, beginning, "Last night, when some one spoke his name, / From my swift blood that went and came / A thousand little shafts of flame," and ending, "O Love, O fire! once he drew / With one long kiss my whole soul through / My lips, as sunlight drinketh dew." We are so accustomed to reading poetry with dry ardor, it's easy to forget how important and sexually charged words could be for those who found voice through them, who found that it answered a longing in lovers forced to forgo physical passion until marriage.

Such marginal intimations act out the dumb show of romantic communion—the marriage of true minds, the silent bond of understanding, and later reminder of the departed as well as solace for the abandoned. Such gestures serve as shorthand for much unsaid, much that does not have to be said, because when lovers speak they so rarely go beyond clichés. Passages marked in each other's presence say what a letter cannot—it's a different kind of telling as well as a different kind of showing.

The couple perhaps leafed through the book, starting with poems already familiar—Libbie may have penciled her approval of some passages in previous readings. (A quatrain from *In Memoriam* is marked once, lightly; then a heavier pencil has gone over the brackets, the date written heavily as well. Something similar happened to the passage from *Maud* dated October 3.) Other lines dated that Sunday are similarly besotted: "A man had given all other bliss, / And all his worldly worth for this, / To waste his whole heart in one kiss / Upon her perfect lips" ("Sir Launcelot and Queen Guinevere"). There are partly legible additions to this thickly annotated passage: "Monroe" in the left margin; beneath the lines a later date, November 3, 1863; and below the October date "I' sposi" ("the newlyweds") and "Nan." Along the right margin Libbie wrote "Dec. 18867 [*sic, for* 1867]" and, after some indecipherable words, "Leavenworth." Below this lies a set of initials.

Nan would be Anna "Nan" Darrah, a childhood friend of Libbie's, who in the fall of 1866 accompanied the Custers across the Kansas plains to Fort Riley, the general's new station. (Custer's rank in the postwar army was lieutenant colonel; but by custom he was called general, his former brevet rank in the regular army.) Autie believed Nan's the "prettiest face in Monroe," according to Lawrence Frost. T. J. Stiles, a Custer biographer, thinks Autie may have had an affair with her. The passage, read with Nan in mind, might be damning, though Libbie's notation probably meant that Nan had written "the newlyweds." She may have borrowed the book for a while—"Anna" is written vertically on the front flyleaf.

At the end of a failed expedition against the Plains tribes the following July, Custer was arrested for abandoning his command, having ridden off to see Libbie at Fort Riley, where a Lieutenant Weir may have been paying her too much attention. (The initials next to the lines from "Sir Launcelot" about the kiss seem to be "T. B. W."—Thomas B. Weir.) The general was also charged with shooting deserters and delaying treatment of the wounded. By December, when Libbie dated the poem, the Custers and Nan were at Fort Leavenworth, where after a court-martial the general had been found guilty. He was removed from command for a year, with loss of pay. Libbie's recourse to this old passage, first noted during her courtship, could reveal some rapprochement between the couple after what Stiles believes were months of marital discord—but it may fix a moment when she found herself looking back sadly on more romantic days.

Four further passages are dated that Sunday in 1863, at the culmination of their courtship, three from *In Memoriam*, including

> So find I every pleasant spot
>> In which we were two were wont to meet,
>> The field, the chamber, and the street,
> For all is dark, where thou art not.

This might recall their somewhat furtive meetings when Custer had not been allowed to call at the Bacon home. Two single lines are also bracketed: "But half my life I leave behind" and "'More years had made me love thee more.'" These are especially touching, the one announcing the end of innocence, the other perhaps looking forward to a long life together. When a reader chooses lines, they assume a character at times different from the work. Context no longer matters.

The final passage marked that day comes from *Maud*: "We stood tranced in long embraces / Mixt with kisses sweeter, sweeter / Than anything on earth." A further pair of lines from "The Day-Dream," dated simply "October 4th," undoubtedly goes with the others: "And on her lover's arm she leant, / And round her waist she felt it fold." Beneath the date she has written "Nan!" but the relation to Nan Darrah is unclear—it may be no more than a passage Nan admired. The quotations of October 3 and 4 suggest the romantic intensity of those two days in October, when the couple probably became affianced, at least in their own eyes. The days were fortunately chosen—the *Detroit Free Press* remarked later that week, "There never was an October which commenced with more glorious weather than this." Libbie's meticulous dating secures their passion in time.

Two additional passages were dated that October. In *The Princess*, Libbie put parentheses around the line "With lengths of yellow ringlet, like a girl," dating it October 15, 1863, ten days after Custer's departure. In April, Nettie had cut one of Custer's locks for her. Beneath the song "Sweet and Low," Libbie has written, "Marie sang October — 63" and "Mrs Varian sang Nov 30. 1863." A contemporary setting of Tennyson's lines by Sir Joseph Barnby had been published that year. Marie is probably Marie Miller, later one of Libbie's bridesmaids. "Varian" would be Madame Charlotte Varian (mother of the actress Nina Varian, then still a child), who according to the *Michigan Argus* had performed in Ann Arbor on October 30.

These nearly exhaust the passages dated precisely, but the death of Judge Bacon three years later, on May 18, 1866, returned Libbie to Tennyson. She was in Monroe attending him during his fatal illness, probably a bout of dysentery or cholera. That day, reading *In Memoriam*, she bracketed the lines lightly marked before:

I cannot love thee as I ought,
 For love reflects the thing beloved;
 My words are only words, and moved
Upon the topmost froth of thought.

The following day, she drew heavy parentheses around one line from "New Year's Eve": "All night I lie awake, but I fall asleep at morn." In the margin, she wrote "Norvell & Conant" as well as the date. John Conant was a young man who the year of Fort Sumter had once walked her home from Bible class, but she also knew his brother Harry. (I have not been able to trace Norvell.) Against a passage from *Maud* (including the lines "But I know where a garden grows, / Fairer than aught in the world beside"), she has added the marginal comment, "Peace to his ashes!" This, and four short undated passages in "The Lotos-Eaters," two poems later, may also be related to Judge Bacon's death. Among them are the lines "Still from one sorrow to another thrown: / Nor ever fold our wings."

Libbie dated a few other lines, almost none of significance. On one page of *The Princess*, however, two passages have been marked: "Two women faster welded in one love / Than pairs of wedlock" and "A word, but one, one little kindly word." In the margin next to the first lines, Libbie has written, "Net + Libbie Dec. 13." Every New Year's Eve these best friends wrote a letter to each other to be read exactly a year later. At the end of 1863, as they sat in the same room, each composing such a letter, they "laid a plan to cheat 'Armstrong' out of his privileges." After the marriage, whenever they all stayed together, Nettie wrote, "We *will* sleep together—won't we Libbie? — Just think, darling, a year ago, you belonged to me as much as to anybody." Like other friends of the time, they shared a bed. The second passage might have been about Nettie; but the December date, if it applies, comes near the time of Custer's brief return east in 1862. The little kindly word might have been "love."

Of the scores of passages marked but undated, most offer insight into Libbie's character only through content. About a quarter are full of love, passion, desire (she liked lines about kissing), but a few lines suggest she was troubled or in despair. She chose some telling passages in "Locksley Hall"—for example, "Love is love forevermore. // Comfort? comfort scorned of devils! this is truth the poet sings, / That a sorrow's crown of sorrow is remembering happier things." In the margin she wrote, "Untroubled night gives counsel best," a variation on a proverb that goes back to Florio. A page later she bracketed the line "I myself must mix with action, lest I wither by despair" and two pages further a pair of lines beginning, "Till the war-drum throbbed no longer, and the battle-flags were furled." All these may reveal her unease during that unhappy year at Fort Riley and Fort Leavenworth—or perhaps she read them during the war, when Custer was on the battlefield. He was a courageous and reckless cavalry commander, always at the front of the charge.

Very few of her selections, however, are martial in character. (She wrote "Je t'aime" against an otherwise unmarked stanza in *The Princes*, beginning "Thy voice is heard through rolling drums / That beat to battle where he stands.") The stanza from "The Charge of the Light Brigade" has been mentioned, dated before the war—some lines she may have marked simply because she loved them as poetry. More interesting, however, are lines here and there that pronounce upon—whether they are the poet's sentiments or not—the proper roles of men and women. She was drawn to lines in *The Princess*: "Men hated learned women" (this underlined), "the tender ministries / Of female hands and hospitality," and a longer passage:

> Man for the field, and woman for the hearth:
> Man for the sword, and for the needle she:
> Man with the head, and woman with the heart.

Such "fixt" roles, as the old king in the poem calls them, Libbie for the most part accepted. The nineteenth century cared more about these roles than the century before or after.

She must have been particularly affected by these lines, as she wrote them on the inside of a rear blank leaf, dating them "Nov. 7. 1867." (The poem "Love and Duty" is headed with the same date.) This falls a month after the close of Custer's court martial, while he awaited General Grant's review of the guilty verdict. It may be a sign of her independence of mind that both quotes stop short of Tennyson's next lines, "Man to command, and woman to obey; / All else confusion." She marked an even longer passage later in the poem, the passage that begins,

> For woman is not undeveloped man,
> But diverse: could we make her as the man,
> Sweet love were slain: his dearest bond is this
> Not like to like, but like in difference.

That extract ends, "Till at the last she set herself to man, / Like perfect music unto noble words." The one line she failed to include lies just between these: "Nor lose the childlike in the larger mind." The vertical mark in the margin simply skipped it—by accident or design.

The great curiosity of the undated passages is how many refer to death. Libbie seems to have combed *Maud* and *In Memoriam* for lines about grief. From the latter, she marked the passage beginning,

> And if along with these should come
>   The man I held as half divine;

     Should strike a sudden hand in mine,
  And ask a thousand things of home;

  And I should tell him all my pain.

Other lines chosen in the same poem are even darker: "But brooding on the dear one dead"; "My paths are in the fields I know, / And thine in undiscovered lands"; "And I shall know him when we meet"; "These two,—they dwelt with eye on eye, / Their hearts of old have beat in tune, / Their meetings made December June, / Their every parting was to die." The two dozen undated passages that speak of love are matched by an equal number on death. These could have been chosen in the wake of her father's death, but their fierce passion suggests that she may have read them after her husband was killed in the massacre at the Little Bighorn in June 1876. In a line from *The Princess*, "And had a cousin tumbled on the plain," she crossed through "tumbled" and wrote "fallen." If the poetry doesn't quite fit, the office of the reader is to rewrite it.

    Officers' wives of the day were allowed to join their husbands at the outposts and sometimes in the field. In their twelve years of marriage, Libbie accompanied the general to posts in Texas, Kentucky, and at last Dakota Territory. When Custer had led his troops out of Fort Lincoln on the expedition against the Sioux, she approached the captain of the steamboat *Far West*, then loading supplies to be ferried upriver for the troops, and begged him to take her as a passenger. The captain politely refused.

    After her husband died in the massacre, Mrs. Custer found herself in financial straits. Though he had purchased a $5,000 life insurance policy, equivalent to a few years' salary, the general had lost a great deal of money in rash stock speculations. After paying his debts, Libbie was almost bankrupt. She survived at first on a small pension and a series of menial jobs. Eventually she took to writing memoirs of her years with Custer. *Boots and Saddles* (1885), titled after a cavalry trumpet call for mounting, proved a popular success, followed by *Tenting on the Plains* (1887) and *Following the Guidon* (1890). Unfortunately they brought little in royalties. Her finances at last restored by lecture fees and an inheritance, she became a canny investor in real estate. Libbie bought a house in New York City, where she died in 1933, days short of ninety-one, defending the reputation of her husband to the last—and leaving an estate worth $13 million in modern dollars. She was buried at West Point near bones that might be, but probably are not, those of the general.

Thoughts of Tennyson remained with the couple. Custer had his own copy of the poems and a decade after their marriage wrote some light verse declining a dinner invitation. The last quatrain read,

> This being written his duty might end,
> With no fear of being called Alfred Tennyson,
> He simply desires, however, to send
> You, the accompanying—Leg of Venison.

Custer was not the only soldier or politician who could dash off verses when required. The poem is dated June 1874, at Fort Lincoln, from which two years later the general and the Seventh Cavalry departed for the fatal rendezvous on the Little Bighorn.

Libbie's battered blue book of Tennyson gives a small glimpse into a once crucial role of poetry. Coleridge touched upon it in his "homely" definition of poetry as the "*best* words in the best order," but that is just an off-the-cuff turn on Pope—"*True Wit* is *Nature* to Advantage drest, / What oft was *Thought*, but ne'er so well *Exprest*." Poetry gave voice—and more than voice, expression—to thoughts difficult for young lovers to put into words. Such passages found a language more elevated than most could manage. It might be tempting to celebrate what we have gained by forgetting that sense of purpose, but it is more interesting to remember what we have lost.

Sent to Coventry (Larkin's "I Remember, I Remember")

"Home is where the heart is," certainly. On the other hand, "Home is the place where, when you have to go there, / They have to take you in" and "You can't go home again." No doubt even before the *Odyssey* the strain of homecoming was troubled by unwelcoming. For every Penelope weaving by day and unweaving by night, there are a hundred suitors waiting to kill you. Ovid was sent into exile on the Black Sea for a "mistake" more tantalizing for remaining a mystery; the letters he wrote Augustus asking for pardon were ignored. Had he returned anyway, the emperor would have put him to death. The longing for home is so universal, rare are the fictions where the prodigal son refuses to return.

No matter how long a maze, twenty yards or twenty years, the Minotaur lurks at the center—eventually you'll end up there, like it or not. Philip Larkin's "I Remember, I Remember" opens with a musty scenario: a man on a train. The train stops. The poem opens before the speaker realizes where he is:

Coming up England by a different line
For once, early in the cold new year,
We stopped, and, watching men with number-plates
Sprint down the platform to familiar gates,
"Why, Coventry!" I exclaimed. "I was born here."

I leant far out, and squinnied for a sign
That this was still the town that had been "mine"
So long, but found I wasn't even clear

Which side was which. From where those cycle-crates
Were standing, had we annually departed

For all those family hols? . . . A whistle went:
Things moved. I sat back, staring at my boots.

The traveler who spent years fleeing his hometown returns by accident. The moment of recognition is for a moment delayed while the passenger takes stock. Once he sees the "men with number-plates / Sprint down the platform to familiar gates," the penny drops.

English train stations look remarkably alike, many of them, their shop-worn, generic architecture so familiar that, finding himself at a station unawares, a traveler might be unable to identify it. The rail platform should have had a station sign at the incoming end; if he wasn't looking as the train pulled in, the passenger might easily have missed it.

The start and end of the journey go unmentioned—the traveler is abandoned between two worlds. However far he has gone from his beginnings, all the effort to escape has only brought him back. "Squinnied for a sign" might seem of necessity metaphoric—though the traveler leans out of the carriage (opening the compartment door or lowering its drop-glass window), even then he apparently doesn't see any station signs. Perhaps the blindness is willful. In his rambling essay on the poem, "Not the Place's Fault," Larkin swears he didn't realize where he was: "Of course the inside of the railway station of one's home town is never very familiar, and I was certainly not likely to recognize mine." He can't mean inside the station building, so he must have in mind what he could see from the tracks of the station grounds.

Photographs of the station in April 1953 show, amid the jumble of advertising signs for cigarettes and light bulbs, chocolates and table water-biscuits, placards for Coventry businesses as well as a handsome old-fashioned sign, suspended above the platform, for the *Coventry Evening Telegraph*, the local newspaper. Though difficult to make out, "Coventry" has been embossed on the top wooden slat of the benches; and the risers of the footbridge steps advertise Triumph Cycles and Motorcycles, a famous local factory. The number and size of lurid signs have been much reduced in a set of photos from November the following year (the riser signs have vanished), but every twenty feet or so a small Coventry sign has been fixed to an openwork girder beneath the platform roof. These signs would have been difficult to miss, had they been installed before the new year. Larkin's trip took place early in January 1954, between the two sets of photographs.

Number plates are what Americans call license plates. Coventry had more than a hundred motorcar factories over the years—Daimler, Triumph, Rover, Morris. In the days before large car-carriers, Larkin explained in a 1968 letter quoted in the notes to *Complete Poems*, employees drove each car or lorry to its destination using temporary number-plates, returning by train with the trade plates in hand.

The sprinting remains mysterious. The entrances to the Coventry platforms were never called gates. I thought the gates might be factory gates or the front gates of the men's houses. Perhaps the drivers were sprinting toward the staff canteen or to a midday meal at home. Perhaps there was some sort of friendly competition. (In his drafts of the poem, Larkin originally had "hurrying past," then "run down"—"sprint down" is more dramatic.) My chance acquaintance Nick Freeman, however, a sheep and pig farmer (and former British Airways engineer), believes the men were paid piecemeal for delivering the cars and that the first drivers to return to the factory had the best chance of a second car that day. This seems far the likeliest explanation. Some high-end cars, he added, are still delivered in that fashion.

The traveler's confusion continues into the next stanza, as he tries to answer the unstated question, "If this *is* Coventry, why didn't I recognize it?" The evidence of the eye is not quite satisfying. Platform signs again go unmentioned. Not "even clear / Which side was which," he can do no more than wonder if near some cycle crates his family had once gone on holiday. A cycle crate today is a box fixed above a tire, but at the time it was the cycle's shipping crate. Larkin calls them wooden crates in the 1968 letter. (A photograph of some decades before shows groups of cycles in open-slatted crates.) From their beginning in the late 1860s, Coventry had been home to more than two hundred bicycle makers. After World War II, only two remained. Many British car factories there, including Triumph, Rover, and Morris, had begun by making bikes.

The crates Larkin saw must lie further along the platform or across the tracks on the down platform. A large consignment would presumably have gone to the goods shed, where it would have been loaded, as the photograph caption has it, on a "rake of open wagons," that is, a line of coupled flat-cars. Damien Kimberly, an expert on Coventry bicycles, suggests that Larkin might have seen a small consignment of cycles waiting for a train's postal van. Passengers going on holiday, however, sometimes shipped their cycles in the van, using Stanley's large wicker crates made expressly for the purpose.

The return home, perhaps inevitably, allows the poet to indulge in the British colloquial lexicon—"squinnied" for "squinted" (as if myopically), "hols" for "holidays," i.e., vacations. Most British men worked six-day weeks of forty-eight hours, with sixteen days of holiday a year (ten days of paid holiday plus six bank holidays—Christmas, Boxing Day, and so forth). The paid two-week holiday was usually taken in summer, when children were out of school—the destination was almost always within Britain, often by the seaside. Larkin's father was the Coventry city treasurer, so his terms of employment may have been more generous.

"A whistle went." This must be a guard's whistle outside the train. From the passenger's point of view, "things moved." The station trundles backward into the past. The speaker reclines in his seat ("slumps" might be accurate), perhaps with some privacy. In British trains of the period, second- and third-class compartments offered a pair of facing upholstered benches sometimes divided by armrests, each compartment with a door that opened outward onto the platform. The separate compartments and opposing benches were inherited from the train carriages of a century before, a series of small linked coaches from a maker of the horse-drawn kind of carriage or coach—the names have stuck.

First-class compartments had separate seats similarly arranged, but first class was almost never used by ordinary Brits, especially during the terrible austerity the decade after the war. The thirty-one-year-old Larkin was barely middle class—his doppelgänger traveler might also have pinched pennies. In long-distance trains, a door opposite led to a communicating corridor that ran the length of the coach. The guard, though equivalent to an American conductor, did not announce the station on arrival, according to railway historian Stephen Parissien. It would seem possible for the traveler not to have known where the train was stopping—and a passenger caught in conversation might not have noticed the sign at the end of the platform. The poem continues:

> "Was that," my friend smiled, "where you 'have your roots'?"
> No, only where my childhood was unspent,
> I wanted to retort, just where I started.

The smile is telling, though an afterthought in the drafts; but what it tells may be amusement that the brief encounter with home has left the speaker, as he records, staring at his boots. The stare is one of exhaustion, shock, concession—or something approaching the leaden gaze of melancholia. He ignores the question.

The two people may be alone in the small compartment—it's hard to imagine middle-class Brits of that day talking so personally in earshot of strangers. (The traveler doesn't reply, so perhaps others are present after all.) Nothing following the question is said aloud until the friend breaks in again at the end. The pun on "started" (to be startled) could be accidental; but the rhyme of *boots* and *roots*—both let something stand, and here the boots seem rooted to the floor—shows how deeply rhyme may be calculated, even if it occurs to the poet in an instant.

He had begun the poem, Larkin explains in his essay, "after stopping unexpectedly in a train at Coventry, the town where I was born and lived for the first eighteen years of my life." He doesn't identify his friend, who as the ghostly auditor necessary for perspective is almost too convenient. The poet would otherwise be forced to add a self-conscious reflection ("I must have looked . . ." or something), removing the tension implicit in the pocket drama. The silent revelation, which for its effect must be held back, would be spoiled by such knowing introspection. The embarrassment is more painful for being unmentioned, the discomfort more devastating for being observed. The traveler's silent demurral balances upon comic equivocation. Larkin criticism could be built on what remains unsaid.

"Coming up England" meant traveling north; "different line," a different route. Larkin was working as a sub-librarian at Queen's University in Belfast. He'd spent the Christmas holidays visiting his mother in

Loughborough, some thirty miles northeast of Birmingham (his father had died two years after the war), then his lover Monica Jones, probably at her home in nearby Leicester, and his friend Kingsley Amis and his wife over in Swansea.

According to Richard Bradford's biography, the young librarian was coming "on the train from Swansea via Bristol to Liverpool," where he would catch the boat across the Irish Sea. (A poem about taking the night ferry to Belfast in 1950 was never finished.) How this is possible is unclear, because the rail route from Swansea to Liverpool runs west to Bristol, by another line northeast into Birmingham, then on to the port further north. Coventry lies in the wrong direction—southeast of Birmingham, some stops short along the London line. Bradford suggests that "perhaps the line was being repaired," but this is not quite satisfactory. Stephen Parissien thinks the route impossible and that Larkin was probably coming from Euston Station in London—on that route, perhaps one Larkin normally didn't take, Coventry was a regular stop. A rough draft has the line, "Coming that way by chance to please a friend." Larkin said a decade later that the trip "was the journey up to Liverpool to get the Belfast boat." Up from where?

The poet could have introduced an earlier experience or perhaps one wholly imaginary, which would make the incident more revealing; but other evidence is contrary. Bradford says, without giving a source, that Larkin was traveling alone, Monica "having, customarily, not accompanied him to Swansea." (Kingsley Amis loathed her.) Reading *The Less Deceived* two years later, however, she wrote the poet,

> *I remember* makes yr "friend" sound a perfect horror! it's quite good in the poem, so long as you never let on it was me in the train with you! I am always proud to see my one contribution, the only one in yr work.

"Always proud"—so she'd seen it more than once, in the magazine *Platform*, where it was first published, or more likely earlier in manuscript. Had she mistakenly expressed such pleasure before, he'd probably have disabused her; but she apparently recalled the incident. We know from Larkin's January 1954 letter to Patsy Strang, with whom until recently he'd been having an affair, that having spent the holiday with his mother he had gone to London: "saw *The confidential clerk* (β–), *M. Hulot's holiday* (α+), the Flemish Exhibition, pictures at the Tate (α), Carlyle's house in Chelsea." Perhaps he had gone with Monica. The loss of Larkin's diaries, burned after his death, makes it impossible to reconstruct his journey. (The Jones letters now at the Bodleian, as yet unavailable for research, may contain a clue.) Somehow, he ended up in Coventry.

In the closed compass of the poem, the traveler has broken his habits, or his habits have been broken for him. This might have been Freudian accident, had Fate a sense of humor. The brief stop now over, the portrait of the traveler staring at his boots tells us all we need know about his boyhood. The body of the poem is devoted not to what the past was but to the pathetic fantasy of what it was not. Provoked by his friend's perhaps innocent question, his reticence seems to betray a childhood of abject misery. It's a shock to discover that the childhood was instead just crushingly dull. For Larkin monotony was the ultimate misery, and so he frequently seemed to embrace it.

The friend's smile perhaps has a glaze of devilishness. "Have your roots," she says (let us say *she*), not "had," as if anyone would still have ties, though the traveler transparently wishes to be shot of the slowly receding city—that is, of the past. ("Have" suggests such ties are permanent, like it or not.) He's lost in mute, sore-tempered reflection. The poem continues again:

No, only where my childhood was unspent,
I wanted to retort, just where I started:

By now I've got the whole place clearly charted.
Our garden, first: where I did not invent
Blinding theologies of flowers and fruits,
And wasn't spoken to by an old hat.
And here we have that splendid family

I never ran to when I got depressed,
The boys all biceps and the girls all chest,
Their comic Ford, their farm where I could be

"Really myself." I'll show you, come to that,
The bracken where I never trembling sat,

Determined to go through with it; where she
Lay back, and "all became a burning mist."
And, in those offices, my doggerel
Was not set up in blunt ten-point, nor read
By a distinguished cousin of the mayor,

Who didn't call and tell my father *There
Before us, had we the gift to see ahead*—

His silence is his answer. The traveler finds in interior musing a dumb-struck way of coping by denial. None of it is true—it does not even try to sound true. This desperate, jealous improvisation mocks the famous victories or fiery achievements of the very young: Alexander the Great; Alexander Graham Bell; Blaise Pascal; even John Stuart Mill, that force-fed goose of a genius who had Greek at three and Latin at eight.

"I Remember, I Remember," a title dyed in either urgency or contemplation, whatever the allusion, redraws the darkened landscape of a boyhood where the boy did not, like Erasmus Darwin or his grandson Charles, cobble up "blinding theologies of flowers and fruits." (In an interview a few years before his death, Larkin said, "When I read accounts of other people's childhoods they always seem more lurid and exciting than mine.") He was granted no religious awakening or philosophical epiphany by a talking hat and knew no big-hearted family of brawny sons and buxom daughters, a family to whose embrace he could flee for solace, a family where his true character could emerge. Standing before his real parents, the boy must have felt a fraud. He invented the childhood promised by Dylan Thomas and D. H. Lawrence, the childhood Coventry denied.

Worse, amid the bracken he never enjoyed an early introduction to what even then was called shagging. "Sexual intercourse began / In nineteen sixty-three / (Which was rather late for me)," Larkin wrote in "Annus Mirabilis." That wasn't true, either; but in "Not the Place's Fault" he admitted, "It now seems strange to me that all the time I lived in Coventry

I never knew any girls. . . . None of my friends knew any girls either."
Blame all-boys schools.

The phrase "all became a burning mist" often confuses readers, but
it's merely an example of the high-caloric prose of popular romances.
More specifically, as the notes in *Complete Poems* relate, it was a catch-
phrase in the 1950s radio comedy *Bedtime with Braden*. (One of Bernard
Braden's regular turns was an extravagant parody of Brando's Stanley
Kowalski.) In short, the traveler suffered a childhood stifling and com-
monplace, lacking those moments broadcast through famous lives. Perhaps it was a childhood without much comfort or warmth, either.

The rough drafts are both more grandiose and more realistic about
this phantasm of youth: "where I charted / Not a single treasure cove,
nor sent / Armies against each other" on the one hand, and, on the other,
"My pursuits / Also included ignorance of birds, / Animals, reptiles,
pond-life, trees and flowers. / Here was the window-seat I never curled
in." To have come from such an undistinguished background, with nothing to predict later success, underlies all the reasons not to return. Ordinary yet not so ordinary, for Larkin was headed to Oxford.

Most difficult childhoods leave a poisonous residue. Time can be spent
but not unspent. Here the years passed yet nothing happened—the traveler might as well have wasted two decades in solitary confinement.
"Unspent" introduces the looking-glass world of this horror, this vacancy,
of all the childhood was not. (It's nonsense, of course. The most tedious
childhood has its days, even if none marked with red letter or white stone.)

Home demands the terror of reminiscence. Larkin wrote decades too
early to be affected by the psychology of repressed memories. Any lapse
of memory, runs that discredited strain, is manifest sign of forgotten
trauma; yet his deflection, sarcastically counterfeiting a past not his to
possess, is far bleaker. What does erasure show when you're conscious of
the lie? Something closer to the pathology of comedy.

Larkin seems to stand naked in his poems—that's the source of the
frisson. Yet why is he not considered, like Lowell and Plath, one of the great
confessional poets? Not necessarily because he stayed loyal to strict
form. So did W. D. Snodgrass, Lowell's major influence; and Lowell
never entirely abandoned form, even in *Life Studies*. Drily conventional,
his modesty a kind of rage, Larkin's poems never revel in erotic candor,

Achillean wrath, suicidal longings, or manic depression—if he was depressed, it was the old-fashioned kind of depressed. (The speaker in "Posterity" is called by his biographer "one of those old-type *natural* fouled-up guys.") His confessions are those of a man who, if he had no cardinal virtues, committed few mortal sins. His three long-term lovers knew little or nothing about one another, and he kept a bumper supply of pornography in home and office. That's old fashioned. His furies were as sealed as a casket. Disappointment and misery were about all he had to confess.

The list of might-have-beens ends with another never-was, the dream-like accomplishment of the young poet, his verse set in type, his greatness predicted by a "distinguished cousin of the mayor." How knowing is that detail about small cities, where influence passes through relatives of local grandees—yet how pathetic the wished-for triumphs. (An earlier and weaker thought in draft was, "some great stranger staying with the mayor.") His homage to his hometown is to rebuild it as a set for a drama of talent recognized and celebrated, except the play was never staged. At the culmination of this wretched catalogue, the friend interrupts:

> "You look as if you wished the place in Hell,"
> My friend said, "judging from your face." "Oh well,
> I suppose it's not the place's fault," I said.
>
> "Nothing, like something, happens anywhere."

So the poem ends. It's God's own territory, to condemn a place to damnation—consider Sodom and Gomorrah. Still, how petty, how far beyond petty into self-damnation, to employ theology for private vengeance. (Larkin's father, an atheist, advised the boy not to believe in God.) Larkin often shared with the confessional poets the reaction of early readers: "Oh, you can't say that in a poem" or "You shouldn't."

Larkin had been more ambitious as a novelist than as a poet. Though *Jill* (1946) received only a smattering of reviews that he later called "no public comment," *A Girl in Winter* (1947), published four months later by Faber and Faber, the famous house that eventually published his poetry, sold very well. The review in the *Church Times* remarked, "We look forward with eager anticipation to further work from the pen of this remarkable young writer." Larkin, according to his biographer Andrew Motion, "cut the piece out and kept it all his life." This may have been the genesis of prediction by the mayor's cousin in "I Remember, I Remember."

At the time of the train journey, Larkin was regarded as a novelist. His thin book of poems, *The North Ship*, had been published in 1945 by a small press better known for pornography. It was reviewed only once, in his hometown newspaper:

> Mr. Larkin has an inner vision that must be sought for with care. His recondite imagery is couched in phrases that make up in a kind of wistful hinted beauty what they lack in lucidity. Mr. Larkin's readers must at present be confined to a small circle. Perhaps his work will gain wider appeal as his genius becomes more mature?

That might have been reason enough to hate Coventry. The book was, in fact, fairly terrible—withered juvenilia with dribs and drabs of Auden and Yeats.

By the time of the Coventry trip, Larkin had abandoned more than one additional novel. He was also writing the poems, collected the following year in *The Less Deceived*, that would make his reputation: "Lines on a Young Lady's Photograph Album," "Reasons for Attendance," "Toads," "Church-Going," and of course "I Remember, I Remember." (The year of Larkin's trip, the manuscript was rejected by the Dolmen Press in Dublin as "too self pitying" and "too sexy.") The almost childish wish to be recognized was, belatedly, about to come true—but foresight does not have 20/20 vision (neither does hindsight, for that matter). Looking back at that faceless childhood in Coventry, Larkin saw nothing to suggest what lay ahead. In 1954, it might have seemed that distinction, much less genius, was beyond his grasp.

There's a curious relation between "I Remember, I Remember" and Auden's sonnet from the thirties, untitled then but later called, not very imaginatively, "Who's Who." (Auden's belated titles for his early poems are often silly.)

A shilling life will give you all the facts:
How Father beat him, how he ran away,
What were the struggles of his youth, what acts
Made him the greatest figure of his day:
Of how he fought, fished, hunted, worked all night,
Though giddy, climbed new mountains; named a sea:
Some of the last researchers even write
Love made him weep his pints like you and me.

The great man has done what great men do, but the sestet reveals that despite the Hemingwayesque achievements he mooned over an unrequited love to whom he wrote long letters she threw away. All the great man's gains cannot conceal a greater loss—both poems turn on the absence of love. The generic recitation of merits seems the direct ancestor of Larkin's comic moaning. The gnawing private dissatisfaction of the honored mirrors the seething *ressentiment* of the unrecognized.

"'Nothing, like something, happens anywhere.'" The line utters a truth so profound it hardly seems profound at all. The resolution of "I Remember, I Remember" resolves nothing—it's merely grudging acceptance of what cannot be changed. "I suppose it's not the place's fault," the traveler sighs, with a hint of bitterness. (The importance of that line was made clear when Larkin chose the telling phrase to title his essay.) "I suppose" gives away how much he wishes to suppose otherwise. Better, perhaps, to have had the utterly miserable childhood of Dickens. The cartoon childhood is emptied out, the shallowness of its comforts shrewdly reinforced—fantasy depends on the lies of myth. This unsettled sort of settlement does not suggest the griping is over, merely that the traveler has reached a temporary impasse, fending off the longings conjured up by the past, longings that cannot be erased or rewritten.

We think of writers as bound by place as much as by time. Reader-tourists gratify their hunger by traipsing to a dead writer's home or grave, even when, as with Yeats, someone else's corpse lies below. Few go to the grove where the poet was guiltily conceived, the hospital where he was untimely hatched, or the church where he was bound to a termagant. "I Remember, I Remember" is antibiography masquerading as

misanthropic growl—it's the revision writers attempt when they ask
heirs to burn their letters. As the traveler lists the events that never happened, the anxiety of presence becomes, in a gratuitous act of efface-
ment, a gratification of absence.

A writer easily becomes a tourist of his own life, teasing from the
cheerless boredom of childhood moments crucial only retrospectively,
where they suddenly assume meaning, every trivial incident an Epiphany if not an Annunciation. Is Larkin dismissing the minor events
that proved necessary to becoming a poet—say, reading Auden for the
first time at seventeen? Is he denying that such nothings happened or
just ignoring them? The benighted childhood was simply dreary, like an
enticing palimpsest that proves no more than a set of bureaucratic instructions. The poem—about nothing much, and everything much, in a
Hardyesque way—conceals a recognition that most lives are composed
of nothings. Childhood's greatest gift to Larkin was self-loathing.

The poem suppresses a very English joke about being "sent to Coventry," that is, given the silent treatment—or, in religious terms, shunned.
Larkin could hardly be unaware that packing his traveler off to Coventry has reduced him to uncomfortable silence. The origin of the phrase
has long been argued, but the *OED* plumps for the evidence in a passage
from Clarendon's *History of the Rebellion* (1703)—some prisoners from
the king's men were sent to Coventry, known for "declaring a more
peremptory malice to his Majesty than any other place."

The source of the poem's title demonstrates the cunning of allusion.
"I Remember, I Remember" is a syrupy lyric by Thomas Hood—the
duplication of the phrase at first seems to gush with Victorian bathos
toward hearth and home. Such homes made homesickness a sometimes
fatal physical longing—the yearning became a call to the grave. Hood
begins, excruciatingly,

I remember, I remember,
The house where I was born,
The little window where the sun
Came peeping in at morn;
He never came a wink too soon,

Nor brought too long a day,
But now, I often wish the night
Had borne my breath away!

Peeping! *A wink too soon*! On the poet goes about the "vi'lets" and "lily-cups" and "flowers made of light" until all that ebullience becomes a catch in the throat—"My spirit flew in feathers then, / That is so heavy now." (Recall the traveler's boots.) The poem ends, however, in a cupful of self-pity, "But now 'tis little joy / To know I'm farther off from heav'n / Than when I was a boy." It's a shortish poem, unbearably twee, yet however heart-tugging not without stirred-up darkness—no longer uplifting, the title becomes a funeral bell. Where Hood scants "childish ignorance," Larkin's traveler laments childish experience, buried within a long list of inexperience and grievance. We have the two sides of Blake here. Even Larkin's rhyme scheme is devious—three rhyme sounds in a nine-line pattern (*abccbaabc*) recast in five-line stanzas, with a last line standing alone. Something is repeated, something squirreled away.

In a letter of 1965 noted in *Complete Poems*, Larkin admitted that his piece "does of course glance at Thomas Hood's poem." Winthrop Mackworth Praed's similar poem of childhood opens with the same line, "I remember, I remember," and closes with a betraying touch that reverberates into Larkin's fallen world. Hood's and Praed's charmless innocence, though both poems sink at the end into despond, is precisely what Larkin makes fun of. His world lives not so much after the Fall as after a Lightness that never existed. Hood retains just a few squibs in anthologies, Praed not even those, which doesn't bode well for a poet entirely undistinguished, as the traveler seems to be.

The brilliance of Larkin's dry salvage lies in the swerve of tone. Until that bleak ending, Hood fairly bubbles over with gap-toothed joy; Larkin throughout is at worst rueful, at best resigned. The earlier poem was more than glanced at—they are poems intimately entangled. Larkin's traveler finds himself at home, less at home than ever; Hood's speaker, done with boyhood, stands "farther off from heav'n." Even had Larkin's traveler survived that preposterous scriptwriter's childhood, he might have been no more happy. It is indeed not the place's fault. The observer, like Milton's Satan, finds below every abyss an abyss still lower.

Part of the irony of the title, but not the whole, is that he might easily have called the poem, after Conrad, "The horror! The horror!" (Recall Quentin Compson's "*I dont! I dont hate it! I dont hate it!*") Even when the traveler is certain of the fatal mise en scène, he is not reminded of his lucky escape—the would-be poet must instead face having returned a failure; indeed, having returned at all. His childhood burns so deeply, his acts of memory become means of erasure.

Larkin takes pains in his essay to state, as if under oath before the city council, that the "poem was not of course meant to disparage Coventry, or to suggest that it was, or is, a dull place to live in, or that I now remember it with dislike or indifference, or even can't remember it at all." This is so lawyerish, battening down every possibility, the reader may feel the poet protests too much. (The essay was written for a Coventry arts magazine.) Larkin's mixed feelings about his childhood, that "forgotten boredom" melodramatically announced in "Coming," tainted the place ever after. Coventry was not the cause, only the metaphor of the condition.

If Larkin suffered that minor revelation at the station, his amnesia may have had a more devastating source, because the Coventry of his boyhood no longer existed. Two weeks after he left for university, on the night of November 14, 1940, five hundred German bombers dropped explosive and incendiary bombs on the city, destroying the famous cathedral, nearly annihilating the town center, causing massive damage to factories farther out, and erasing part of the rail station. There were further raids over the next two years. Joseph Goebbels afterward talked of other cities being "Coventried" (a usage missing from the *OED*), and the ravaged cathedral was left as a skeletal reminder of the destruction. "This was still the town," then, retains an ambiguous air—desire, happy or not, that some scrap apart from the running men had remained, or nervous anxiety that not everything had been smashed. There's a mild irony in the running men being the only immediate sign of old Coventry, since the major reason for the bombing had been to wipe out the factories.

This explains the most curious implication of the traveler's inability at first to recognize part of his home town. Why leave out the obvious, that the city had been bombed and that, whatever the damage to the station, the unseen surroundings (the "town that had been 'mine'") no longer survived except in a ghostly past? Even had the station been more or less unchanged (the main building suffered little), once he knew it was Coventry he could not help but recall the almost total obliteration.

Larkin mentions the bombing only once in his essay, almost as an afterthought. He ends by saying, "I never went back there to live again." No, but two days after the bombs fell he hitchhiked home to search for his parents, only to find their house abandoned. (They'd gone to a nearby village for safety.) He saw the result of the terrible raids firsthand. Buildings may still have been burning. It's tempting to see the memory as so traumatic, it must be the horrifying specter at the heart of the poem. Still, recalling in the poem that November night of the Blitz would have turned the subject from the lasting pain of childhood to the terrors of war, even at home.

There was a better reason for Larkin not to say a word. Given how much he seems to detest the city, whatever his protestations, its ruin might have seemed wish fulfillment. The Luftwaffe had done the job for him.

The State of Criticism (On Being Asked to Write on the "State of Criticism")

The State of Criticism lies somewhere between New York and New Jersey. Its wetlands and rocky shore have long been scarred by chemical factories and oil refineries, close to waste ground whose rusting signs announce, "Bird Sanctuary." Shore birds flock there, the guidebooks say; but no snipe or plover have been seen in living memory. That hardly matters, since the state bird is the vulture, which flourishes; and the State of Criticism is widely celebrated for the quality of its carrion.

I'm wary of conferences, or round tables, or conference calls on the State of Criticism, because I'd rather be writing poetry than writing criticism, and I'd rather be writing criticism than criticism about the state of criticism. Randall Jarrell remarked, sixty years ago, that the "ambitious young intellectual . . . buys himself a new typewriter, rents himself a room, and settles down to write . . . book reviews, long critical articles, explications." Rather than risk writing poetry or fiction, he meant.

That is, alas, no longer true. The ambitious young intellectual buys himself a laptop, rents himself some friends, and settles down in Brooklyn to write poetry, poetry, and more poetry. He blogs, and tweets, and puts his new poems on Facebook or Twitter. Everyone loves him. Everyone whispers in his ear how brilliant he is. Meanwhile, magazine editors complain that if you ask poets to write a review, they fall all over themselves making excuses. There's no way to clear a room faster, at that endless cocktail-party that is poetry, than to announce that the last man standing will have to write a review of it.

It's not that poets lack opinions. Get to know a poet and he'll eagerly tell you that A is shockingly overrated, B hasn't written a good poem since

Nixon was impeached, and C won the Pulitzer because his best friend was a judge. Poets are violent in their tastes (not that you'd know this from reading the reviews they so rarely write), but they're nocturnal animals—their real feelings come out only when the lights go off.

It never occurred to me until far too late that poets could be unhappy about a review—I mean a serious review, one that spoke to the various flaws of a book as well as to its occasional virtues. Let's face it, the vast majority of books published since Gutenberg started to ink his movable type in Strasbourg and Caxton got his thumbs dirty in London have possessed few virtues and all too many flaws. Even if you refuse to review the tired, the poor, the huddled masses, and the wretched refuse of the trade, the remainder are still books unlikely to be read or remembered a decade later. Perhaps every year two or three new books appear that will grace a shelf awhile, and every five years or so some sod writes a book worth reading in a century.

The critic's job is to point out which books those are and give some coherent reason why, or fail to do so. I've written about the wrongheaded reviews of brilliant books. Many critics saw, with a high degree of accuracy, what the poets were doing in *Lyrical Ballads*, or *Leaves of Grass*, or *The Waste Land*; but they thought what the poets were doing wasn't poetry. The failure was not in their eyesight but in their taste—or their philosophy.

Given how critical poets are, why don't they write more criticism? Even if you make the usual arguments—that criticism is woefully ill paid; that criticism interferes with those narrow shop-hours the poet is open for business (the poet might as well padlock the door, those days he's scribbling reviews); that, since criticism is so rarely like lust, few poets can muster the desire to write about poetry—even if you rally the old apologies, you haven't mentioned the one poets rarely speak of, that writing criticism is a mug's game. If you write a bad review of X—indeed, if you write a good review of X that isn't quite as good as X thinks he deserves— why, X will be delighted to be your enemy forever. You also incur the lifelong hatred of X's bosom friends, and his beloved mother, and his distant cousins, and his dog. (No review could ever be as good as X deserves, so all the X's of the world feel.)

A reckless young poet may be cheerfully willing to endure the wrath of X; but sooner or later he will find himself applying for a job or a grant or hoping for an award (something foolish poets do every day, and some not so foolish), little knowing that X's friends have been sharpening their knives a very long time. The one truth of criticism is, the wounded bear never forgets.

Poetry, at least for a few years, is kind to that minor Machiavel, the literary politician. The glad-handing hail-fellow-well-met sort who kisses babies at every whistle-stop, keeps in his back pocket a little patronage to hand out, and praises older poets to the skies usually thrives, until one day he dies quietly in office and is promptly forgotten. The rewards of poetry may seem meager enough, yet I've heard that a certain poet in the Ivies makes $300,000 a year and that another at a rich Southern university makes $250,000. I've been told that a young poet whose first book was rapturously received, and whose criticism has stung a few, has been unable to find a job. The poet who didn't need to write criticism would scarcely see much advantage to doing so.

The critic is a Diogenes in a world where everyone else is Rebecca of Sunnybrook Farm. In that utopia that is poetry, all the poets are wonderful poets—no, brilliant poets, so brilliant your eyes hurt to look upon them. Every book a poet writes is better than his last. Every word the poet speaks is engraved upon marble walls lining the leafy boulevards of the utopia of poetry, and if not the boulevards then no worse than a palm-lined avenue nearby. (In the utopia that is poetry, work crews day and night build more broad boulevards and more sunny avenues, even if no one actually lives there, for the utopia of poetry bears an uncomfortable resemblance to the village of Potemkin.) The poets cover their limbs in velvet robes and top their heads with golden crowns. Like heads of state, they never carry money, for in the utopia of poetry everything is paid for by the utopia of poetry. They travel in golden carriages, though these may look like pumpkins to everyone else.

In the utopia of poetry, no accountant is ever permitted to examine the GDP or the national debt, for the major export of the utopia of poetry is poetry. It may not sell very well; and there are countries that want no more of it, that will never again ship sugar or slaves or rum for a little poetry, or even a great lumpish heap of it. No matter, because it's widely known that the citizens of this utopia are perfectly happy to eat poetry, and drink poetry, and give each other gifts of poetry; and somehow they thrive and beget baby poets who run about unclothed until they too are old enough to don the velvet robes and grip the golden tiaras.

In the utopia of poetry, every poet wins every award every year. It's simply not true that all the poets are better than average. No, each is unique, more unique than anyone else. Every poet is getting better and better. The one question banned in the utopia of poetry is who pays for the utopia of poetry. The utopia of poetry runs a deficit every year yet every year somehow produces more poetry. It is said that when Stalin wanted to run a country, he first consulted the poets.

But enough. That is the world of which most critics of poetry write, and the only thing that distinguishes most critics of poetry from a publicity department is that the critics often write for free. Indeed, they're so widely known for their charity, even poets who don't write criticism often stop now and then to scribble a blurb or two. I have always suspected that those who write blurbs never read the books, because there is nothing more threatening to the utopia of poetry than to read the poetry. The definition of a blurb is a "brief recommendation by an author more famous, a compliment that moves everyone to tears though no one believes a word of it."

Then there is that other sort of criticism, the sort PhDs write while they're waiting for the tenure-track jobs rarer than the ivory-billed woodpecker, the criticism that speaks of "liminal surfaces" and "transgressive interrogation" and "free-floating something-or-others"—the sort of criticism no one but a PhD would read and no one but a PhD would write. I feel sometimes like a traveler who, every time a stranger from the land of theory opens his mouth, runs in the opposite direction. Those who love that language love that language, though it seems so badly translated out of some arcane dialect of Ruthenian that the shifts and dodges and crotchets that make poetry interesting are no longer interesting.

It's worth remembering that the world Randall Jarrell complained of in his essay—it was called "The Age of Criticism"—was often wonderful. To go back seventy or eighty years to *Partisan Review* and *Hudson Review* to see what Blackmur or Empson or Jarrell himself was writing is to be astonished. When literary magazines come thudding onto my porch now, there are criticism and reviews enough; but the criticism is rarely equal to what was published two or three generations ago, and the reviews—oh, oh, the reviews, having overdosed on high-fructose corn syrup—make earnest cases for books so dull the quotations beg you never to read another line.

These days, with the internet open at all hours, there is more criticism than ever and more poetry than ever. If the criticism published in magazines has often been bad, or bad enough, the criticism on the internet has rarely been good, or good enough. Opinion you will find in Maecenean abundance, opinion with all too much enthusiasm and all too little taste or judgment. A few of these critics are rabid; most are rhapsodic—but the usual sins do not attract the rare virtues. On occasion, you will find a reader dogged with purpose, one who scours the poetry carefully, has an idea or two, and who can write a few sentences that don't make your eyes bleed.

Such critics, in the old days, would have written for magazines and been paid; and they will thrive writing criticism on the internet for free. I am glad for them. They are obviously men and women of leisure. For a poet, the only reason to write criticism is the excuse it gives to think about poetry. No doubt critics write criticism for different and often perverse reasons, but I write to find out what I have to say. I am too lazy to have any other excuse.

As for the State of Criticism, rumors that it is severely depopulated are exaggerated. It isn't true that the factories are about to close or that the cities have declared bankruptcy to relieve themselves of the burden of paying pensions to retired critics. It is patently false that the leaders of the State of Criticism have stored their wealth in Swiss banks under assumed names. It is still a fine state, welcome to all. If I sent you a postcard, it would say, "Wish you were here."

The Perils of Reviewing (On Being Asked, "What Are the Perils of Criticism?")

Perils? Pauline suffered perils (train track, ropes, 4-2-4 loco bearing down), but about all a poetry reviewer can fear from fellow poets is a little squinty-eyed distaste and some unconcealed hostility. The obvious complaints—that the poor reviewer didn't get this plum or that shiny brass ring—are no worse than those all poets grouse over in the privacy of their cold retreats.

What earthly use would criticism be if it didn't require such penalties? Would we really want to live in Poetry World, where the banners have slogans in Basic English ("Write what you know! Write what you know!") and the bronze statues all honor mediocrities? ("Let us go then, you and I," one of its honored poems begins, "to Edwin Guest Plaza.") Where every poet marches up and thanks the critic for the mud and brickbats and begs for another helping? I learned long ago, when I happened to mention the plagiarism in John Gardner's *Freddy's Book* and Paul Mariani's *Robert Lowell*, that the whistleblower might as well swallow the whistle and choke on it, if he expects authors to be grateful for having their misdemeanors exposed. I've been threatened with lawsuits more than once. And, as some may know, one poet offered to beat me up—and another to run me over with his truck.

When poetry's latest mini-celebrity parades forth, the critic is obliged to say that the poor dolt paid for his fancy boots with counterfeit bills—or that she doesn't realize her von Fürstenberg has a rent in the rear. Poets write what they write, and critics say what they say—since the day some Middle Eastern fabulist scribbled the tale of the scorpion and the turtle, the poet can hardly grumble that he wasn't warned.

The real perils of reviewing are quite different. Just as you can look at only so many paintings in a mediocre gallery without wanting to swear off art forever (there's nothing like a room full of daubers to make you hate Rembrandt), reading a hundred or more new books of poetry every year makes you wonder if reading the backs of pesticide boxes might not be more gratifying. The reviewer is in peril if he forgets that he's breathing the pure serene not to tell readers which contemporary poet has flat tires on the drive up Parnassus (though his job is that, that too) but to cast a spotlight on that rarest of things, the astonishing book that might otherwise pass unnoticed.

The sense of possibility is what keeps the critic—what ought to keep him—opening each new book with a little tremor of delight, even if the tremor immediately gives way to dismay. When he loses that shudder of potential joy, the critic might as well retire the acid pen and sit in his porch rocker, waiting for the hearse. The only peril a critic faces is the peril of forgetting why he began to write criticism.

Verse Chronicle: Home and Away

JOHNNY CASH

Fans of Bob Dylan found it impossible to understand why he would sing a duet with Johnny Cash, at least until they heard "Girl from the North Country." I recall the kitchen where *Nashville Skyline* played almost half a century ago but not who owned the house or even where it was—only that I'd hitchhiked there. That was the year Cash became best known for the chintzy novelty song "A Boy Named Sue." Still, my ears perk up when "Folsom Prison Blues," "I Walk the Line," or "The Man Comes Around" crackles through my car radio. If there's an American song book a century from now, they will probably be included.

Cash was a mythic figure in American folk culture long before he died in 2003. He was not the outlaw he pretended to be (he never spent longer than a night in jail), just a hard-working alcoholic country-singer who tried to commit suicide and found religion. The movie script could have written itself.

Forever Words is part of a cache of lyrics discovered after Cash's death at seventy-one, lyrics he never turned into songs. Like the bureau drawer of poems left by Emily Dickinson, his papers give a good name to the hoarding instinct. These scraps are no more "unknown poems," as the subtitle has it, than the Man in Black's grocery lists—they're just lyrics without his whiskey-tinctured voice or whiskey-fueled guitar. The lightweight introduction provided by the editor, Paul Muldoon, enters with clichés and takes its bow in breathless awe. He's aware how much of country derives from the Scotch-Irish folk songs of Appalachia and, to a lesser extent, Southern blues. (Gospel hymns go unmentioned.) Cash borrowed the blues's simplicity, often adding the nightmarish narrative of the border ballads, to make something as close to poetry as lyrics come.

> The lights are on past midnite
> The curtains closed all day
> There's trouble on the mountain
> The valley people say.

Auden mastered that sense of foreboding in the thirties, and the delicate play of antithesis would have pleased Pope. Or take this:

> The war has come
> And the growing is hard
> The soil is tough
> As our front yard.

How different the lyric would be had it ended "In our front yard," more pathetic rather than boastful and aggressive. Hard-bitten was the tone Cash aimed for—otherwise his lyrics overdosed on the rancid syrup that makes country difficult to take. He knew that real pathos *comes* hard. He wasn't the kind of country singer who resorted to yodeling—except once, badly.

Lyrics without music are no better than dead trout mounted in some man cave. Cash might have felt the influence of tradition had he known nothing about it; but a man can't write, "I need my biscuit buttered, Babe" or "Who's gonna grease my skillet / When you're gone?" or "You've done every dirty thing / That a woman shouldn't do" without having the blues growling in his ear. The brutal, the unforgiving, the knife edge of misery—that was where Cash came into his own:

> Job was a wealthy man
> He had a lot of kids and a lot of land
> He had cattle on a thousand hills
> He lived every day to do God's will
> Satan came with the sons of men
> The Lord said Satan where you been?

Bitter, and dry. Facsimiles of a dozen manuscripts let the reader see Cash in the midst of revision—changing "mystic horseman" to "spirit rider," say—but also show what appear to be frequent inaccuracies in the transcriptions. Muldoon admits having used numerous manuscripts to concoct a "finished" version. Lyrics are often fluid from performance to performance; but, much though I sympathize with the editor's tinkering, there's a lot of tinkering. A few questions remain. Why arrange the lyrics alphabetically by title when chronologically would have been more telling? Why, in "I'm Comin', Honey," does the editor expand "Tenn" to "Tennessee" but not "Penn" to "Pennsylvania," which fairly wrecks the line's rhythm and sense?

There aren't more than three or four good songs here, alas; and too many lyrics collapse into gooey blather ("I would be gentle and I would never hurt you / And God might send a moonbeam / And lay us down to pleasant dreams"). Worse, the baldly autobiographic lyrics are excruciating ("I was born to sing / But not to the wind and space / But to people's hearts / And people's ears"). Good songwriters don't need to be considered poets—they're walking the other side of the street. Words matter there, but they matter more with music.

This unnecessary book has no doubt been pitched as poetry because poetry is rarely so "relatable," the saddest word in the language. Nick Carraway is relatable, but *Gatsby* a great novel because Gatsby is unknowable. Hamlet is not relatable. Achilles is not relatable. Sometimes we understand the plight of a character, sometimes the necessity of tragic action—but, if a character is no more than our mirror, there's nothing left to know. Great fiction depends on the gap of the unknown—the characters we know best often serve as mere comedy. We know Rosencrantz and Guildenstern, but we laugh at their deaths.

ADAM FITZGERALD

Adam Fitzgerald's silly, gadabout poems manage to be demented and dorky at the same time. If there's a notion that ties together all the foolery in *George Washington*, his second book, it's the oppressive drivel of American life. "Nothing succeeds like excess," said Lord Illingworth in *A Woman of No Importance*; and I'm sure Congress might yet adopt that as our new national motto.

The criticism of excess doesn't demand excess, however—like the quote, it needs parsimony; but Fitzgerald's idea of an argument is just to let her rip:

Pharaonic Tarheel Bobbysoxers
cannot undo solace that comes
alone in accusative plural.
Plywood dentures ungulate
trinal outliers. Oceanic
sensibilities edify and expunge
crisp figments.

The title is "Big Data," so the poem must be an example or just what happens when a tsunami of phenomena has no organizing principle. After sixty lines, either a lawsuit or suicide seems required.

Sometimes there's an idea buried in the rubble. "Leaves of Grass" presents four slices of American life that read like mini-essays cobbled from Wikipedia: "The internet replaced stores owned by men in splotched overalls / that once inspired Norman Rockwell," "*The Private Lives of Elizabeth and Essex* was a 1939 Hollywood / historical romance," "Walt Whitman Shops formerly known as Walt Whitman Mall / is a commercial center located in South Huntington, New York." The younger poet's numbed delivery could have been invented by Walmart for uplifting readings in the break room. He makes the mistake of quoting three lines of Whitman that have more life than the four pages of the poem.

Fitzgerald has a taste for the mangled or recycled touchstone: "sufficient / unto no tomorrow," "Linoleum not to be remembered if outlived," or "I contain immortal lodgings," respectively clumsy, lame, hilarious. His gift for rollicking humor is otherwise rarely in evidence. I thought his early poems showed promise, but not all promises are kept—or, to take a leaf, not all premises are swept, either. The most interesting poem here is the second titled "George Washington," which comments in sly if slightly plodding fashion on the composition of the first. It's a meta-poem, but when the meta-poem is more interesting than the poem, you wonder.

When he can't get the point across about the inner despair of capitalism or the flummery of American culture, Fitzgerald resorts to shouting:

"MT DEW DANK IN THE MOUTH / DEADLY COCKSPANIEL HEDGES / TRENCHCOATS ICE CUBES SUCK." Here sentences and phrases have dissolved into word soup. The trouble with such poems is that the giggling behind the arras turns out to be so dull. When a poet writes lines like "I inject chlorine into my memory-parts with lady satisfaction" or "I short shrift on gummy rafts" or "Slimy stolid parts slither through your airy creases / while your lemon skull ricochets alien brain patter," perhaps it's time to revive the stuffed owl anthology. If there's anything here not in the *Avant-Garde Playbook for 1922*, I can't find it.

Too much of *George Washington* is third-generation Ashbery—Ashbery the Inimitable, because you can't fake a faker (a problem the older Ashbery knows too well).

How does one grow the cojones to celebrate a Fudgsicle?
I'll tell you, and won't begin by mentioning trellises forsooth.
The items on the register are mechanisms inscrutable, yes.
But they sway in the doubled-up air with a sense of lucidity,
A kind of gong affect that chiggers as it steamrolls forth.

This has all the Great Pretender's mannerism and none of his lightness of touch. Fitzgerald isn't the worst Ashbery imitator out there—and he's a lot better than Conrad Aiken trying to do Eliot. Still, I wish this poet would spend more time trying to be himself.

"Gong affect" must be a mistake—I hope it's a mistake—for "gong effect," but there are other lines in this long and wearying book where English seems to go astray. Experimental poetry encourages all sorts of contortions of manner and meaning; but a poet who says, "FDR brandished a Brooks Brothers collared cape and / fedora," doesn't know what "brandished" means. My favorite line comes from the biographical note, "Adam Fitzgerald is the previous author of *The Late Parade*." Who the hell is the current one?

The occasional charm of *The Late Parade*, Fitzgerald's first book, has been lost here in ideas old in the days of Thorstein Veblen. A death is sometimes mentioned; but it has been forcibly removed from the world of these poems, crowded out by all the dreck that takes the place of feeling. "I say a bunch of shit without thinking," the poet says. It sounds like an indictment, but it's the beginning and end of an ars poetica.

JANA PRIKRYL

The After Party, Jana Prikryl's canny, knowing first book, seems stateless at times, like a clutter of blue-ribbon translations. Poetry in which different manners clash is not necessarily a mish-mash. Early Eliot found style in mixed styles, as did early Pound (though much less successfully, since one of his manners was cod-medieval).

The density of intelligence in Prikryl is at war with the slackness of architecture, as if the perceptions had been caught on the fly, the poet a Nabokov with a giant butterfly net. (Was that a butterfly or a mot juste floating by?) Whatever the local delights and privileges, they're diluted by the scattershot lines before or after.

> The dwarf maple caught my attention
> in an ominous way, its purple,
> its deep purple leaves shredded gloves
> that gesture "Don't worry, don't worry,"
> among floating albino basketballs of hydrangea
> among other things the people landscaped
> like fake lashes.

The angular description of the opening, that hesitant stuttering over color and that not quite believable note of reassurance, is wrecked by the albino basketballs.

Prikryl can channel Paul Muldoon at the drop of a hat:

> The city's an amphora, broken-dishy.
> The bits were nicked to model demolition.
> Stacked and drowning, stacked and drowning.
> The qui vive is the salt spray owning
> knowing bunkers defunct since Vichy.

Still, such trivial party-pieces seem beside the point. Her sentences love to balance on tiptoe, the syntax uncoiling like rope; yet their devil-may-care self-indulgence has an inherent modesty, the high spirits never tipping into arrogance or self-regard:

It's a costume drama of uncertain date; be not too dogmatic
in your visualization but do picture us
looking fabulous.

Prikryl's stronger work benefits from focused, even slightly absurd
ideas: a package tour with her thirty-two great-great-great-great-
grandmothers, romance at the funeral of a young politician, a portrait of
the women who distribute fluoride in grade schools. Marianne Moore
had the same donation-box sense of what a poem might contain—
Prikryl is not afraid to tear up the rule book. They both possess a poet's
sine qua non, a way of seeing that peers beneath the skin.

Some poems in this grab-bag book are dull, some weightless as
meringue, some cunningly original. The latter half is wasted on a loose
sequence about a character named Mr. Dialect, who offers little challenge to Berryman's Henry or Zbigniew Herbert's Mr. Cogito. Each
mini-section is an island of sorts—perhaps the theme is exile, perhaps
what it means to be Canadian. (Prikryl's family escaped from Czecho-
slovakia to Canada when she was barely of school age.) The collection of
jigsaw pieces turns into James's loose, baggy monster; but the writing
can be meticulous and thrilling: "Mr. Dialect pauses on a bluff / twice
pink in the spreading lakes, / his suit bespoke / and out of style":

> Compulsive translator, in time he'll slip
> the modesty that's his;
> he too
> reaches for effects.

> And the other one
> who is not upside down
> in the lake, rippling,
> with almost the same intensity

> sends regrets.

You know she's been reading Stevens or Ransom, but not without deliberation or effect.

Prikryl's strength is putting mismatched parts together. She knows to end a poem before she's said everything—she's a specialist in cliffhangers, and even in the dithery pieces her last lines can bring you up short: "I don't have anywhere / to be except this unambiguous shore," "Goodness that shows / every sign of being also / resourceful has always been so / difficult to refuse," "I was susceptible to the consolations / of analogy," "I have a perpetual feeling / a lake ought not to be this size." If too much of this book is insouciant, or fey, or simply annoying, if there's a chilly affectlessness borrowed from Moore and Anne Carson (as if the sentences had been written on Mars), the best poems are intimate, sprightly, and darkly insinuating. This debut seems oddly mature and immature at once. That's not the worst way for such a shifty and striking intelligence to begin.

LARRY LEVIS

Chatterton died at seventeen, Keats at twenty-five, Shelley at twenty-nine. Now a poet may be called young until Social Security kicks in. When he dies in middle age, the Romantic mythos of the poetic life—burning out with incandescent brilliance, major poems still unwritten—makes it difficult to see the poet plain. Larry Levis died of a heart attack in 1996, months before turning fifty. After his death, Philip Levine and David St. John edited a posthumous book of his poems, *Elegy*. St. John has now produced a second volume with poems left out or in one case presumed lost.

The Darkening Trapeze inherits the half-visionary, half-kooky flourishes that in the late sixties and early seventies defined American poetry. In Merwin, Bly, Kinnell, and James Wright, a deeper strain of imagism found literary form; but at this distance its bardic yawp looks closer to Carl Sandburg and Robinson Jeffers than to Whitman. (The "stones and bones" school might well have been called "stoners and boners.") Levis's poems, though they caught the breeze of the zeitgeist, were much toned-down versions, though he suffered from the melancholia of poets who overdose on Vallejo, Lorca, Neruda, and Rimbaud. He lived in a world too numinous with meaning:

Before all the trees became bibles,
The forests & fields were pure,
The river sometimes forgot
That it was only a river,
And the tiger sometimes felt
It stood for more than itself,
More than the zoo all around it,
And the stone wished to be more
Than another stone among stones
In a building no longer there,
In a building made of stones.

The trouble with such a poetic stance is that it doesn't leave much room for anything else—every dead flower, every broken wine-glass, every passing cow must be given a coat of romantic varnish, the thicker the better. Every incident must be honeyed with regret—or, worse, remorse. The subject is the aftermath of a bombing; but we get no closer to terror in the following lines, "In the bomb-magnified quiet, / Their flesh spilled out of their gowns." The only horror lies in the preciousness of artistic detachment. The poem ends with a line indebted to Auden, but Auden wrote about war with chilling moral savagery. With Levis, detachment seems the cocoon in which the poems have wrapped themselves.

Much of this uncollected work feeds on the sorrows of ordinary life, but the ordinary life is given a sugary glaze that makes it unbearable:

Who reads beside the faint hymn
Of seven flies clustering
Over her bowl of overcast
Soup gone cold by now?

Faint hymn of seven flies? Bowl of overcast soup? This is studied without being sad, saccharine where it might have been bitter. Levis's poems are too often drenched in a morbid sentimentality that afflicts and flattens every contour of emotion. Only a reader with AMD (Acute Mawkishness Deficiency) could be moved by one more lyric poem about the fellowship of alcohol, the glory of women, or the wretched despair of even the over-paid and overfed. The poems possess what he calls the "overcast melancholy of a cheap / Utrillo print." They have written their own epitaph.

I prefer the Levis who surprised himself, who could write a disturbing whimsy about Van Gogh's ear or a soft-core erotic fantasy about Wallace Stevens and a manicurist:

> she dusted his nails & blew
> Hot little breaths on each one of them,
> "So you wanna floor show with your manicure."
> The next time she undid a button on her blouse.

Levis could end a poem with a bizarrely cheerful shrug, "Well, / It seemed quite funny to us at the time," or "Chin up? Ready?" or "No? *No* hunh? No." He could bring all the winsomeness to an abrupt halt: "She moves her hips forward until / They touch the sink, withdraws them slowly, pushes them / Close again. *Some enchanted fuckin' evening*, she says." The contempt succeeded where the manner did not. Unhappily, the breast-baring, the romantic guff, the shambling and monotonous talk usually got the better of him. Edward Hopper could have done the illustrations, but one Hopper is company and two is a crowd. With their free-floating lugubriousness, these are the poems young Werther might have written, though it's surprising how rarely you find this tone among the true Romantics.

I knew Levis a little at Iowa, forty years ago. Stocky, a heavy smoker with wide-set eyes, he had a more than passing resemblance to Ernie Kovaks. His sad-sack manner belied a sardonic, dark intelligence—he moved in chiaroscuro with slothlike deliberation. The poems have been made no better by the hyperkinetic blurbs pasted to the book: "In poem after thrilling poem, Levis manifests . . . the pity and the penetration that made him of such consequence," "The work of Larry Levis has steadily gathered a kind of literary cult," "He was our Whitman for the late twentieth century." The editor calls him "one of the truly major American poets of his time." Levis has suffered what is not the worst memorial, to be overrated by his friends.

SHARON OLDS

What scientist wouldn't give his eye teeth for a longitudinal study of Sharon Olds's sex life? Over the past four decades, her books have made a start; but in *Odes* she presents the forensic version, an encyclopedia of the body. After the odes to the clitoris, the penis, the condom, the tampon, to withered cleavage and menstrual blood, to the blow job and the douche bag, and of course to the vagina, there's little left to the imagination.

We live in an age when Whitman's paeans to the body electric would not raise an eyebrow, much less cost him his government job. Olds has long been praised for her unashamed nakedness, her unsparing examination of the body sexual. She has decorated her clean, prosaic line—the kind cats and dogs used to read—with the confetti of metaphor, like sequins on a mourning dress. Here's the clitoris:

> Little eagerness;
> flower-girl basket of soft thorn
> and petal, near the entry of the satin
> column of the inner aisle;
> scout in the wilderness; wild ear
> which perks up; tender dowser, which points;
> imp; shape-shifter; bench-pressing biceps of a
> teeny goddess who is buff,

and so on. And on. *Odes* is as choked with metaphor as a Christmas goose with stuffing; but there's a despairing emptiness to these endless Circean transformations, rarely the exaction or rightness images demand. Then there's the Baby Snooks baby talk—here the "teeny goddess," there the "teentsy hymens," over yonder a "weentsy Minerva." (Note to her publisher: please fire the copy editor who let "miniscule" slip by, twice—or was that Baby Snooks, too?)

Too many of these odes remind me of eighth-grade health class, the overworked bespectacled teacher slamming her pointer into the blackboard, raising a cloud of chalk dust as she explains "vestibular bulb" and "alveolar valve," "Malpighi's layer" and "fimbrial fringe." All appear in poems here, yet despite Olds's suburban smugness and endless shopping lists of metaphor, the dark mysteries of sex are missing, along with any visceral sense of longing, compassion, compulsion, or lust. Some of her biology is bizarre or preadolescent, indeed, lost in the medieval world of the homunculus—does she really believe her eggs had "teentsy hymens" in them?

The relentlessness of these poems could have been devastating or ennobling—instead, they're just exhausting. For all their overeager metaphors and tabloid sensibility, with a how-to guide for good sex added, the poems seem to have been thrown together by a junior accountant. Then come the fantasies:

> Once, in a dream, I wandered in one,
> my oldest home, my hobo-sack home,
> I underwater-breaststroked through
> the dessert of it, like the inside
> of a tongue, and light came through into the pink
> male sewing reticule.

Olds is dreaming of her father's balls. I like the primness of "male sewing reticule," but isn't her vision a bit too close to Raquel Welch floating through the arteries in *Fantastic Voyage*?

The poet doesn't flinch from the effects of age; and many of these odes are odes to loss, especially loss of beauty: in addition to her withered cleavage ("the snakes, / the ripples, the nest of nestlings's necks!"), she writes to her wattles, her stretch marks, her hip replacement, and her cellulite. Olds is now seventy-four, but the geriatric poems are surprisingly girlish, and more than a little vengeful. How else explain, when she recalls her mother's douche bag, "I'd been some kind of catsup Halloween / costume in her, almost before I was / bipedal"?

Olds has always been a confessional poet, specializing in confession lite. She's not afraid of thoughts that might embarrass others, not afraid to mention the unmentionables; but Lowell revealed something crippled in the least gesture of expression, and Plath's every metaphor was a quiet act of psychosis. Olds's reports on her safari-park tour through the body have a monotonous sameness—knowledge of the mechanics is not the same as knowledge of self. Some poets are all surface, and some have depths where you never hit bottom. Olds is a poet of the shallows.

She has been doing this sort of thing a long time. The writing is as always professional, slightly aloof, antiseptic; but where it goes wrong it's hilarious. Olds is addicted to ridiculous euphemism: blood becomes the "bright arterial / ingredient," the vagina variously the "nether pate," the "nether face," the "between-my-legs," and "my / *there*." (How oddly prudish these seem.) Her metaphors at their worst are revved a little high—"each nipple . . . like a / rose-red eraser come alive and starvacious," "blobulettes / of fat," "they creatored my spirit," "he did not uncare for / his eyes in me," and (of her cleavage) "now my own declivity is / arroyo-ing." Then there's the romantic gush hurled at the poor reader. After a good douche:

> Lo!, you are
> a night clearing, in which a fountain
> of Aphrodite leaps up, and cascades
> down, making her notes, her brine
> sea chanty, her sparkling douche-bag song.

These odes would have benefited from an index, with entries like "*blow job*, Deep Throat technique for, 56"; and "*mother*, pubic hair of, 62." Very little of the outside world seeps in, except when the poet mentions ash trees, the baseball bats made from them—and then, in a dumbfounding non sequitur, the "ashes" of the dead at Nagasaki and Hiroshima. The unfathomed neediness of these poems, their hunger never assuaged, makes it easy to mistake self-obsession for bravery, desperation for risk. "I love to be a little / disgusting," Olds declares, and it's hard not to agree.

GEORGE HERBERT

The market for devotional poets may be at an all-time low. Apart from Hopkins, in the past century or more the flares of Christianity have produced little devotional verse beyond Eliot's devious religious poems and Berryman's "Eleven Addresses," written during his late access to faith.

Devotion is not a mode harmonious with poetic skepticism—in the quarrel with the nature and conscription of the profane, there seems no room for theology.

George Herbert was reluctant to choose the religious vocation. At Cambridge, he was known as a wit with an unusually keen intellect. Izaac Walton, in his life of the poet, says that the Bishop of Winchester, the formidable Lancelot Andrewes, debated predestination with Herbert, receiving "some safe and useful aphorisms in a long letter written in Greek . . . so remarkable for the language and reason of it that after reading it, the Bishop put it into his bosom and did often show it to many scholars . . . but did always return it back to the place where he first lodged it and continued it so near his heart till the last day of his life." This was no mean compliment—Andrewes was one of the most brilliant men of the day.

Seemingly destined for great things, Herbert sought preferment at the court of James I. No doubt carbonated humor came at a premium there— and the poet loved fine clothes. He did not take holy orders until he was thirty-one. (Donne, whose career bears some relation, was not ordained until his early forties.) Herbert in time became rector of a small parish church at Lower Bemerton, near Salisbury. Gathering his poems shortly before his death (tuberculosis, thirty-nine), he called them a "picture of the many spiritual conflicts that have passed betwixt God and my soul, before I could submit mine to the will of Jesus." His sole volume of poetry, *The Temple*, was published posthumously.

100 Poems is part of a series presenting poets too little read, at least beyond the scattered works, like Herbert's two shaped poems, "Easter Wings" and "The Altar," that have taken root in anthologies. He does not have the density, the erotic darkness, the impacted wordplay of Donne. Herbert worked a thinner vein, but with exquisite drollery and a delicacy that give domestic character to the privacies of seventeenth-century faith.

Herbert could rise to Donne's manner when he wished:

Engine against th' Almightie, sinners towre,
        Reversed thunder, Christ-side-piercing spear,
        The six-daies world transposing in an houre,

A kinde of tune, which all things heare and fear.

Usually, however, he preferred to borrow images from the rural land-scape or the flotsam and jetsam of the household: "We are the trees, whom shaking fastens more, / While blustring windes destroy the wan-ton bowres"; "My thoughts are all a case of knives"; "Parrats may thank us, if they are not mute"; "we can go die as sleep . . . / Making our pil-lows either down, or dust." In *The Country Parson*, his handbook for rural clergy, he advised taking spiritual lessons from everyday objects: "things of ordinary use are not only to serve in the way of drudgery, but to . . . serve for lights even of Heavenly Truths."

Though Herbert was a more restricted poet than Donne, he possessed greater sweetness of character. He was deeply conscientious as a rector, where his radiant humor must have been welcome. The conflicts of faith recorded in the poems may have come before ordination, as he claimed; but there's no reason to think his faith was always easy. The poems are sometimes playful, and for that we sacrifice the violent dramatics and superb arrogance of Donne. Herbert's snapshots of private life are like Rembrandt's little sketchbooks of the passing scene.

> The nimble Diver with his side
> Cuts through the working waves, that he may fetch
> His dearely-earned pearl, which God did hide
> On purpose from the ventrous wretch;
> That he might save his life, and also hers,
> Who with excessive pride
> Her own destruction and his danger wears.

Pearls then were still drawn from British waters.

The editor of this edition, Helen Wilcox, has unforgivably chosen to produce Herbert's poems in old spelling and without notes. Spelling and meaning have changed enough in four centuries to make his poems a thicket of barbed wire. The casual reader is unlikely to know that "Ieat" is "jet"; "sent," "scent"; "owes," "owns"; "cares cops," "care's copse." Her-bert's vocabulary is scarcely less obscure: "relishes" means "musical embellishments"; "curling," "hairdressing"; "outlandish," "foreign"; and "pull'st the rug," "pulls the blanket over his head." Old spelling is admirably stringent and pure but as much practical help in reading as a blindfold. (If you're going to be pure, bring back the long *s*.) No one would think of presenting a popular edition of Shakespeare this way.

Herbert loved complex stanzas, varying line lengths, poems that rang virtuoso changes on form and expectation—some of his forms have never found a name. His sensibility was that of a man who likes to juggle chainsaws while doing crossword puzzles—the bravura display was almost his only vanity (there were those clothes at court), but his hard honesty makes human a style often crotchety and fidgety. The poet, all too aware of the brevity of life, seems grateful to be alive, grateful and good humored. "Let a bleak palenesse chalk the doore," he wrote, "So all within be livelier then before."

Verse Chronicle: Hither and Yon

JOHN ASHBERY

John Ashbery turns ninety this year, an astonishing thing in itself; and the ability of old Puck to write poems as good as those he wrote half a century ago is either testimony to a well-oiled imagination or a revelation that all along he's been writing poems the way a butcher stuffs sausages. The sausages aren't half bad—but I suspect that, like the butcher, the poet doesn't give a hoot what critics think. Or the pigs, for that matter. A typical mid- or late- or later-than-late-Ashbery poem runs like this:

> It wasn't always this way.
> Somewhere, ants were taking control
> of earth's blistered pulse.
> Peanuts were jettisoned from the nacelle
> of the montgolfière, all moyenâgeux and thrifty
> as it came to be about. I ask only for staples
> for my staple gun.

How peanuts dumped from a hot-air balloon became medieval is anybody's guess. Those who expect logic or intimacy or the whisper of a point will be confounded by such poems, even with garlic and pepper added.

Commotion of the Birds is Ashbery's umpteenth book since *Self-Portrait in a Convex Mirror* (1975), still his finest work. His early books (and the occasional outlier later, like *Flow Chart* [1991]) were rip-roaringly avant-garde, but soon he nestled into a cozy absurdist style like a pair of bunny-rabbit slippers.

It's hard to dislike a poet who starts a poem,

> We're moving right along through the seventeenth century.
> The latter part is fine, much more modern
> than the earlier part. Now we have Restoration Comedy.
> Webster and Shakespeare and Corneille were fine
> for their time but not modern enough,
> though an improvement over the sixteenth century
> of Henry VIII, Lassus and Petrus Christus, who, paradoxically,
> seem more modern than their immediate successors,
> Tyndale, Moroni, and Luca Marenzio among them.

Perhaps this is a parody of a witless art-historian—or a sneaky way of situating Ashbery's work in a poetic tradition now moribund for many readers. For Webster and Shakespeare and Corneille, read Pound and Eliot and Stevens. Or is it a meditation on the rise of the baroque, a style that might with a little squinching inform Ashbery's own? There are no curlicues without a lot of waste, both in the carving and in the looking. Besides, the double-tongued Ashbery always has one tongue in cheek and one sticking straight out at you. (His chronology is out of whack, though—Henry VIII and Tyndale were contemporaries; Orlande de Lassus was born a decade after Giambattista Moroni and outlived him; and Petrus Christus painted in the fifteenth century, not the century after.)

You can no more say what an Ashbery poem is about than you can say what a laughing hyena is about. The limits of sense, the tomfoolery that isn't quite foolery, the impending doom that never pends—all the poems are about poetry, more or less. They're like watching a man on a distant breakwater. From his panicky gestures and his leaps and caracoles you know something is terribly wrong, unless he's just rehearsing the fencing scene in *Hamlet*. The tension between the coherence of the parts and the sheer nonsense of the whole has informed Ashbery's career, which puts him in a long line of American charlatans and Ponzi schemers. Imagine a Bizarro World where Ashbery made perfect sense, and Billy Collins and Mary Oliver—the Southeys of our day—were incomprehensible.

I'm not sure I'd want to live in that world, but a vacation there would be a relief.

For those who like Ashbery's silliness—delivered with the aw-shucks, gee-willikers grin of a Gomer Pyle flâneur—there are poems enough here. The best have a tale sputtering beneath the surface of comprehension, never to be spoken. Many poems seem a bit more discombobulated than usual, as if the dark matter that once provided invisible glue had dried up. There are too many passages like

> (You always need to get somewhere,
> civil engine,
> some more dumb bunny cheesecake.)
> Thanks for having me
> slipshod and enjoy
> his undistinguished underwear.

Is "dumb bunny cheesecake" a loose reference to *Playboy* centerfolds (those would be Playmates, then, not Playboy bunnies) or just, well, dumb bunny cheesecake? Then again,

> Rainbow pencils retracted.
> Next, a group of officials withdrew support
> of accident forgiveness, and I'm like
> Comrade Fuzzy, my gaydar's
> gone berserk the way it messes.

If Ashbery's elusiveness, his endless deferral of meaning, is one of the reader's guilty pleasures, the hope that at the end of the next sentence, or the next, all will be explained is here often crushed at the outset.

Poems don't owe us a thing—they don't exist to gratify our idea of what a poem is or should be. Yet in the two thousand pages of poetry Ashbery has published since the title poem of *Self-Portrait*, I can scarcely recall a single poem. That magnificent one-off, as provoking and indelible now as then, was obviously a mistake he decided never to repeat. In his reckless embrace of the folly of life, his love of foreign tongues, his harvest of the slang of the hour ("gaydar," "it went viral," "enuf"), the

Old Master of delayed gratification has inherited the spirit of Whitman. You can love Ashbery and find him preposterous. You can hate him and wish he'd never stop.

ALICE OSWALD

Alice Oswald's most recent book, *Memorial*, concocted obituaries for the obscure warriors who died in the *Iliad*. Her narrow talent burns like a hot needle—it's hard to predict what this quirky poet will do. The book that brought her attention, *Dart* (2002), followed the course of an English river through the voices of those who lived or worked on its banks. *Falling Awake*, her new book, is broken into halves, first a group of poems in discomfiting conversation with the natural world, then a long poem on the coming of dawn.

Oswald has the stunning off-kilter eye possessed by Moore, and Bishop, and Plath:

> This is the day the flies fall awake mid-sentence
> and lie stunned on the window-sill shaking with speeches
> only it isn't speech it is trembling sections of puzzlement which
> break off suddenly as if the questioner had been shot

Casting the flies as political hacks should not go unnoticed—but perhaps she means that any schmuck who gives speeches bears passing resemblance to those Valkyries of the windowsill. Her work displays the long inheritance of nature-obsessed Romantics like Clare and Shelley, and the longer inheritance of the Greeks. Oswald and Anne Carson both trained as classicists.

The Romantic strain makes her sound at times like Ted Hughes, though in acts of description she teases out a nature gorgeous rather than brutish:

> Old scrap-iron foxgloves
> rusty rods of the broken woods
>
> what a faded knocked-out stiffness
> as if you'd sprung from the horse-hair

of a whole Victorian sofa buried in the mud down there

or at any rate something dropped from a great height

The natural world is instinct with life, but the poet—like Persephone—finds beneath it the house of the dead: a rotting swan imagines herself "climbing out of her own cockpit"; the badger "shuffling away alive // hard at work / with the living shovel of himself" cannot know that the dead hear him overhead.

Little raptures of sentiment often trail such meticulous acts of witness; yet it's easy to forget the soft tears when along the way Oswald makes nature so raw and fresh: the lark with a "needle / pulled through its throat," the dawn that can "fasten the known to the unknown / with a liquid cuff-link," a bat that "swooped in like a pair of leather gloves," and a "flower / turning its head to the side like a bored emperor." Oswald does more for animals in clothes than anyone since Grandville—when she notices a "fox in her fox-fur," it's hard not to picture Ava Gardner or Joan Crawford.

At home with plants and animals, as Eden was before God snatched up the gobbet of clay, Oswald proves ill at ease in the world beyond nature. "Village" is an updated *Spoon River Anthology* spoken by the living, but gossip about fellow town-folk ("somebody on her knees again not what she was / somebody screaming again last night being strangled or something") has none of the sympathies evident elsewhere. Oswald's design may be intentionally grim and unforgiving, but something goes dead when she leaves the comforting society of field and wood. Whatever poetic intelligence drives the poems vanishes when she confronts men and women.

"Tithonus," the long poem that closes the book, is divided from the others by a page black on both sides, a leaf of night between the days. Eos, the dawn, asked Zeus to make her lover Tithonus immortal. She was just as ditzy as you imagine, since she forgot to ask for eternal youth—as usual, when a mortal is granted a favor, the god screws him completely. Tithonus grew older and older, but he could not die. None of that makes its way into the poem, a moment-by-moment account—or "performance," as the poet has it—of the coming of dawn. Each page has been dressed with a vertical scale, down which the verse has been spaced according to some obscure system of pauses.

Mostly the poem confines itself to half-thoughts and observations as night hardens into day. (Two facing pages, blank except for the scale, end with a simple "Etc.") In the stirrings and rustlings that accompany the shift to the crepuscular, the animal world steals from the human. Whether it's the wood doves who "start up litigations in the trees" or a lark that "in a prayer-draught / shakes the air," Oswald loves this mingling of realms. Though the "performance" is rather stillborn, her devilish turns of phrase make an outdoor concerto of bird and bug noise. In her introductory note, the poet explains that the poem starts "when the sun is six degrees below the horizon, and stops 46 minutes later, at sunrise." When she reads the piece, it takes exactly that long. It could be read in jig time—if you're offered a ticket, you might consider watching paint dry instead.

We're in no danger of returning to the fifties, when so many poems dragged in Achilles or Odysseus, Orpheus or Narcissus, or some other refugee from *Bulfinch's Mythology*. Nevertheless, it's not the worst thing to be reminded of the Greek antiquity to which we owe so much, the lost world that has never quite vanished. It rises in ghostly fashion in our museums, our architecture, in the metaphors of psychology, as it has risen in a weary string of Hollywood blockbusters.

VERA PAVLOVA

Translation is a bugger. A competent line-by-line rendering of the *Iliad* will give the reader without ancient Greek the gist of the original. The losses of meaning may not be minor; but the losses of music, tone, and force (form is always force) will be almost crippling—translation can do only so much, and that so much usually gives no more than the ghostly outline of the original. Pushkin is famously untranslatable. Joseph Brodsky in English, even in poems he translated himself, sounds like a man with a wooden ear or two. (I make an exception for the very few poems translated by Hecht, and Heaney, and Walcott, none of whom knew Russian.)

Vera Pavlova is a Russian poet, librettist, and music scholar now living in Toronto. She writes short poems, really no more than squibs— trivial observations, snippets of faux wisdom, winsome notes about clouds and children. *Album for the Young (and Old)*, her second book in English, was translated by her late husband, Steven Seymour; at times an air of melancholy hangs over the poems, suggesting a foreknowledge that poetry could not assuage.

Pavlova manages to capture the odd unlikelihood and quiet horror of children's play:

> Guess what me, Inna, Katia, and Rita
> were doing yesterday at the playground!
> We were playing the Crucifixion. I was
> Jesus the Saver. They called me
> all kinds of names, like "dumbhead," "idiot,"
> whipped me with nettles about my legs,
> beat me manually and with a stick, then
> tied me to the cross with a skipping rope.

The innocence of the opening, the sublime mishearing of "Jesus the Saver" (I wonder what the phrase was in Russian), the attempt to reproduce the Passion with a child's limited resources (nettles for scourges, skipping rope for nails)—these reveal the darkness beneath childhood. That the children are ignorant of the implications of their play contributes to the sense of unease.

At times Pavlova sidles toward the Russian past that except in whispers long went unmentioned. With defensive wryness, a grandmother keeps alive memory of the terrible days after the Revolution. Her favorite toy was a rag doll: "I called her Nell. / Eyes with lashes. Pleated hair. A skirt with frills. / In nineteen twenty-one we ate her. She was / stuffed with bran. A whole cupful of bran." Elsewhere:

> *"It was a famine, for months and months we had*
> *no bread at all, I have no idea what we lived on,*
> *but for some strange reason my tiny legs were plump.*
> *'Mommy, let's cut them off, cook them, and eat them.'"*

"She laughs joyously as she tells it," the poet remarks. That's the nervous laugh of a survivor.

Unfortunately, few poems in this long book of short poems possess such darkened passions. Pavlova's sugar-coated wittering infects even subjects more adult.

All summer winds come from the sea,
all winter snows come from mountain caps.
If you expand your soul to the limit,
you will discover: space has no bounds.

Apart from the meteorological defects, this cutesy twaddle might have been dropped by some dime-store guru. Or consider: "Sulking is ugly! Instead / why don't you learn / to say THANK YOU / in every tongue that exists." Or: "Honest, I do not miss my childhood, cross my heart. / I wonder if my childhood misses me, if only a bit." Or: "lawn please forgive me / only one leaf of your grass / will be a bookmark." Readers with high cholesterol or high blood-pressure should not go near this book.

Patches of unconvincing translation turn up, like "What fun it is to be feasting, / stooped up in the dark!" *Stooped up*? ("Curled up" or "crouched" would probably come closer to the mark.) In a poem about chess, the "Four-knight debut" should surely be the "Four Knights opening." (I suspect the word mistranslated is *debyut*.) There are many lines no doubt better in Russian—among them, "the unhatched breasts painfully itched." The problems, however, run deeper than translation. Had Little Miss Muffet grown up to write poems, they could not have been more tooth-grindingly precious.

DANIEL NADLER

In these days of vanishing attention spans, the merciless distractions of media, and flash fiction, why not flash poetry? There's a long tradition of short poems in other languages; and some of the greatest modern English poems are miniatures, so well known their authors don't need to be named: "I never lost as much but twice," "Down by the Salley Gardens," "In a Station of the Metro," "Epitaph on an Army of Mercenaries," "Fire and Ice," "The Red Wheelbarrow," and of course "Poetry" in its final and most memorable version.

Short poems often come in gouts, a form of repetition compulsion. When Lowell started scribbling a handful of sonnets a day, poetry became an obsessive act of elation. Daniel Nadler's first book, *Lacunae: 100 Imagined Ancient Love Poems*, is a stampede of shorts, the great majority half a dozen lines or fewer. Love poems, those invitations to suffering, often seem in translation a gallery of clichés (the poems in Dante's *La Vita Nuova*, for instance, come badly into English). Whether Nadler's subtitle is meant to suggest that the poems are fictive strays from the *Greek Anthology* or phony Sapphic fragments from the waste dumps of Oxyrhynchus, they look about as ancient as a Grecian urn that spent yesterday on the shelves at Costco.

Nadler has something of a talent for similes, as well as a taste for soft-focus romance and the American folk wisdom varnished onto wooden plaques and hung in dry-cleaning shops. Much of the book might be called a paean to the simile, the little brother of metaphor rarely given the respect its big brother commands. I know poets who loathe similes, though Homer did pretty well by them, and a lot of poets since have shown how subtly they can be employed. Even good figures, after all, may come to bad ends:

> As you sleep
> the early sky is colored
> in fish scales, and you open your eyes
> like a street
> already lined with fruit.

The striking metaphor for a mackerel sky is weakened by the extravagant nonsense that follows. It's not that Nadler thinks in platitudes, not exactly—it's that he's a true believer in the soppiest kind of puppy love: "You are as happy as a waterwheel / when the earth is flooding," "I waited for you like vines around a house that was never built," "My lips are shy, / like a candle that will not flicker." These would be no better had they been inked onto papyrus two millennia back. Too many sentences drag a simile behind them like an anchor, which is unhappy if you're a trireme, disastrous if you're Leander. It's hard to imagine these phrases exciting a lover to passion; but you should wait for the

Hollywood version, preferably with Angelina Jolie in peplos and Brad Pitt in chiton.

There are occasions when Nadler's poems possess the ghost of an idea, but he has no ear for his absurdities: "Beside you I sleep with difficulty— / a cherry rolling along the stem of its thought" (how a cherry rolls along a stem is beyond me). Or: "Your dark breasts glow, / the pan crackles"—this might have been like Pound's Chinese had the juxtaposition (as if the breasts were just waiting to be grilled) not been eyerollingly silly. Whenever Nadler starts the heavy breathing, the poems go all to hell: "Need I open a sky / to find the last soft shame / in your nakedness?", "Between kisses the air is quiet, / like trees after a snowfall. Talking softly, after, / a branch is shaken loose."

It's an axiom that the would-be profound is often ridiculous:

> Sister, the terror
> at this immense nudity of unknowing
> will in time subside
> like a sea burying a billion colored corals with its name.

This immense nudity of unknowing? That the poet is referring to a baby is no excuse.

> Islands are pronounced by the ocean without bubbles.
> Sometimes the ocean chokes on an island
> as it tries to take it back;
> these are left alone.

Perhaps such lines pass for wisdom in Silicon Valley or its rivals (Nadler is CEO of the Cambridge startup Kensho, which specializes in data analytics), but they look like rejects from the Hallmark Cards R&D lab out in Kansas. A poet who traffics in fake *sententiae* not surprisingly adores lugubrious guff like "Leave me the moon / to reflect certainty / the way a child's face reflects its mother" and "I crystallized my eyes with the liquor of the seed I planted in my mouth. / I cut my destiny in two and kept the heavier one." The jacket copy calls the book an "exercise in poetics of vital import."

JORIE GRAHAM

Jorie Graham's new book, *Fast*, is a very slow read—it hurts to make the joke. Ages ago, in *Erosion* (1983) and *The End of Beauty* (1987), her darkly allusive poems, embedded in the long history of Western culture, showed a deep and insinuating eye for nature. Their dramatic juxtapositions fed on lush imagery. Not until *Materialism* (1993) did the poetry begin to suffer from grandiosity—long passages of Plato, Wittgenstein, Brecht, and Jonathan Edwards were posted like manifestos between the poems. As her subjects became the Great Issues of the Day, the style degraded into a twitchy, obsessive record of thought, not a stream but a stuttering of consciousness, like Joyce without brains:

> Ode to Prism. Aria. Untitled. Wait. I wait. Have you found me yet.
>   Here at my screen, can you make me
> out? Make me out. All other exits have been sealed. See me or we
>   will both vanish.
> We need emblematic subjectivities. Need targeted acquiescence.
>   Time zones. This is
> the order of the day. To be visited secretly. To be circled and
>   canceled. I cover my
> face.

Emblematic subjectivities? Targeted acquiescence? At times Graham writes like a PhD in Theory Theory. A few lines cannot convey the dreariness of the whole, every page like a midnight talk-show fading in and out on a car radio. Whatever subject she turns to, whether the ecological collapse of the oceans or the definition of the human, the result is frenzied and mind-numbing.

Graham has become queen of run-on thought, her poems now no more than phrases strung along the line, with punctuation for clothespins. Her books continue to be visited by outbreaks of bizarre punctuation, and *Fast* will be no disappointment to virologists—the new poems are frequently infested by little arrows (Times New Roman, the colophon helpfully informs us) no doubt meant to speed the reader's eye from phrase to phrase.

another mind, prefigured by drones → algorithms → image
vectors → distributive consciousness → humanoid robotics → what is
   required now →
is → a demarcation → what is *artificial* → technological end-times
   now only
just beginning → along the watchtowers → pleasures of nihilism,
   speechlessness,
incredulity →

The lines seem to have stumbled into a museum devoted to the martyrdom of St. Sebastian. Nothing ties the tsunami of phrases together except the big-box themes. Graham is good at drift-netting the divagations of thought (the semblance is at best counterfeit), but the writing cannot escape the misery of detours within detours. At one point she gives her credit-card number and expiration date. The reader may be tempted to use them.

Every stratagem to hold the attention—freakish punctuation, uneven leading, juddering line-breaks, shifting margins—only distracts the reader further from what she has to say. Poems that resort to the dialect of "a post industrial cock or a derivative / cunt," "Chemsex," and "death in hyper-drive" need all the help they can get. The language is so desiccated, so lacking in rendering, so removed from the pleasure of words that an attempted bit of wordplay is almost too embarrassing to quote: "But what if I only want to subtract. It's too abstract. I have no contract. Cannot enact impact / interact. Look: the mirrored eye of the fly, so matter of fact."

Graham has come to treat crumbs of basic science with a fangirl's awe:

Teasing out the possible linkages I—no you—who noticed—if the
   world—no—
the world if—take plankton—I feel I cannot love anymore—take
   plankton—that
love is reserved for an other kind of existence—take plankton—that
   such an
existence is a form of porn now—no—what am I saying—take
   plankton—it
is the most important plant on earth—think love—composes at least
   half
the biosphere's entire primary production—

The private here seems ill at ease with the public. These new poems possess the empty urgency and vacant mutterings of a stranger's deranged cell-phone conversation. Graham's world is always in crisis, but poetry remains a terrible medium for ideas. (Hers offer nothing not already plastered on op-ed pages.) The exceptions are poems on her aging mother and dying father, as well as on her own bout with cancer. The airless and harrowing style has unfortunately removed every dreg of emotion—and the poems are never warmed by the whisper of mortality at the edges:

> you earthling—awaiting your biochip—
> they are taking tranches of the body which is one—which has been
>   one all of my life—
> can you hear me, he says, squeeze this if problems arise he says, ok?
>   ready? *if if if if*
> if yes if yes—here's this to worship—hi hi hi hi—hi hi high high—

That's inside an MRI scanner, with sound effects.

As Graham's style collapsed, she started writing books devoted to the big picture, with titles like *The Errancy, Swarm, Never,* and *Overlord,* which could have been straight-to-video horror films. When you've won the Pulitzer, the MacArthur, and a raft of other prizes, you may imagine that whatever you write is flawed only by its brilliance. I admire the poet's resolve and even her desperation, but the endless blithering and the dense pages of scat-writing confirm the other signs. One of the major talents of the eighties has become an old bore.

ANNE CARSON

Anne Carson's eerie, sometimes creepy poems confound expectation—they may confound others things as well, like the reader. Her latest project, *Float,* consists of twenty-two chapbooks jammed into a clear plastic case, meant to be read in no particular order. It's an idea, like many of Carson's, at once compelling and daft. The obvious question, "Why shouldn't the reader take control of his reading?" may be answered, "Who the devil cares?" If subjected to enhanced interrogation (that place where critical theory and the CIA meet), Carson would probably declare the reader, not the author, the final arbiter of order. She may eventually hand out bags of shredded paper, a single word on each scrap of confetti, the reader to organize them as he likes.

Over the past two decades, Carson has become one of the most inspired and infuriating of poets. The idiosyncratic designs of her work—the odd-ball premises, the even odder presentations—have produced one of the most important millennial poems, *Nox*, as well as a hurrah's nest of dil-ettantish fiddle-faddle. If the reader feels that critical essays have no place in a book of poems, Carson has found the place here. (Think of the even more radical strategy of Lowell inserting the memoir "91 Revere Street" into *Life Studies*.) Some of these chapbooks are poems, some are lectures, some are—well, I'm not sure what to call them: Carsonograms, perhaps.

Carson loves to mess with the reader's expectations. The poetry is as ever elliptical, irritating, uncanny, and frequently as mechanical as one of Yves Tanguy's contraptions. There's a goofy list-poem called "Eras of Yves Klein" ("The Era of One-Minute Fire Paintings," "The Era of Being Flattered by Camus") and another on the Cycladic people ("To the Cycladic people is ascribed the invention of the handbag," "The Cycladic people were very fond of Proust"). There's also a series of increasingly deranged translations of a short lyric by Ibykos, the sixth-century BC Greek—the first is more or less literal, but those following are limited to the vocabulary of (I'm not kidding) Donne's "Woman's Constancy," or Brecht's FBI file, or the instruction manual for a microwave: "bubbling, / spattering, / accompanied by you rubbing your hands together, / without venting the plastic wrap." One uses just the "stops and signs from the London Underground":

Nay rather, like the seven sisters
gardening in the British Museum,
accompanied by penalties,
tooting,
turnpiked,
hackneyed,
Kentish,
cockfostered,
I am advised to expect delays all the way to the loo.

The translations are hilarious, but you wonder if Ibykos might not be justified in rising up and strangling Carson in her sleep. She treats poems like an Erector Set—sometimes she makes something you'd never have thought possible, sometimes she leaves a jumble of gears and girders on the floor.

The most interesting piece in this gallimaufry of chapbooks is the essay from which those translations come, "Variations on the Right to Remain Silent" (a typically sly Carson joke), a knowing discussion of the silence of absence (as in Sappho's fragments) and the silence of the untranslatable (Homer's moly or the Bible's apple). She might have added the accidental silence of the hapax legomenon, or the silence of the familiar word used in an unrecorded way, or the complete muteness of a language like Linear A. Those are all problems of translation. Carson's arguments are more teasing than convincing. (Who else would write an essay on Homer, Godard, and Bardot?) She says of moly and other words only gods know,

> Linguists like to see in these names traces of some older layer of Indo-European preserved in Homer's Greek. However that may be, when he invokes the language of gods Homer usually tells you the earthly translation also. Here he does not. He wants this word to fall silent. . . .
> What does this word hide?

Moly, Carson suggests, might conceal the gods' secret knowledge of immortality. This makes a great deal of Homer's failure to provide a translation, though that failure is an old scholarly crux—it's possible that he didn't need to, that everyone in Homer's day knew what moly was, even if the herbal knowledge was later lost. (The plant is thought by many scholars to have been the snowdrop.) What the gods alone possess, she fails to say, is matched by what humans alone possess—they live knowing death awaits them.

This poet is always worth arguing with—she states in the same essay that the French word "cliché" was "assumed into English unchanged, partly because using French words makes English-speakers feel more intelligent." The word strolled into English as a technical word in printing, however, not because English speakers were ga-ga for French but because there was no English word available. ("Stereotype" was also printer's French.) When she claims in one poem that the Phoenicians, after inventing the alphabet, wrote on the "back / of / envelopes," you know she's kidding—unless she means the hollow clay envelopes (*bullae*), precursors of the written tablet, that held tokens used to keep track of a merchant's cargo. When she remarks about the sonnet, however, that "your eye enjoys it in a ratio of eight to five," you wonder about her math skills. Despite their weirdness, her sonnets mostly employ the normal Petrarchan octet and sestet.

Carson's poems are designed rather than driven—indeed, they're cold as a row of marble columns. That they don't seem like poetry is their claim on the poetic. She herself has an abstract relation to the world—it's no surprise that she likes Iceland. Despite her sometimes wearisome games, emotion still struggles forth, the more powerful for having been resisted. Carson's a slant poet. Emily Dickinson was another.

Pound's China / Pound's Cathay

Half a century ago, I was given a private tour of the Beinecke Library in New Haven. As we walked between two ranges of books, the librarian remarked that after reading *Barnaby Rudge* Edgar Allan Poe exclaimed, "I can write a better raven than Dickens!" Pausing, the guide turned and said, "Here is the original raven." There on a shelf stood Grip, Dickens's own pet, stuffed and preserved in a wooden case, staring out with a glassy black eye.

Nothing was said about the pile of seventeen steamer trunks, each bound in twine with sealed knots, lying between two basement elevators. These mysterious, unlabeled trunks were surrounded by the fog of forbidden knowledge that gathers about the surviving blocks of Plato's Academy and the ruins of the ruins of Palmyra. They contained Ezra Pound's papers, awaiting the end of a lawsuit over ownership.

Among the books and manuscripts in those trunks lay notebooks kept by a Massachusetts art historian who, at the end of the nineteenth century, had recorded his sessions with two scholars of classical Chinese poetry. Ernest Fenollosa had graduated from Harvard and at twenty-five begun teaching at the University of Tokyo. Before he was forty, he'd become curator of Asian art at the Boston Museum of Fine Arts. Following a divorce and a lightning remarriage to his assistant, herself a divorcée, he lost his position—Boston society disapproved. It's the stuff of *The Age of Innocence*. The Fenollosas moved to Japan.

Patience is a virtue, but for a writer impatience often a necessity. Ezra Pound's ambition to reform English verse began crudely and absurdly in poems of some late-to-the-party jongleur who hadn't read much past

Chaucer. That medieval jingling and clanking persisted a long while ("What thou loveth well remains, / the rest is dross"), but it became more an affection than an affectation of style. In his early years, in Italy and then London, he wrote poems in gouts and published books rapid-fire: *A Lume Spento* (1908), *A Quinzaine for This Yule* (1908), *Personae* (1909), *Exultations* (1909), *Canzoni* (1911), *The Sonnets and Ballate of Guido Cavalcanti* (1912), *Ripostes* (1912), and *Des Imagistes* (1914, editor), all before *Cathay* (1915). A man on the make, he was making his way—Pound learned on the fly, as brilliant poets often do. When he collected his early verse in *Personae* (1926), a year after turning forty, he dropped over a hundred scraps of juvenilia, if juvenilia include the verse of early middle age. He'd have needed to drop many more to purge his beginnings of all the pretensions of style that had made him a goad, and a joke, to critics.

The notebooks of Chinese glosses and paraphrases lying among Fenollosa's manuscripts helped change English poetry. Without them, Pound might not have pursued the new style that made free verse, rather than some idiot grandchild of Martin Farquhar Tupper and Walt Whitman, a change of sensibility that used modern language in a modern world. Imagism, the movement he founded on the hop, was in flight by the time he published "A Few Don'ts by an Imagiste" in the March 1913 issue of *Poetry*. Whether Imagism drew him to the Chinese poetry or the poetry deeper into Imagism is unclear, but Imagism was embodied in *Cathay*. Pound discovered how to put the shimmer of the real into modernist verse, and other poets took note.

A writer's life has moments of pure good fortune, and good usually means undeserved. Pound already had a leaning toward the Far East, having begun to write haiku, probably the spring after his arrival in London in 1908, after he'd joined a breakaway group from the Poets' Club. *Japonisme* was not quite dead. He first drafted "In a Station of the Metro," one of the first glimmers of modernist poetry, soon after visiting Paris in 1911. Its relation to classic haiku is as striking as it is obvious, though he measured the lines to a form quite different. In the fall of 1913, Pound had placed thirty "Chinese" poems in *Poetry*—really short prose sketches, apart from two set as poems—by his friend Allen Upward. Pound wrote his wife, Dorothy, "The chinese things . . . are worth the price of admission":

On the way I saw the parrots of dusty crimson feathers wrangling over a piece of flesh, but on account of the perfume of thy scented billet I was unable to hear their screams.

A potter, who was creating the world, threw from him what seemed to him a useless lump of clay, and found that he had thrown away his left hand.

When the delicious verses of Li Po were praised in the Court of Heaven an envious mandarin complained of the poet's scandalous life. The Divine Emperor, who was walking in his garden, held out a rose and asked him, "Do you smell the gardener's manure?"

Upward hadn't translated the poems from Chinese—he'd just made them up. The mystique of China began to infect Pound's verse before he possessed any decent knowledge of the real thing.

During this period of musing about the Orient, Pound met Mary Fenollosa, Ernest's widow. Pound's friend Laurence Binyon, then assistant keeper of the Department of Prints and Drawings in the British Museum, arranged the occasion. Not long after Pound came to London, Binyon had shown him Japanese ukiyo-e prints from the museum's extensive collection. The meeting with Mrs. Fenollosa in September 1913, when the Upward poems had just been published, went well. She apparently told Pound of her husband's deep interest in the poetry of ancient and medieval China. Pound must quickly have boned up on the subject, because soon he had so impressed her that in December she handed him most of Fenollosa's remaining notes and manuscripts, saying, as he recalled almost half a century later, "You're the only person who can finish this stuff and [as] Ernest would have wanted."

Pound found among those papers Fenollosa's record of his close examination of classical Chinese poetry. The American poet at first immersed himself editing Fenollosa's translations and analysis of Noh plays, published as *Certain Noble Plays of Japan* (1916) and *"Noh" or Accomplishment* (1916). It took nearly a year for Pound to get round to the poetry. Fenollosa, who had little or no classical Chinese himself, had studied the poems in 1899 with Mori Kainan, perhaps the most important *kanshi* poet of the day, that is, a Japanese poet who wrote in classical Chinese. (Three years earlier, Fenollosa had a less accomplished teacher, Hirai Kinza, whose errors in reading Chinese look embarrassing now. Pound drew on Hirai's cribs for only one poem, so his misadventures are almost irrelevant to *Cathay*.)

As Mori's English was poor and Fenollosa's Japanese probably not advanced, an expert in both, the professor of international law Ariga Nagao, was employed as a translator. Also fluent in classical Chinese, he prepared the crib for one of the most important poems in the book, "Song of the Bowmen of Shu." Mori and Ariga used what is called the *kundoku* method of reading and translating. This is Timothy Billings's quite remarkable discovery in this extraordinary edition of *Cathay*. *Kundoku*, a kind of "gloss-reading," allowed scholars who couldn't speak Chinese, who could pronounce the characters only in the Japanese fashion, to read the texts closely. This is reminiscent of the study of Latin in the West, where for centuries the texts were pored over by students and scholars who sometimes could not speak the language and whose pronunciation would undoubtedly have driven ancient Romans mad— though in their polyglot city ancient Romans were used to foreigners mangling their tongue and delighted in making nasty remarks about it.

Most of the poems that drew Pound's interest were by Li Bo, one of the most beloved of Tang poets. Pound knew him as Rihaku, his Japanese name; but until the Chinese adoption of the Pinyin system, which altered Peking to Beijing, he was called Li Po in English. Pound believed that all the Chinese poems in *Cathay* were Li Bo's, though three were by others. Transmission of the mostly eighth-century poems, borrowed from an eighteenth-century anthology, proceeded through this gloss-reading. Mori, the editor believes, would first read a line in Sino-Japanese pronunciation. (Sometimes the old Tang dynasty pronunciation had frozen sounds later altered in Mandarin, keeping ancient rhymes that could otherwise no longer be heard.) After reading the line, Mori would interpret the Chinese characters one by one. Ariga would render each gloss in English while Fenollosa jotted it down. Having moved through the whole poem, Mori would return to the beginning and parse each line, the paraphrases sometimes differing significantly from, even contradicting, the word-by-word explanation. Context alters sense.

Mori would add notes on allusion, history, and technique, and again Ariga would translate and Fenollosa serve as amanuensis.

The method reveals as much about the Japanese study of classical Chinese poetry as the finicky care and self-correction about the teaching itself. Pound, however, rarely saw the Chinese originals and often favored the glosses over the paraphrases, which gave him dangerous leeway. Most of his errors, where there were errors, came because he never realized that the glosses were not translations per se, just potentials sometimes rejected in the paraphrase. A translator, *kun*-reading Prospero's "And rifted Jove's stout oak / With his own bolt," might have glossed "bolt" as: *"short arrow / discharge of lightning / sudden spring or start / act of gorging food."* One can imagine what Pound would have made of that.

The method is best illustrated by one of the short poems, perhaps that most frequently anthologized, "The Jewel Stairs' Grievance." I have skipped the Sino-Japanese pronunciations, so what follow are Mori's gloss readings, his paraphrase (both as translated by Ariga), then, in bold, Pound's later translation.

jewel   steps   grow   white   dew
The jewel stairs have already become white with dew.
            (dew was thought to grow on things)
[The jewelled steps are already quite white with dew,]

night   long   permeate   transparent   stocking
                      attack   gauze
Far gone in the night, the dew has come to my / gauze sock.
[It is so late that the dew soaks my gauze stockings,]

let ~~down~~   down   water   crystal   sudare
                          crystal
So I let down the crystal curtain
[And I let down the crystal curtain]

transparent clear   look at   autumn   moon
And still look on the bright moon shining beyond.
[And watch the moon through the clear autumn.]

Gloss and paraphrase were followed by Mori's long note:

> *Gioku kai* [the poem's first two ideographs] means here—a place where
> court ladies are living, one of the imperial mistresses. The subject of
> the poem is that one of them was waiting in vain for the lord to come.
> The beauty of the poem lies in not a single character being used to
> express the idea of waiting + resenting; yet the poem is full of them.
> the idea. This is how. Thinking that the lord will come, she was com-
> ing out to meet him at the entrance, a flight of steps ornamented with
> jewels. She was standing there till the very dewiness of night wets her
> stockings. She lets down her curtain already despairing of his com-
> ing. And yet she can see the moon shining so brightly outside, and
> had to think of the possibility of the lord's still coming, because it is
> so fine a night; and so passes the whole night awake.

Given the slight clumsiness and halting character of the English, the
lines are no doubt more or less verbatim from Ariga. Pound was drawn
to poems whose meaning could be worked out only through hints and
whispers. Indeed, his attraction to Chinese poetry was, beyond what in
1911 he called "Luminous Detail," the demand placed on the reader to
detect what lay beneath the surface. Hints become wholes. He remarked
about the poem in his later essay "Chinese Poetry," "You can play Conan
Doyle if you like." Pound appended his own note in *Cathay*.

> Note.—Jewel stairs, therefore a palace. Grievance, therefore there is
> something to complain of. Gauze stockings, therefore a court lady, not
> a servant who complains. Clear autumn, therefore he has no excuse
> on account of weather. Also she has come early, for the dew has not
> merely whitened the stairs, but has soaked her stockings. The poem
> is especially prized because she utters no direct reproach.

This is the only note of any length in *Cathay*.

Largely ignorant of Chinese culture and art, without Fenollosa's notebooks Pound could never have penetrated the sense of a poem relying so
much on gesture and custom. Billings observes, "The Jewel Stairs' Grievance" was "based on one of the ancient topics for folk tunes, the 'palace

complaint.'" A Yuan dynasty scholar commented, "There is not a single character expressing resentment, yet we see the idea of hidden resentment between the lines."

The final sentence of Pound's note seems to show uncanny intuition, though it's merely a paraphrase of Mori's "the beauty of the poem lies in not a single character being used to express the idea of waiting + resenting." One of the themes of this critical edition is how mistaken many scholars have been in finding just such Holmesian deductions throughout *Cathay*—yet here Pound does go further than his source. Mori never mentions a palace, does not associate gauze stockings with court ladies, does not say the clear skies deny the tardy lover any excuse, and does not infer that the lady has come early. Pound shows what elsewhere he has wrongly been given credit for, the power of deduction. (That does not mean his deductions were right. The tardy lover may have had a different excuse; the lady may have come on time and simply waited in disappointment.)

The editor's notes make clear how much was lost in the Chinese whispers from scholar to translator to Fenollosa to Pound. The "jewel stairs," for instance, were jade steps, though according to Billings they would have been marble. The Chinese word for jade meant "jewel" in Japanese. Japanese borrowed numerous Chinese words during the Tang period, and sometimes meanings gradually changed. "Sudare," one of the few Japanese words in the glosses (a sign that Fenollosa had some Japanese), meant bamboo curtain or screen. If lowered, then a curtain, the precise translation of the Chinese character. "Crystal" probably meant "beaded," the word Billings uses in translating an earlier poem by Xie Tiao. Were moiré not the invention of a later day, I'd wonder if the character didn't mean watered silk, crystalline by moonlight.

There were many classes of error for which the *kundoku* method and the men involved stand responsible. Many things could have gone wrong in the daisy chain of such transmission. As Murphy's Law demands, in *Cathay* they did. The corruptions in modern Japanese of classical Chinese words are more than matched by blunders of the translators, mishearings by Fenollosa, and misreadings by Pound—and then the dozens of places where Pound, mistaken or not, mucks with the original for a stronger poetic effect.

Among the most famous of Mori's and Ariga's lapses was translating the Chinese characters for "elephant (ivory) bow" (a bow, as Billings notes, merely "decorated at both tips with ivory") as "ivory edge of arrow." The faulty paraphrase that followed became Pound's "the generals have ivory arrows." Later, in one of the Chinese poems he added to *Lustra* (1916), "ridge beam" becomes "tile," the result of a false friend in Japanese. Similarly, the Chinese word *qing* marked off a range of color from blue to black, picking up along the way, as one scholar put it, "cerulean, azure, perse, leek-green, peacock-blue, cyaneous, bice, verdigris," among others. The word in Japanese generally meant "blue," and so it was glossed and paraphrased. This gave Pound reason enough for blue grass, blue willow-tips, unripe blue plums, and a blue gate. He could have driven a herd of blue cows through one poem, though he rejected the idea. It's odd that Mori did not consider the oddity of it all.

These are missteps, certainly; but they led to effects difficult to quarrel with. The gear of generals might well be, like General Patton's ivory-handled Colt .45s, expensive, unlikely, even dandyish. Flamboyance is recognition of power. It's not even clear what an ivory arrow would be—an ivory shaft would have been almost impossible to manufacture (elephant tusks have too much curvature). An ivory point could be sharp but, because lighter, far less penetrating than bronze. Ivory arrows are unknown, so far as I can discover. Other inventions, however, compensate for qualities in the Chinese line lost in translation—inaccuracies may repair what's missing.

Pound has been the lightning rod for those who despise the school of Imitation, the weak little brother in Dryden's genealogy of translation. Every method has its exemplar, and Pound showed all that imitation could do that metaphrase and paraphrase cannot. He's also responsible for the wild liberties that followed from translators far less gifted. In the end, Pound's fancies led to Christopher Logue dragging Uzis, helicopters, and spaghetti shoulder-straps onto the Trojan battlefield.

Fenollosa sometimes found Ariga's English difficult, though fortunately the mistakes had little effect. The American's handwriting was a greater problem. Thomas Pynchon once remarked, by way of apology for exasperating stretches of dialogue in his early work, that he suffered from a malady known as Bad Ear. Many an editor—perhaps most recently that of *The Notebooks of Robert Frost*—has torn out his hair struggling with the scrawl of some long-dead worthy afflicted with Bad Hand. Fortunately, Fenollosa managed to correct the worst, so Pound was not stranded in the middle of translation wondering what "ship's intestines" were. Fenollosa had fortunately emended it to "sheeps' [*sic*] intestines."

Fenollosa's penmanship, though a little better than Frost's, is full of snares, particularly with short words lacking context. One of the scholar's most crippling vanities is hubris—and that Pound lived in such vanity is no reason for critics to follow him. Billings takes forgivable pleasure pointing out the stumbles of poet and scholar alike. Pound, for example, probably read "from the West" as "for the West" (and Hugh Kenner later as "further West"), dispatching the poem's traveler in the wrong direction. "Sitting" became "fill full"; "outsiders," "outriders"; "housegates," "banquets"; and, in a stunning act of misprision, "to no purport," "howl portents," allowing Pound to invent the delightful but errant line, "For them the yellow dogs howl portents in vain." Some misreadings may have been bumbling accidents, others deliberate—Billings is smart not to play umpire.

Do these instances matter? Most do not. One exotic detail can be much like another, so far as effect is concerned. Mori paraphrased the opening line of "The River Song" as "A (fine) boat of shato wood, with sides of *mokuran*," glossing "moku ran" as magnolia. Pound, ever looking for the concrete detail—one of his demands in "A Few Don'ts"—translated the line, "This boat is of shato-wood, and its gunwales are cut magnolia." "Gunwales" is a nice touch, acting like darkroom fixative. Unfortunately, there's a rat's nest of error here. Mori thought shato very like a long-lived flowering tree resembling an elm; instead, it's a pear tree whose wood is as water-repellent as teak. Worse, though early commentaries, as Billings notes, proposed conflicting glosses of "side of a boat" and "oars" for the middle character of the line, scholars for the past thousand years have leaned toward "oars." Whether the boat's sides or oars are made of magnolia may be crucial to the sailor, not so much to an audience with no idea what shato wood or "moku ran" is. The exoticism is what sells the line. Pound's makeshift shifting works, so long as you don't try to set out to sea using his instructions. (Perhaps it wouldn't matter even then. I shall have to ask a Tang boat builder.)

Last, we have the wrenching contrivances of Pound's translations themselves, rich and astonishing in some ways, bastardizing in others, sometimes both at once. (If anyone was willing to abuse poetic license for the master touch, it was Pound.) He was guilty of appalling acts of ignorance—not knowing the Chinese ideogram for "river," he invented the "River Kiang," that is, the "River River." Billings implies that putting the name of a river last is unknown in modern American English. Not in Boston, where the River Charles is sometimes still referred to. Such names—River Hudson, River Potomac—were once common, probably vanishing only toward the end of the nineteenth century, along with constructions like "Washington City" and the "City of Mexico."

Pound treated gloss and paraphrase as equals—elsewhere in "The River-Merchant's Wife: A Letter," he combined the characters for "ride on," "bamboo," and "horse" with the paraphrase, "When you came riding on bamboo stilts," to cobble together the suggestive line "You came by on bamboo stilts, playing horse." I've always found the line mystifying, probably with good reason. The Chinese characters for "bamboo horse"—that is, a hobbyhorse—were borrowed by the Japanese for "bamboo stilts." Mori's paraphrase was simply wrong. Pound's bullheaded ignorance was at other times a poetic advantage when he muddled gloss and paraphrase into brilliance. *Cathay* would lack many of its most affecting lines had he been more cautious, more austere.

T. S. Eliot said that Pound was the "inventor of Chinese poetry for our time." Pound's genius was not to be in the right place at the right time but to make time and place right for him. What he did for Chinese poetry, and translation as a whole, perhaps could have been done sooner or later; but he sensed that by inaccuracy he could sniff poetry out. No one more stringent has managed to give a glimmer of the depth and intimacy of the original. What's lost in translation can never be found—but Pound's method, however cranky and conniving, made Tang-era poetry again a living art. The rasps and chisels he took to Mori's paraphrases show his extraordinary eye for editing—a decade later, he took the junk heap of *The Waste Land* drafts and saw within, as Michelangelo did in a naked block of marble, the figure struggling to get out.

Perhaps the most interesting poem in *Cathay* is not Chinese at all. Years before, Pound had translated "The Seafarer," one of the Anglo-Saxon poems rescued in the Vercelli codex, a rare survivor of dozens or hundreds of Old English poems now lost. The manuscript, copied by a scribe during the latter half of the tenth century, has been housed in the Biblioteca Capitolare in Vercelli for nearly a thousand years. Pound translated the poem by taking down from the shelf his college Anglo-Saxon textbook, often employing the glossary, as Billings recounts, the way he later did the glosses of Mori and Ariga—that is, as a tray of sweets. Pound lopped off the last two dozen lines of the poem as later Christian "guesses and 'improvements.'" (The debate over the affinity of the secular and homiletic passages, begun before he was born, is still alive.)

Pound's translation was published in the *New Age* in 1911, three years before he began work on *Cathay*. His method was to imitate the two-beat hemistiches and alliterative line of Anglo-Saxon poetry. The transformation sometimes wanders off the path of meaning, yet what emerged was the most convincing imitation of Old English half lines in modern translation, raising again the language of the dead:

> May I for my own self song's truth reckon,
> Journey's jargon, how I in harsh days
> Hardship endured oft.
> Bitter breast-cares have I abided,
> Known on my keel many a care's hold,
> And dire sea-surge, and there I oft spent
> Narrow nightwatch nigh the ship's head
> While she tossed close to cliffs. Coldly afflicted,
> My feet were by frost benumbed.

Thus begins ninety-nine lines of translation in "thud metre" (as Berryman said of Lowell's early poems), with steam-hammer alliteration and English syntax twisted into the appearance of antiquity. Pound's willful way with meaning used approximation, distortion, and genial fraud. Among other things, "song's truth" would more accurately be rendered "truth-song" or "true tale"; "reckon," "express"; "jargon," "narrate" or "relate." Even so, a case can be made for all these leaps of faith. (Billings is meticulous in marking Pound's nods and winks.) The flights of fancy elsewhere might on occasion make a strict constructionist drop dead, but the performance remains a tour de force. It's a pity Pound didn't pursue the manner through, say, "The Battle of Brunanburh," "The Finnsburg

Fragment," and a long section of *Beowulf.* His contortions are rarely overly gymnastic and never outright crazy—his use of "benumbed" for "bound, fettered" and the hoary word "scur" for "showers" are fine examples of archaizing.

One method Pound used to striking effect, to the horror of translators with a theological belief in accuracy, was the calque, that is, literal but unidiomatic translation—or, even better, "exotically literal translation," as Billings puts it. What he terms "concocted calques" ("deliberately unidiomatic phrases . . . that create the illusion of 'faithful' translation") fabricate, often dramatically, tone or mood. Often this was done to make a plain phrase florid or vivid: "trees fall," in Li Bo's "Lament of the Frontier Guard," instead of "trees drop leaves"; or, in "The Seafarer," "Caesars" for "*cāseras*," the latter meaning just "emperors."

A more radical method, which Billings calls "homophonic substitution," willfully uses often accidental similarities between words. Pound was a prodigy at this, though his translations have been attacked by those who think local shifts and dodges can never serve the whole. The dark shelves of dull translations of *Beowulf* and its blood cousins argue otherwise.

Such substitution, evident everywhere in Pound's version of "The Seafarer," shows how far he was willing to stray from the original to make a deviant, theatrical version, literal sense be damned, or at least darned. The editor's notes, as full and gratifying as I can imagine, reveal in fine detail how such a poet uses his talent—and why great translations almost always come from the desk of a poet. There are places in "The Seafarer" where Pound simply nudges the original ("benumbed" for *gebunden* ["bound, fettered"]; "care's hold" for *cearselda* ["cares throne/abode"]— and what a splendid sailor's pun on "ship's hold"!) while keeping the roughneck Anglo-Saxon manner, often tucking in a layer of meaning beneath the literal. In this tale about sailing through miserable, icy weather (or sailing through figurative seas toward doctrinal shores), he often cuts more deeply into Anglo-Saxon than mirror translation could.

I might cross broadswords with the editor just once, over his note to the hemistich Pound renders as "Corn of the coldest." The full thought is "*hægl feoll on eorþan, / corna caldast*" ("Hail fell on earth, / the coldest of grains"). Billings comments, "Pound was probably thinking of the general archaic sense of 'corn' as a 'small hard particle, a grain, as of sand or salt.'" Possibly—but he might have been recalling corn not in the English sense (that is, wheat or oat grain) but as dried American corn (maize), which would very much resemble pellets of hail.

Classical translation often requires a poetic swerve in order to exist simultaneously as an original frustratingly opaque to readers and a counterfeit shining as boldly as did the source to those who first heard it recited or sung. The translator becomes a persona, both guardian of the temple and collector of night soil—Pound was a man of many masks. A reader who disapproves of his tools may still admire his reckless daring. The startling thing is how frequently his feints and niggles can be justified.

Where Pound goes astray, rendering "There storms beat on the stone cliffs, there the icy-feathered sea-swallow answered them" as "Storms, on the stone-cliffs beaten, fell on the stern / In icy feathers," the warping seems almost forgivable if we recall that "stearn" or "stern" was an Anglo-Saxon name for the tern (sea swallow). Exaction comes at the cost of good poetry—to please the professor, you must plug your ears with wax. Even Pound's famous howler, turning "cities" into "berries," can be defended though not excused. Billings ably lays out the evidence. (The Anglo-Saxon words were "*byrig*" and "*berige*"—Pound's glossary was misleading.) The poet's substitution of "English" for "angels" (*englum*) has less to recommend it, except as part of his scheme to cleanse the poem of what some have felt to be Christian mangling. Sam Johnson said of a now obscure translation of Aeschylus, "We must try its effect as an English poem; that is the way to judge of the merit of a translation." Had the Great Panjandrum been born later, he might have been speaking of Pound's *Cathay*.

The scholars who had no access to the Fenollosa papers, or who apparently saw them and did not know what they'd seen, do not get off lightly. Billings, his knowledge of Chinese and paleography in full feather, can afford to have a little fun with academics who overestimated their skills.

If no less a scholar than Ronald Bush transcribed "drum" as "dream" because he didn't know that the word being glossed was *gu* (drum), and no less a scholar than Hugh Kenner transcribed "red / (of beni)" as "red / (of berry)" because he didn't know that *beni* means "rouge" ·

in Japanese, is the fault truly Fenollosa's for not having better handwriting?

"To be sure," the editor dryly remarks, "it also helps to know some Chinese when attempting to copy lecture notes on Chinese poetry, and a little Japanese if the notetaker was studying in Japan." Billings's paragraphs on the faux pas compounded by other critics—sometimes the misreading of one becoming the basis for another's errant speculations—are the saddest and most hilarious in the book.

The major revelation of this critical edition is that Pound, though not an impeccable translator, made few outright mistakes. His artistic choices can be quarreled with, his poetic license withheld when due for renewal; but, however often he pushed license to the limit, he made only a smattering of boneheaded errors—and even some of those might be called artistry. (One scholar could find only eight actual slips in "The Seafarer," a poem often reviled by academe.) Pound saw advantage in what I once called the "right wrong word." He's sometimes guilty of the genius of mistake, but forcing translation into new territory prevents it from being sealed in the tomb of the scholar's dullness.

A good translation is like brokering a trade deal between hostile neighbors, a great one like waging a war. In the century of translation since *Cathay*, a century fruitfully and even madly encouraging to translators who knew not a scrap of the language with which they were wrestling, there have been few major successes. (Later homophonic translations, like the absurdist renderings of Catullus by Louis and Celia Zukofsky, have usually been nutty or worse.) None has been so perfect, not in but because of its inadequacy, than *Cathay*. None has given readers such direct access, however imperfect, to an alien world. Pound's dreams of eighth-century China may have been no more accurate than his fantasies of twelfth-century Périgord—but neither were anyone else's.

Poets do not become themselves all at once. They proceed crabwise, by small advances and reversals, and their gifts come into focus through the cryptic, piecemeal evolution described by Stephen Jay Gould as punctuated equilibrium. "The Seafarer" in 1911 was one kind of advance; "In a Station of the Metro," finished the following year, another; but the subtle artistry in scenes of complaint and affection, of doubt and consequence in "The River-Merchant's Wife: A Letter," "Song of the Bowmen of Shu," "Lament of the Frontier Guard," "Exile's Letter," and other poems in *Cathay* were a great leap toward the broad sweep of history, the clatter of different tongues, the painterly landscapes and spotlit details that marked his poetry ever after. *Cathay* showed how to let one world be penetrated by the literature of another, the driving mechanism behind *The Cantos*. The poet who emerged from the Chinese poems was not yet whole; but the Pound of 1910 and that of 1920 would hardly have recognized each other, and *Cathay* was largely responsible.

What if Mrs. Fenollosa had returned to America after her husband's death and laid his papers to rest in a dusty archive? What if Pound had departed for France in 1912, not 1920, and remained a latter-day medievalist, still raging against the Georgians? What if Harriet Monroe's 1912 letter inviting Pound to submit to the fledgling *Poetry* had been lost and Pound never become the magazine's truffle hunter for new talent? What if he'd then missed meeting Frost in 1913, who without Pound's prodding might have continued in the vein of *A Boy's Will*, no more than a minor New England pastoralist? What if the assassination of the Archduke Ferdinand in Sarajevo had failed in 1914, and the Great War been postponed? What if, not meeting Pound, Eliot had settled in at Oxford and, the war not preventing it, returned to America to defend his PhD dissertation and become a professor of philosophy at Harvard? Perhaps from time to time he would have written a few quatrains about the odd characters of South Boston but never married Vivienne Haigh-Wood, never suffered neurasthenic collapse, never written *The Waste Land*. What if, without Pound's Imagist poems, without Eliot to rail against, Williams had done no more than scribble occasional juvenilia on his prescription pad, remaining a small-town obstetrician? The modernist wildfire might have burned itself out, or never begun.

Timothy Billings has given us a stunning, masterful edition of a book that reinvented two worlds and made modern poetry possible.

Interview with Jonathan Hobratsch (2015)

I have strong interest in the history of Boston and Massachusetts. The state has provided scores of American poets such as Emily Dickinson, Edgar Allan Poe, Martin Espada, Ralph Waldo Emerson, Jones Very, and Elizabeth Bishop. Do you take any particular pride in having been born in Boston? Does this connection influence you?

My mother's ancestors were Pilgrims, their descendants mostly small-town types scattered along Massachusetts Bay: Scituate, Cohasset, Marshfield Hills. Her great-grandfather was a packet captain on the North River. Of her grandfathers, one was a livery-stable owner in Marshfield, the other an estate gardener who owned an eighteenth-century house in Marshfield Hills. As a young man, he kept a general store that failed because he gave credit to anyone who walked through the door. It's now the town library. I inherit such mild ironies.

I feel more affinity to the fishing village where I first went to school, Westport Point. My father honored in engineering at Yale after failing a physics lab freshman year during World War II. He'd been in officer training, but after failing the lab he was forced to join the navy as a rating. After the war he returned to Yale and later worked as a salesman for Alcoa. In the mid-fifties he became a low-level executive in Providence, absent on business trips as often as present. I grew up knowing the river and the sea, always the sea. I don't take pride in the Boston roots—after sixteen generations of cross-breeding, and not a little inbreeding, you're left with no more than a homeopathic dose in the blood. That's probably a disappointment to the DAR.

I went to a two-room schoolhouse a few doors down from my parents' house in Westport. I'm grateful for that backwater upbringing. My mother let us roam the cowpath roads, the skunk-cabbage swamp, the rocky outcrops. The bachelor who lived behind us, down a woodsy hill, was happy for us to visit. (Our sledding slope ended in his yard.) A rough sort who showed off his brass knuckles, he helped me with my modest stamp collection. Later he was charged with murder (argument over a boat, revolver), but my father flew back eight hundred miles to be a character witness at his trial. I grew up making friends with older neighbors. The bachelor's brother and his wife lived in the house across the street. Retired, swanning off to Hawaii or other places during the winter, they sent back postcards and brought home little treasures for us—a piece of lava, a quartz crystal. A lesbian sculptor lived next door, though we didn't know her beyond picking the dandelions in her yard at a penny a dozen. She had once, it turns out, been highly praised by Lachaise. Her uncle, I found out weeks ago, was the philosopher Charles Peirce.

I had school friends, of course. One's now a lawyer in Sacramento who on occasion plays golf with Clint Eastwood, another a surgeon in Seattle. Another works for the state, another married a preacher, and another owns a bargain warehouse in Elmira. When I think of my childhood towns, I think about people rather than history. Later my parents moved to Pittsburgh, then Long Island.

You went to the Iowa Writers' Workshop, which has helped produce at least eleven Pulitzer Prize–winning poets, not including faculty. Considering this, and the ongoing debate on the merits of MFA programs, did you find your MFA experience useful?

I knew nothing about MFA programs until I was casting about for something to do after college. I was music director, then program director, of the student radio-station at Yale—we were longhaired types with a pathological addiction to rock 'n' roll. I'd been hacking at poetry in a hapless way, despite the best efforts of a string of poetry workshops (taught variously by a Yale Younger Poet who wore a beret and smoked cigarillos, an Old English professor, and a minor member of the O'Hara circle). I was smart off the page, perhaps, but on it hopeless until two workshops my final semester, one by Richard Howard, who took the train up from New York each week. He was in his early forties and had taught his first workshop only the previous spring. He gave us quirky assignments, in equal parts demanding and infuriating. After the first, I knew how to approach a poem. I'd been trying to write by listening to the muse, but my muse was deaf and dumb. The assignment offered a set of problems, and I was good at problem solving (calculus and chemistry had been almost my sole delights in high school). Howard almost never allowed us to speak in class. He was a superb monologist, reading poems by Bishop, Lowell, Jarrell, poets foreign and domestic. Three striplings from that seminar went on to publish books.

The other workshop was nominally in fiction, taught by a young would-be novelist—he was only twenty-six—who a few years before had been the favorite student of Robert Penn Warren and Cleanth Brooks. He'd gone to Iowa, giving it up after a year for Hollywood, where he wrote for *Peyton Place*. (He finished the Iowa degree by mail.) He returned to Yale for law school, a decision that ended abruptly after an unhappy incident involving alcohol, a shotgun, and the light bar atop a police car. He'd bully into the seminar room, sit down, and talk about the book of the week, talk brilliantly without notes: *The Great Gatsby*; *The Sun Also Rises*; *Absalom, Absalom!*—and novels we might never have known, Leonard Gardner's *Fat City* and Richard Yates's *Revolutionary Road*. The seminar was supposed to last two hours, but he rarely made it past fifty minutes—the psychological hour. Students almost never spoke. It was an extraordinary set of performances. He went on to create *NYPD Blue* and *Deadwood*. That was David Milch.

From Howard I learned how form and manner drag inspiration from the imagination, from Milch how the depths of language and character create feeling. This may sound mechanistic; but these are ways of tapping the cask or drawing off water from the dam, at least for a certain kind of imagination.

David Milch may have told me about Iowa. Later that term, in his office, he asked if I'd heard the decision. I shook my head. "Let's call!" he said brightly, terrifyingly. He picked up the receiver of the heavy desk-phone and dialed the number—which, on a rotary phone, took forever. Finally it rang. It rang. Someone picked up. "This is David Milch," he said. "Yeah. I'm sitting here with my student Bill Logan, who applied. Yeah. Yeah.

OK." He slammed down the phone. "You didn't get in." He then offered to make me his assistant the following year, splitting the small fee he received for the seminars. The workshops were in the college-seminar program, taught by freelancers, guns for hire, for $2,000 each. It was a remarkable act of generosity, and I almost took him up on it. To my regret, I didn't.

I was admitted to Iowa a year later. The reasons for my previous rejection were plain. That class had been overstuffed with talent and included Debora Greger, Tess Gallagher, David St. John, and Laura Jensen, among others. My class was not so talented. Donald Justice taught my first workshop. He was a teacher of finesse, of small choices rather than large ones, nudges rather than broad strokes—a perfect graduate-school teacher, in other words. Iowa was competitive, but I thrived on competition.

People have been arguing about writing workshops for half a century, and they'll be arguing about them half a century from now. Some poets and critics are fixed on the idea that writers must be self-made, must rise from below to live in garrets, starving for their sestinas—that's a cheerfully safe romantic fantasy until you're hungry. Chatterton might have lived had he been given a little more money. Byron, Keats, and Shelley never had regular jobs—but they had enough to get by, Byron more than enough.

What is your general impression of MFA programs and the poets they produce?

In a world where we don't inherit wealth (my parents lived an upper-middle-class life on credit), the arts can't exist without patronage, and the minor patronage of writing workshops partly recreates the atmosphere in the little bohemias of a century ago or in the courts of Renaissance princes. I spent my years at Iowa filling the gaps in my college education (Dante, Old English, *Beowulf*), trying to write poems that pleased me.

Certainly, Iowa was a hotbed of fashion, but the students trying to write in the style of the moment—the stones-and-bones movement—were late running to catch that bandwagon. I wish there had been more interest in form and meter—even Justice wasn't interested then; though a decade later, when I joined him at the University of Florida, his interest revived. At Iowa I had a few teachers charming but lazy, at least one who couldn't write his way out of a paper bag, and one who was smart but more than a little evil. I don't regret a day I spent there. Justice and I became good friends, and I've been in love with Debora Greger ever since.

We live in a world on fast-forward, compared to the early seventies. Students know about dozens of writing programs now, who's headlining the AWP Conference, who's up and who's down in the stock market of fashion. That first year I applied to two writing programs; I was offered a place at Columbia, which I couldn't afford. I've heard of students now who applied to eighteen.

There are perhaps a dozen strong MFA programs, another dozen with one good poet and some mediocrities. The rest are mostly local affairs, with weakish poets and not much reason for existing. Even in the best programs, probably sixty percent of the poets stop writing seriously once they graduate, perhaps seventy. They learn during the program that they don't have the stamina, or the curiosity, or the anger to be writers (or perhaps what Eliot called the writer's "necessary laziness," which is very different from normal laziness). MFAs have the same dropout rate as Hell Week in SEAL training. No MFA program can make a poet out of someone who can't persevere, can't stand to fail. The only sign of later success is the willingness to submit poetry to magazines. A student who can do that, and who possesses some native gifts, can go somewhere.

What advice do you have for younger poets entering or exiting an MFA program?

Coming or going, a student should not be afraid of reading, afraid of being influenced by the dead. Most students haven't read nearly enough; and too many have been badly taught in college, with books briefly in vogue or courses like "Post-Colonial Chaucer" or "Jane Austen Among the Animals." Such students have had one or perhaps two inspiring teachers and gained from them—but contemporary English departments want to fill students' heads with theory and ignore what young writers need: great books, not great theories, and some understanding of why great books are great. I was not an English major—I drifted from American history to political science (sophomore year I took graduate courses in probability and game theory) and, later, American history and literature. I had to catch up, but I was a reader.

Try to ignore fashion. Read. Read more. "Read or die." Richard Howard said that.

You teach in Florida and live part-time in Cambridge, England. Would you consider yourself a transatlantic poet? Would you say your poetry is received differently in the United Kingdom than in the United States?

My sweetheart and I went to English on Amy Lowell Poetry Traveling Scholarships in 1981 and stayed two years. (I had the fellowship, then Debora.) After I was hired at Florida, we returned every few years, finally buying a house in Cambridge. We've had seven stays of a year or so, going every summer for the past two decades. Three of my books have been published there, the most recent a selected poems. I wouldn't call myself transatlantic—that would require too fancy a self-opinion—but I write a fair amount about England and the rest of Europe. I like having a desk drawer with a few pounds and euros and dollars in it. I like clearing my desk in the States and starting afresh in England.

I knew more poets in England thirty years ago—I've lost track of some, and many have moved on, a few to America. The first year we lived in Cambridge, I met Michael Hofmann, for a long while now my colleague at Florida. Debora and I mostly hunker down and write. Twice a week I walk across Cambridge to play chess with George Steiner, and afterward we join Debora and his wife, Zara, for tea. Every week or so we go to London for the art.

The reviewers have been kind to me in both countries. A few brickbats have been thrown, but what fun would writing be if every review were a shout of joy?

You have written six books of criticism and have received awards for them. What living poet today do you think is highly undervalued? Also, who do you think is the most valuable literary critic for American poets today?

I'll take "living poet" in a broad sense. Robert Lowell, then. By "most undervalued," I mean in relation to his poems. That may seem an odd choice, since before his death he was considered the best of his generation. A lot of readers have been turned off by the high-flown manner, which remained empyrean even when more colloquial. They prefer Elizabeth Bishop, whose poems are comfy but never dowdy. Fashion is a strange beast, and perhaps Lowell will never be loved as he was; but, when the fashion of being out of fashion stops, we may realize what an extraordinary artist he was, one who changed the course of American poetry twice and who was even more influential in his day than Pound and Eliot in theirs. If you mean a poet *still* living, I'll let my reviews answer that.

As for critics, a young poet could do worse than read R. P. Blackmur, the best poetry critic we've ever had; or Eliot, who possessed extraordinary, almost unnatural gifts as a critic. I learned much from Randall Jarrell, whose reviews and essays are a model for high standards, wicked humor, and a working poet's sensibility. Among contemporary critics, I've learned far too much from Christopher Ricks, George Steiner, and Geoffrey Hill.

Billy Collins is a former U.S. poet laureate. I've heard that he makes more money from his books of poetry than most other poets. I have read that you do not value his work with the same esteem that many of his readers do. Why do you think he is so popular? What are his faults as a poet?

Collins is popular because his poems take no effort to read, offer the pleasures of high-caloric junk food, and require no thinking at all. There's nothing wrong with that. Readers buy the easy, the polemical, the sentimental—and why shouldn't they? Few readers, even among poets, have a taste for verse that makes them work. If it weren't Billy, who has written some very funny poems about writing poetry (oddly, his only interesting subject), it would be someone worse, another Rod McKuen or Anne Morrow Lindbergh. I forgot, we already have another Rod McKuen—it's Mary Oliver.

You were once called "The Most Hated Man in American Poetry" by the Hudson Review. *You seem likable enough. How do you handle such criticism?*

On hearing that, my mother said, "It's good to be the most of something." I've never been bothered by the antagonism my criticism arouses. Indeed, I'm not sure criticism would be worth doing if it didn't make a few poets tear out their hair. Critics aren't in business to be publicity agents, though many seem to think there's no higher calling than shilling for bad poetry.

It's not the critic's job to lay down laws. Shelley said wittily that poets were the unacknowledged legislators of the world. Poets don't really want to be legislators—all those tedious committee meetings!—and neither do critics. The critic's job is to say something about a poet that isn't utterly stupid. That so many critics fail suggests that it's not rocket science. It's harder.

Afterword: The Way We Live Now

We live in the age of grace and the age of futility, the age of speed and the age of dullness. The way we live now is not poetic. We live prose, we breathe prose, and we drink, alas, prose. There is prose that does us no great harm and that may even, in small doses, prove medicinal, the way snake oil cured everything by curing nothing. To live continually in the natter of ill-written and ill-spoken prose, however, is to become deaf to what language can do.

The dirty secret of poetry is that it is loved by some, loathed by many, and bought by almost no one. (Is this the silent majority? Well, once the "silent majority" meant the dead.) We now have a poetry month, and a poet laureate, and poetry plastered in buses and subway cars like advertising placards. If the subway line won't run it, the poet can always tweet it, so long as it's only twenty words or so. We have all these ways of throwing poetry at the crowd, but the crowd is not composed of people who want to read poetry—or who, having read a little poetry, are likely to buy the latest edition of *Leaves of Grass* or *Paradise Lost*.

This is not a disaster. Most people are also unlikely to attend the ballet, or an evening with a chamber-music quartet, or the latest exhibition of Georges de La Tour. Poetry has long been a major art with a minor audience. Poets have always found it hard to make a living—at poetry, that is. The exceptions who discovered that a few sonnets could be turned into a bankroll might have made just as much money betting on the South Sea Bubble.

There are still those odd sorts, no doubt disturbed, and unsocial, and torturers of cats, who love poetry nevertheless. They come in ones or twos to the difficult monologues of Browning, or the shadowy quatrains of Emily Dickinson, or the awful but cheerful poems of Elizabeth Bishop, finding something there not in the novel or the pop song.

Many arts have flourished in one period, then found a smaller niche in which they've survived perfectly well. More than a century ago, poetry did not appear in little magazines devoted to it but on the pages of newspapers and mass-circulation magazines. The big magazines and even the newspapers began declining about the time they stopped printing poetry. (I know, I know—I've put the cause before the horse.) On the other hand, perhaps Congress started to decline when the office of poet laureate was created. The Senate and the House were able to bumble along perfectly well during the near half-century when there was only a Consultant in Poetry to the Library of Congress—an office that, had the Pentagon been consulted, might have slapped the acronym CIPLOC upon it.

Poetry was long ago shoved aside in schools. In colleges it's easier to find courses on gender, or race, or class than on the Augustans or Romantics. In high schools and grade schools, when poetry is taught at all, too often it's as a shudder of self-expression, without any attempt to look at the difficulties and majesties of verse and the subtleties of meaning that make poetry poetry. No wonder kids don't like it—it becomes another way to bully them into feeling "compassion" or "tolerance," part of a curriculum that makes them good citizens but bad readers of poetry.

My blue-sky proposal: teach America's tots to read by making them read poetry. Shakespeare and Pope and Milton by the fifth grade; in high school, Dante and Catullus in the original. By graduation, they would know Robert Frost and Elizabeth Bishop by heart. A child taught to parse a sentence by Dickinson would have no trouble understanding Donald H. Rumsfeld's known knowns and unknown unknowns.

We don't live in such a world, and perhaps not even poets alive today wish we did. My ideal elementary-school curriculum would instead require all children to learn: (1) the times tables up to, say, twenty-five; (2) a foreign language, preferably obscure; (3) the geography of a foreign land, like New Jersey; (4) how to use basic hand tools and cook a cassoulet; (5) how to raise a bird or lizard (if the child is vegetarian, then a potato); (6) poems by heart, say one per week; (7) how to find the way home from a town at least ten miles away; (8) singing; (9) somersaults.

With all that out of the way by age twelve, there's no telling what children might do. I have thieved a couple of items from W. H. Auden's dream curriculum for a College of Bards. If the elementary-school students are not completely disgusted by poetry, off they could go one day to that college, well prepared.

The idea that poetry must be popular is simply a mistake. Yet who would have suspected that the Metropolitan Opera and the National Theatre in London would now be broadcast to local movie-theaters across America? The cigar-chewing promoter who can find a way to put poetry before readers and make them love it will do more for the art than a century of hand-wringing. He might also turn a buck.

You can live a full life without knowing a scrap of poetry, just as you can live a full life without ever seeing a Picasso or *The Cherry Orchard*. Most people surround themselves with art of some sort, whether it's by Amy Winehouse or Richard Avedon. Even the daubs on the refrigerator by the toddler artist have their place. Language gainfully employed has its place. Poetry will never have the audience of *Game of Thrones*—that is what television can do. Poetry is what language alone can do.

Permissions

"Dickinson's Nothings": *New Criterion*, April 2014

"Verse Chronicle: Song and Dance": *New Criterion*, December 2012

"Verse Chronicle: Collateral Damage": *New Criterion*, June 2013

"The Iliad, Reloaded": *New York Times Book Review*, December 23, 2012 (as "Plains of Blood")

"The Beasts and the Bees": *New York Times Book Review*, April 14, 2013 (as "Heart's Desire")

"Two Gents": *Poetry*, July/August 2014

"Kipling Old and New": *New York Times Book Review*, December 1, 2013 (as "Imperial Rhymes")

"Frost at Letters": *New York Times Book Review*, June 22, 2014 (as "Early Frost")

"Verse Chronicle: Seeing the Elephant": *New Criterion*, December 2013

"Verse Chronicle: Civil Power": *New Criterion*, June 2014

"Seven Types of Ambivalence: On Donald Justice": *As We Were Saying: Sewanee Writers on Writing*, ed. Wyatt Prunty, Megan Roberts, and Adam Latham (Baton Rouge: Louisiana State University Press, 2021)

"A Literary Friendship": Foreword to *A Critical Friendship: Donald Justice and Richard Stern, 1946–1961*, ed. Elizabeth Murphy (Lincoln: University of Nebraska Press, 2013)

"Randall Jarrell at the Y": *92nd Street Y Online* (online), August 2015 (as "William Logan on Randall Jarrell")

"Flowers of Evil": *Partisan* (online), June 2015

"Verse Chronicle: The Glory Days": *New Criterion*, December 2014

"Verse Chronicle: Doing as the Romans Do": *New Criterion*, June 2015

"Meeting Mr. Hill": *Poetry*, April 2012

"The Death of Geoffrey Hill": *New Criterion*, April 2014 (as "On Geoffrey Hill, 1932–2016")

"Two Strangers": *New York Times Book Review*, October 28, 2016 (as "Lonely Bloom-
    ing"); and November 27, 2016 (as "Subdued Exuberance")

"The Jill Bialosky Case": *Tourniquet Review* (online), October 2017

"Jill Bialosky, New Revelations": *The Walrus* (online), November 10, 2017 (as "New
    Plagiarism Accusations Against Bestselling Author Jill Bialosky")

"Verse Chronicle: Under the Skin": *New Criterion*, December 2015

"Verse Chronicle: Foreign Affairs": *New Criterion*, June 2016

"Mrs. Custer's Tennyson": *New Criterion*, April 2014

"Sent to Coventry: Larkin's 'I Remember, I Remember'": *New Criterion*, April 2014

"The State of Criticism": *Battersea Review* (online), October 2014

"The Perils of Reviewing": *New Walk* (Spring/Summer 2015)

"Verse Chronicle: Home and Away": *New Criterion*, December 2016

"Verse Chronicle: Hither and Yon": *New Criterion*, June 2017

"Pound's China / Pound's *Cathay*": *New Criterion*, April 2019

"Interview with Jonathan Hobratsch (2015)": *Literati Quarterly* (online), Spring 2015

"The Way We Live Now": *New York Times*, June 15, 2014 (as "Poetry: Who Needs It?")

Books Under Review

Dickinson's Nothings

Emily Dickinson. *The Gorgeous Nothings*. Ed. Marta Werner and Jen Bervin. Christine Burgin/New Directions, 2013.

Verse Chronicle: Song and Dance

Anne Carson. *Antigonick: Sophokles*. New Directions, 2012.
Frederick Seidel. *Nice Weather*. Farrar, Straus and Giroux, 2012.
Jorie Graham. *P L A C E*. Ecco Press, 2012.
D. A. Powell. *Useless Landscape; or, A Guide for Boys*. Graywolf Press, 2012.
Natasha Trethewey. *Thrall*. Houghton Mifflin Harcourt, 2012.
Averill Curdy. *Song & Error*. Farrar, Straus and Giroux, 2013.

Verse Chronicle: Collateral Damage

Paul Muldoon. *The Word on the Street*. Farrar, Straus and Giroux, 2013.
Matthew Dickman. *Mayakovsky's Revolver*. W. W. Norton, 2012.
Jane Hirshfield. *Come, Thief*. Paperback ed. Alfred A. Knopf, 2013.
John Ashbery. *Quick Question*. Ecco Press, 2012.
Adam Fitzgerald. *The Late Parade*. Liveright, 2013.
Anne Carson. *Red Doc>*. Alfred A. Knopf, 2013.

The Iliad, Reloaded

Alice Oswald. *Memorial: A Version of Homer's* Iliad. W. W. Norton, 2013.

The Beasts and the Bees

Carol Ann Duffy. *Rapture*. Faber and Faber, 2013.
——. *The Bees*. Faber and Faber, 2013.

Two Gents

August Kleinzahler. *The Hotel Oneira*. Farrar, Straus and Giroux, 2013.
William Stafford. *Ask Me: 100 Essential Poems*. Ed. Kim Stafford. Graywolf Press, 2013.

Kipling Old and New

Rudyard Kipling. *100 Poems Old and New*. Ed. Thomas Pinney. Cambridge University Press, 2013.

Frost at Letters

The Letters of Robert Frost. Volume 1, 1886–1920. Ed. Donald Sheehy, Mark Richardson, and Robert Faggen. Harvard University Press, 2014.

Verse Chronicle: Seeing the Elephant

Will Schutt. *Westerly*. Yale University Press, 2013.
Victoria Chang. *The Boss*. McSweeney's, 2013.
Vijay Seshadri. *3 Sections*. Graywolf Press, 2013.
Clive James. *Nefertiti in the Flak Tower*. Liveright, 2013.
Ange Mlinko. *Marvelous Things Overheard*. Farrar, Straus and Giroux, 2013.

Verse Chronicle: Civil Power

Charles Wright. *Caribou*. Farrar, Straus and Giroux, 2014.
James Franco. *Directing Herbert White*. Graywolf Press, 2014.
Spencer Reece. *The Road to Emmaus*. Farrar, Straus and Giroux, 2014.
Linda Bierds. *Roget's Illusion*. G. P. Putnam's Sons, 2014.
Geoffrey Hill. *Broken Hierarchies: Poems, 1952–2012*. Ed. Kenneth Haynes. Oxford University Press, 2014.

Flowers of Evil

David Lehman. *The State of the Art: A Chronicle of American Poetry, 1988–2014*. University of Pittsburgh Press, 2015.

Verse Chronicle: The Glory Days

Louise Glück. *Faithful and Virtuous Night*. Farrar, Straus and Giroux, 2014.
Joshua Mehigan. *Accepting the Disaster*. Farrar, Straus and Giroux, 2014.
Matthea Harvey. *If the Tabloids Are True What Are You?* Graywolf Press, 2014.
Edward Hirsch. *Gabriel*. Alfred A. Knopf, 2014.
Paul Muldoon. *One Thousand Things Worth Knowing*. Farrar, Straus and Giroux, 2015.
John Berryman. *The Heart Is Strange: New Selected Poems*. Ed. Daniel Swift. Farrar, Straus and Giroux, 2014. Note: A year after the review of this book, it was reissued in a "revised edition" with the gaps mentioned now filled.

Verse Chronicle: Doing as the Romans Do

Rowan Ricardo Phillips. *Heaven*. Farrar, Straus and Giroux, 2015.
Dorothea Lasky. *Rome*. Liveright, 2014.
John Ashbery. *Breezeway*. Ecco Press, 2015.
Eavan Boland. *A Woman Without a Country*. W. W. Norton, 2014.
Rowan Williams. *The Other Mountain*. Carcanet Press, 2014.
Henri Cole. *Nothing to Declare*. Farrar, Straus and Giroux, 2015.

Two Strangers

Marie Ponsot. *Collected Poems*. Alfred A. Knopf, 2016.
Ishion Hutchinson. *House of Lords and Commons*. Farrar, Straus and Giroux, 2016.

The Jill Bialosky Case

Jill Bialosky. *Poetry Will Save Your Life*. Atria Books, 2017.

Verse Chronicle: Under the Skin

Lavinia Greenlaw. *A Double Sorrow: A Version of Troilus and Criseyde*. W. W. Norton, 2015.
Yusef Komunyakaa. *The Emperor of Water Clocks*. Farrar, Straus and Giroux, 2015.

John Crowe Ransom. *The Collected Poems of John Crowe Ransom*. Ed. Ben Mazer. Un-Gyve Press, 2015.

Juan Felipe Herrera. *Notes on the Assemblage*. City Lights, 2015.

Claudia Emerson. *Impossible Bottle*. Louisiana State University Press, 2015.

Verse Chronicle: Foreign Affairs

Frederick Seidel. *Widening Income Inequality*. Farrar, Straus and Giroux, 2016.

Maureen N. McLane. *Mz N: the serial: A Poem-in-Episodes*. Farrar, Straus and Giroux, 2016.

Les Murray. *Waiting for the Past*. Farrar, Straus and Giroux, 2016.

Melissa Green. *Magpiety: New and Selected Poems*. Arrowsmith Press, 2015.

Marianne Moore. *Observations*. Ed. Linda Leavell. Farrar, Straus and Giroux, 2016.

Christopher Logue. *War Music: An Account of Homer's Iliad*. Farrar, Straus and Giroux, 2016.

Verse Chronicle: Home and Away

Johnny Cash. *Forever Words: The Unknown Poems*. Ed. Paul Muldoon. Blue Rider Press, 2016.

Adam Fitzgerald. *George Washington*. Liveright, 2016.

Jana Prikryl. *The After Party*. Tim Duggan, 2016.

Larry Levis. *The Darkening Trapeze: Last Poems*. Graywolf Press, 2016.

Sharon Olds. *Odes*. Alfred A. Knopf, 2016.

George Herbert. *100 Poems*. Ed. Helen Wilcox. Cambridge University Press, 2016.

Verse Chronicle: Hither and Yon

John Ashbery. *Commotion of the Birds*. Ecco Press, 2016.

Alice Oswald. *Falling Awake*. W. W. Norton, 2016.

Vera Pavlova. *Album for the Young (and Old)*. Trans. Steven Seymour. Alfred A. Knopf, 2017.

Daniel Nadler. *Lacunae: 100 Imagined Ancient Love Poems*. Farrar, Straus and Giroux, 2016.

Jorie Graham. *Fast*. Ecco Press, 2017.

Anne Carson. *Float*. Alfred A. Knopf, 2016.

Pound's China / *Pound's* Cathay

Ezra Pound. *Cathay: A Critical Edition*. Ed. Timothy Billings. Fordham University
Press, 2019.

Index of Authors Reviewed